Birth Signs

Birth Signs

The Unique New Guide to
Your Planetary Influences
by DEBBIE FRANK

VERMILION
LONDON

First published in 1992 by Vermilion
an imprint of Ebury Press
Random Century House
20 Vauxhall Bridge Road
LONDON SW1V 2SA

A catalogue record for this book is available from the British
Library.

ISBN 0-09-177062-9

Set in Joanna and Gill

Printed and bound in Great Britain at The Bath Press, Avon

Book content designed by Derek Westwood

★

My thanks to two lovely Librans who have helped to keep a
balance in my life while I have been writing this book - one gave lots
of hugs and the other wagged his tail - Michael and Oliver. Also to my
mother, who although no longer in this realm still added her
Virgo touch enabling things to fall into place.

★

CONTENTS

Why you need to know your birth signs

One of the reasons people from all walks of life come to me as personal clients is that they want to know what astrology can tell them about their lives in much more detail and with much more insight than they find they can get from reading their horoscopes in newspapers or magazines.

What most of us think of as our astrological sign is in reality our Sun sign - that is the sign of the zodiac with which the Sun was aligned on the day of our birth. The Sun sign is, of course, an extremely important factor in determining our essential character. On the other hand, the positions of the nine other planets at the time of birth have a more direct bearing in some key areas. In order to get the complete picture we need to know how the nine other Birth Signs figure in certain aspects of our lives otherwise it is like trying to recognize ourselves through a description of the colour of our eyes alone.

Although the Sun sign reveals what is important to a person and what kind of identity he or she is likely to have, if we want to know, for example, about the inner person we should look at the Moon sign. Knowing this will reveal what a person is like in private, how he or she feels about things, and what he or she might be like to live with. If we want to know how people think then we need to look at their Mercury sign. It is helpful to know the Venus sign if we want to get an insight into people's love lives and see what attracts them and what they want from their relationships. The sign position of Mars will tell us about their drive, assertiveness, and ways of getting things done. We can understand people's outlooks on life more easily if we see the birth signs of Jupiter and Saturn; then we realise if it is important to them to maintain a sense of humour or a sense of duty. The sign positions of Uranus, Neptune and Pluto reveal the background influences at work in their childhood - the dreams, new ideas and turning points that shape an era and a generation of people.

All of these insights can be gained from knowing the position of the ten Birth Signs; these give us the particular blend or astrological mix that makes up each unique personality. In addition, we need to recognize the packaging of people, that is, how they present themselves to the world. The sign which is on the Ascendant or 'rising' at the time of birth is very important in determining how we actually come across to others. It is the mask which we wear and, because it is so visible to others, it is easy to spot.

This then, is the reality of astrology: the Sun sign, while vital, is only a part of your astrological profile - and this is why people often find that analyses of their personality in books, newspapers or magazines which are based entirely on Sun signs are disappointingly inaccurate and misleading. It may be a puzzle to learn that as a Libran you should be easy-going, lazy and affable when in fact you are driven to achieve your ambition, frequently argumentative and simmering with passion – these other qualities come to light when you see the positions of the some of the other planets. Perhaps, in this case, you have Mars in Scorpio and an Aries Ascendant.

Once we know the individual placements, we have the key to interpreting the interplay of the various energies in life. I hope that you will find Birth Signs a useful book for understanding not only the threads that weave your own patterns of behaviour, but also those of other people.

It is important to remember that astrology is a skill that relies on the interpreter to evaluate the various contradictions of the human psyche. None of us is completely one thing or the other but, through astrology, we can gauge how we may act differently in various situations. Once the Birth Signs have been ascertained, another layer of interpretation can begin using the aspects between the planets and the house positions. However, that is another stage. Here you can begin a fascinating exploration of yourself and others, and the blending of science and art that is astrology can grow.

HOW TO FIND YOUR BIRTH SIGNS

In order to find tour own birth signs you need to look them up in the tables at the end of each chapter. The tables in this book have been simplified from their calculated astronomical form to make them easy to use and concise enough to reproduce in a book of this size. However, they are intended as a guide for those born in the United Kingdom. Only by having your own chart calculated with respect to the exact time, date and place of your birth can the positions be gauged with total accuracy.

The Ascendant table gives the rising signs for a year in three day blocks. Firstly, find the block that relates to the date of your birth and then find the timeband within which you were born. Next to the relevant timeband is your Ascendant.

The Moon table is explained within the Moon chapter.

Mercury, Venus and Mars signs are found by following the line of your birthyear across the table until you come to a range of dates that includes your birthdate. The column heading that this range of dates.is in gives you the planets sign. In these tables there may be more than one line for a year. This is because a planet may have passed through some signs more than once in twelve months.

Jupiter, Saturn, Uranus, Neptune and Pluto all have much briefer tables. Once again, for each planet find your birthyear and date within the range of dates given.

CHAPTER ONE

The Ascendant and the Descendant

The Ascendant: your image

How do you introduce yourself? What sort of impression do you make? What does your appearance say about you?

The Ascendant, or rising sign as it is also known, is the point on the individual birthchart that is determined by the moment of birth. The sign of our Ascendant is the one that is positioned on the horizon when we enter the world, consequently it imprints a certain way of approaching life.

Our birth is our first step into the outside world – it is the entrance we make on the stage of life. Later on, when we greet something or someone new, we tend to expect the same kind of scenario and re-enact 'the script' from this earlier time. It is as if the parts in the play are handed out at birth and we unconsciously assume the role we feel expected to perform. It might be the hero or heroine (Aries rising), the sensible one (Taurus rising), the chatterbox (Gemini rising), the helper (Cancer rising), the prince or princess (Leo rising), the organizer (Virgo rising), the sweet one (Libra rising), the dark horse (Scorpio rising), Mr or Miss Happy-go-Lucky (Sagittarius rising), the responsible one (Capricorn rising), the independent one (Aquarius rising) or the romantic (Pisces rising). Through the rising sign, other people become aware of who we are.

Psychologically, the pattern that we expect to see continues. We perceive the world in a particular way – is it a friendly place (Sagittarius rising), or should we exercise caution (Capricorn rising). We behave according to our perception each time we go for a job interview or meet someone at a party. The Ascendant describes how we introduce ourselves. It is what we want others to see about us. We may be quick to convey the fact that we are straight forward and reliable (Taurus rising), or sympathetic and caring (Cancer rising). We want to make these qualities visible. We give away clues all the time – carrying messages via our clothes, our hair, our body posture, that make up a particular image. Other factors play a part too, such as our taste, which is reflected in the Venus sign, and the extent to which we embody our Sun sign. However, the Ascendant leaves an unmistakable kind of impression, based on how we appear to be. Underneath the presentation lies another layer to the story.

Along with the Sun sign and Moon sign, the Ascendant is of vital importance in understanding the inner and outer person. If you like, the Ascendant is what we play on full volume, the Sun sign is 'our tune', and the Moon is our background music. So, if we take the sign of Gemini for instance, it could manifest itself on the Ascendant as appearing to be full of nervous energy; as the Sun sign it yields a flow of communication and an essential versatility, whilst as a moon sign it gives an inner quality of alertness.

The Descendant: your partner

What sort of partners do you attract? What do you need from other people? How do others complement you or irritate you?

The Descendant is the opposite point to the Ascendant; whichever sign is rising will find its exact opposite in this position. It is interesting to note that whatever qualities we give out to others via the Ascendant, we tend to attract the opposite qualities in others to balance us. Analytical, cynical Virgo rising requires accepting Pisces, its opposite on the Descendant, to complete the rest of the picture. The Descendant point symbolizes our 'other half'.

The sign on the Descendant describes the partner who offers us the alternative viewpoint. We see in others a different way of doing, approaching and being that can be developed in ourselves. The Descendant sign does not necessarily manifest itself in real life terms as the partner. Not all Scorpio Ascendants marry Taureans, but they are likely to marry people who have a strong earth sign emphasis in their charts. The Descendant is related to the *type* of person, the kinds of qualities and attributes that we unconsciously seek out.

The Descendant relates to significant others in our lives. It can be seen as the marriage angle, the angle of business partners, the point where we come into contact with the public, or someone whom we feel opposes us. Not only can the sign correspond to more than one person, it can also express itself on different levels as can all the signs. For instance, Capricorn on the Descendant could describe the marriage partner as being a secure rock or a bringer of responsibilities. But Capricorn here could also manifest itself as the cautious business partner, or the 'cold fish' who rubs you up the wrong way. In some form or other, the qualities of Capricorn will be met. This sign tends to come into our lives through the behaviour of others. We 'project' (see in others) qualities that we do not recognize in ourselves. This is what they do, say and believe, not us. It is difficult to acknowledge that other people are mirroring back to us something that is latent or unconscious in ourselves.

ARIES ASCENDANT

Aries rising types are likely to make an impact. They want to be noticed and will dress accordingly – brightly, loudly at times. The fieriness is evident immediately as their presence crackles with energy. They have that action man or girl look, and give the impression that you had better not hold them up. They give off strength and vitality and their presence makes things happen.

Men with Aries rising can be prone to balding – this sign is associated with the head and heat, a combination that seems to burn off hair. Their hot-headedness can also translate into fevers and headaches.

When Aries is rising at the moment of birth, the individual is in a hurry to make his mark on the world. Sometimes this coincides with a quick or early delivery – Aries wants to be first. Later in life, Aries is never one to hang around; he pushes forward in any new encounter.

The image that is created by this sign on the Ascendant is one of assertion and independence. Ariens knows their own minds and are forthright about expressing them. They are daring and at times reckless in their desire to have their own way. And, because this is the sign of the self, it is important for them to be in the driving seat and not one of life's passengers.

LIBRA DESCENDANT

When Aries is the sign on the Ascendant, then its opposite sign Libra is to be found on the Descendant. The forcefulness of Aries rising attracts a partner that complements and balances. What is required is a diplomat to smooth over the troubled waters churned up by Aries. The impulsiveness of Aries is tempered by the logic and perfect timing of the Libran type of partner.

EXAMPLES OF ARIES ASCENDANT

HRH PRINCESS MARGARET

In true Aries fashion, Princess Margaret has exhibited her independence through her choice of partners. The fact that her amours may not have been

seen as suitable royal matches at the time did not prevent her from pursuing love with a divorcee, a commoner and a landscape gardener. She is now solo again, a state that people who have Aries rising handle with panache enabling them to sparkle and call the shots. Note the defiantly defined eyebrows of Aries rising which resemble the glyph for this sign.

JOHN LENNON
John Lennon exhibited the strong Aries nose and brow and exuded the audacity of this sign on the Ascendant. Lennon was keen to prove himself and prepared to go out on a limb in the process. He wouldn't compromise for the sake of the Beatles and arguments surrounded his decision to go solo with the album Imagine. His marriage to Yoko Ono marked a further split as he forged ahead with his own personal and professional life, independently of the others.

TAURUS ASCENDANT
Taurus rising can be spotted through his or her generally solid appearance. Although not necessarily heavy, this Ascendant tends to be well-built, and the neck, which is the area of the body associated with Taurus, is often especially strong looking. It is as if the earthiness of Taurus manifests itself in the body to keep the subject firmly on the ground. As Taurus is ruled by Venus, the planet of beauty, the appearance radiates a certain voluptuousness or healthy ruggedness.

The image that comes across in those with Taurus on the Ascendant is one of prosperity. Certainly, their appearance usually gives the impression of luxury as they dress in the best quality clothes, preferring natural fibres such as silk and linen. Venus usually girds her loins with something beautiful and likes to wears jewellery.

Taurus exudes satisfaction and an enjoyment of the material plane, particularly the body and the senses. Security is sought through external means, bringing about an attachment to people, money, or possessions that makes it difficult for this rising sign to let go of the past and move on in life both literally and metaphorically.

Where Taurus is found on the Ascendant, individuals are concerned with building stability and establishing a sense of permanence. They enter into new arrangements with deliberate steadiness and cannot be rushed. They are cautious but they are also reliable and capable. It may take longer to leave no stone unturned but you can be sure that the job gets done.

SCORPIO DESCENDANT
With Scorpio on the point of partnership, the Taurus rising habit of maintaining the set-up at all costs is challenged. The type of partner that Taurus rising attracts is more familiar with the angst that this Ascendant prefers to keep at bay. Where Taurus wants to keep the boat steady, Scorpio will rock it just to provoke change. Through other people, the Taurean Ascendant breaks out of his safe container, confronts emotions and examines life on a deeper level.

EXAMPLES OF TAURUS ASCENDANT

CHRISTINA ONASSIS
The wealth surrounding Christina Onassis is a classic example of the external circumstances that provide security and sometimes a prison for Taurus rising. Physically, Christina Onassis displayed the Taurean tendency towards a solid appearance, yet retained her earthy sensuality.

LIZA MINNELLI
Despite the insecurities of her early years, and subsequent personal battles, Liza Minnelli radiates the Taurean capacity to keep going and look good with it. The sign of Tauraus is connected with the throat area and throughout her long career she has made use of the gift of her beautiful voice.

GEMINI ASCENDANT

The agility, litheness and constant movement of this rising sign is a give-away. Sitting still makes Gemini rising fidget. Physically, they seem to have the elixir of eternal youth. Like Peter Pan they never seem to grow up, and the clothes they wear are usually designed to feed the impression of youth. Gemini rising still looks good in jeans at 60 – with the mobility of a kitten rather than a dozing moggie. A lively, questioning mind also keeps them attuned to the present rather than the past.

They can give the impression of a highly strung race-horse champing at the bit and at times can appear rather nervy. Geminis have to keep on the move. The air quickly gets stale for them and they need to alter the atmosphere in order to breathe. Gemini rising needs to be around different types of people – too much sameness clogs their system.

Communication is of the utmost importance. There is a need to exchange ideas, news and opinions as if this Ascendant is permanently operating a mental market stall. The changeability of Gemini on the Ascendant is an asset when adaptability and versatility are needed. They make transitions in life easily and willingly, their curiosity calling them forward. However, there are times when their restless attitude inhibits the ability to settle.

SAGITTARIUS DESCENDANT

The sign of the archer is on the Descendant when Gemini is rising. Encounters with others of a more Sagittarian nature helps people with Gemini rising to thread together the variable bits of their lives into a meaningful goal. This type of partner can encourage Gemini to look beyond what is in front of his nose towards a broader perspective. Sagittarian partners can manifest themselves as travellers, seekers, the people who go far and believe in capitalising on their opportunities. They encourage Gemini rising to raise their sights.

EXAMPLES OF GEMINI ASCENDANT

AUDREY HEPBURN

Audrey Hepburn exhibits the elfin-like quality which is often evident with the sign of Gemini rising. The bone structure is petite and her agile manner like a gazelle that gives the impression of girlish youthfulness. Her looks encapsulate both the innocence and intelligence that are the hallmarks of Gemini on the ascendant.

LAURENCE OLIVIER

With sprightly Gemini on the Ascendant, Lord Olivier was still treading the boards into his 80s. His extraordinary power of communication was expressed through his acting career on stage and film, making him one of the most versatile and mesmerising performers of all time. Olivier was always on the hop from one place to another, on tour and between homes. He rarely stood still, reflecting the Gemini adaptability and tendency to be constantly on the move. The capacity for change is useful in the acting profession, and Gemini can quickly alter its stance to embody another character. Lord Olivier's Geminian-slim figure contributed to his trim appearance. In his later years he was quite at home performing with young people – the Geminian boyish sparkle still twinkling.

The emotional state of people with Cancer rising is usually conveyed through their appearance. Despite the protective shell of the crab, feelings tend to seep out through a look or a gesture. The face inclines towards roundness and openness, as if to register the fullness of emotional expression.

Cancer rising people give the impression of vulnerability. In a sense they are looking for someone to take care of them yet, with their instinctual concern for others, they also need to get in touch with their own need to nurture. They pick up emotional undercurrents and enable others to open up. When someone with this Ascendant asks you how you are, they mean emotionally – not bodily, financially or occupationally.

Home is of the utmost importance to Cancer rising types. They need to establish a retreat which acts as a safe place when the going gets tough. They can never feel entirely comfortable in surroundings that are devoid of personal touches and it is sometimes possible to spot those with this rising sign purely by the way they have 'Cancerianized' their environment.

With Cancer on the Ascendant, people feel their way through life, one day feeling confident and outgoing, the next withdrawing back into their shells. In their daily lives, they need to allow for these fluctuations in mood, yet Cancer rising must find ways to channel their sensitivity constructively rather than just wallowing in them. A balance must be struck between valuing their ability to move through life on the basis of what they feel about things, and containing the feelings in order to prevent drowning on the high seas of emotion.

CAPRICORN DESCENDANT

Capricorn on the Descendant provides a backbone for Cancer rising. Although at times practicality and realism may bring Cancer down to earth with a bump, this type of partner can hold and sustain. Cancer supplies the structure and organisation which helps to provide the security that is essential for Cancer rising.

EXAMPLES OF CANCER ASCENDANT

JILLY COOPER

As a sensitive Cancer rising, it is the personal rather than the public side of life that Jilly Cooper writes about. Her own home and family form a strong part of her identity and her image is one of sensitivity and wearing her heart on her

sleeve. There is nothing stiff or formal about her appearance; she has the Cancerian open face which tends to draw others and their private lives out.

RICHARD BURTON

Richard Burton's looks were distinctly Cancerian – he had the classic 'moon face' and a sensitive appearance that gave the impression of a man in touch with his feelings. Burton's voice was capable of portraying powerful emotions leaving the audience with a sense of involvement. In Cancerian fashion his personal life seemed to spill out all around him, and was inseparable from his public persona. When he died, people felt they really knew him – he was not someone who kept his distance or hid himself.

LEO ASCENDANT

It is usually possible to spot Leo rising by the mane of hair, and the proud bearing. This Ascendant always puts on his or her royal attire to meet their audience. The Leonine image exudes quality. It is definitely a case of cashmere and caviar. People with Leo rising are marked out by their 'cut above the rest' style and their desire to dazzle.

They cannot help seeming to stand permanently in the spotlight. They actually need plenty of hours of sunshine to bring out their best. They are performers at heart and like to catch the attention of other people. Their ability to express themselves however, depends on an appreciative audience. It is a sad lion who does not receive the praise he thinks he deserves. It can come as a surprise to see how easily Leo rising is crushed by indifference.

Master of the grand gesture, Leo rising individuals are generous and warm-spirited but never let their standards slip. They will not stoop to conquer – it is beneath their dignity – and they equally expect others to treat them with respect. Leo rising signs live in a special world, and can create a rarified atmosphere around them where everyone is made to feel important, but, of course, they remain number one, the king pin.

AQUARIUS DESCENDANT

The sign of Aquarius is on the angle of partnership when Leo is rising. Leo needs to counteract his or her emphasis on directing things from the centre through a partner that understands the importance

of standing back. Leo seeks an unusual partner, someone who is confident enough of their individuality not to score points. A little detachment and objectivity can help Leo to cool it.

EXAMPLES OF LEO ASCENDANT

MARILYN MONROE

Marilyn Monroe epitomized the Leo look, complete with lioness's mane and a glamorous personal presence. She always managed to make an entrance that drew attention to herself and her powerful image was created as a result of a performance that didn't stop at the end of the film. At any time she was able to simply light up and radiate the 'look at me' magnetism that is the essence of Leo.

HRH PRINCE CHARLES

Perhaps Prince Charles can be excused from the Leo habit of expecting to be treated like Royalty! Whether he is arriving in a stylish car or playing polo on the finest horse, his appetite for high standards is evident – and architecture is no exception. Everything for Leo rising must be the best. His expression is dignified and he has the Leo pride and self-consciousness that will not allow him to don a factory hat without worrying that he might look 'silly'.

21

VIRGO ASCENDANT

Virgo Ascendants give themselves away through crisp presentation. Their perfectly polished, immaculately ironed, colour co-ordinated looks make other rising signs feel they have been dragged through a hedge backwards. Virgoans look elegant and well-groomed rather than sexy. When they buy clothes, they look for the label with the washing instructions rather than the designer's name. Mainly they go for clothes that are well-cut, preferring simplicity to frills and furbelows, although they love accessories which enable them to achieve a perfect match.

Virgo rising people have an alert, intelligent look and a youthfulness in common with Gemini the sign that shares Mercury, the planet of the mind as a ruler. They exude an energy that is busy and thorough. Virgos like to be seen to be doing something useful.

Virgoans cannot help but notice where improvements might be made. They are not loud, or attention-seeking but they make their observations, criticisms and suggestions known. These Ascendants live in a 'could do better' world. Their penchant for organizing and arranging the details is immediately apparent, and they generate a general feeling of having things under control. Scratch the surface to their other birth placements and you might find out that this is not the case, but they always make it look good.

PISCES DESCENDANT

If Virgoans lived in a Utopian world of efficiency they would lose their raison d'etre. This Ascendant needs others to create the conditions that bring out the best in Virgo. In partnership terms this means that Virgo attracts partners of a more chaotic nature and attempts to 'sort them out'. The nebulous quality of the sign Pisces encourages Virgo to relax and accept.

EXAMPLES OF VIRGO ASCENDANT

MADONNA

Although Madonna is no Mary Poppins, she shares the same finicky Virgo Ascendant as Julie Andrews. She is constantly analysing and refining her image, going to great efforts to get the effect just right. Her stage act comes under her never-ending critical appraisal as she strives for improvement. Madonna exhibits the 'studied' Virgo appearance that never looks careless or thrown together.

NIGEL HAVERS

Nigel Havers always exudes an air of careful presentation. His clean cut look is typical of Virgo rising who wouldn't dream of appearing with dirty fingernails or a button missing. Physically he has the alertness and youthfulness associated with Virgo.

LIBRA ASCENDANT

The impression given by Libra rising signs is one of good grace, consideration for others and equanimity. An image of social acceptability is important to them. Their style is essentially non-confrontational as they prefer to negotiate and avoid unpleasant scenes. In fact the outer persona can be so glossy and poised that there is no hint of what troubled waters may lie underneath. Like Taureans, who are also ruled by Venus, Librans are concerned with creating a beautiful appearance. They usually have more than enough clothes to choose from and revel in the whole process of 'getting ready'. Selecting the right hairstyle, tie-pin or brooch is raised to an art form.

A major issue for Libra Ascendants revolves around relationships. They feel most comfortable when they are connected to a partner. Not just one either; this is a need for companionship that extends far beyond a desire for love and encompasses a desire for company on everything from business to shopping trips. These Ascendants often get into the situation of buying the shoes or dress because a friend says it suits them, thus tipping the scales of indecision.

Although the need for relationships is so strong

with this Ascendant, Libra is an air sign and tends mentally to rationalize rather than passionately consume love. People must play fair and keep to their side of the bargain when they enter into agreements with Librans. If the refinement and beauty is tarnished or soiled by the uglier emotions, such as jealousy and rage, Libra rising wants to exchange the goods.

ARIES DESCENDANT
Librans are often attracted to assertive types who know

their own mind and challenge them to come off the fence.

Through the give and take of partnership, a Libran learns when to adjust and when to stand up for his or her share. An impulsive partner helps Libra to get moving and combat the paralysis of indecision.

EXAMPLES OF LIBRA ASCENDANT

ELIZABETH TAYLOR
Libra rising is a lover of beauty, and Elizabeth Taylor

is no stranger to the art of adornment. She has made jewellery her trade-mark. Whether it was Liz's sparkling eyes or her sparkling diamonds that made the headlines, she was always able to mesmerize others with her luxurious Libran presence. The need for partnership has also been a central theme of her life, making her more famous for her private life than her movies, which have also echoed Libra's call for romance.

ROD STEWART
An eye for beauty is again very much apparent in another Libra rising. Rod Stewart's accessories have always included attractive women. Love songs and love life form a strong part of his image. He is perceived as a man who has searched long and hard for the perfect partner.

SCORPIO ASCENDANT

There is an intensity about Scorpio rising that is immediately apparent. Not only are the eyes penetrating, the entire presence is powerful. Scorpio on the Ascendant loves to make a dramatic impression with deep, rich colours. Preferring clothes that hint at sexuality but never quite expose it.

Scorpion looks are usually highly defined – mousey hair is definitely not allowed in the Scorpio palette of colour which concentrates on dramatic shades. The magnetic attraction of Scorpio ascendants radiates enormous pulling power but, at the same time, there is a strong desire for personal privacy. They may appear to be ice-cool or highly seductive, but they will never fade into the scenery.

The Scorpio emphasis on transformation is highly evident with this rising sign. The image that is put across will usually change radically in a lifetime, mirroring alterations in their status, values and attitudes. Scorpio is a survivor of life's challenges, and with each drama that unfolds this rising sign sheds another skin to reveal something else from underneath.

The legendary secretiveness of Scorpio can close the door of communication with this Ascendant, blocking the two-way flow of interaction with others. Scorpio rising people must learn to release their intense emotions and let go of the need to control everyone, including themselves. Once repression is converted into expression, Scorpio rising signs discover themselves and their unique ability to reach deep inside other people.

TAURUS ON THE DESCENDANT

Scorpio rising needs the stability of a partner who creates a constancy and order in life to balance the highs and lows. A Taurean type of partner will see the molehill for exactly what it is, rather than agreeing with Scorpio rising that Mount Everest has appeared. Scorpio needs to be reminded of the here and now, to take a look at the surface before automatically scratching below it.

EXAMPLES OF SCORPIO ASCENDANT

MARGARET THATCHER

The piercing eyes and aura of power give away Margaret Thatcher's rising sign as a Scorpio. Her general presentation is of a strong lady – even an iron one. At times Scorpio rising can appear almost hawk-like, and when Prime Minister, Margaret Thatcher's looks were a picture of control as she gathered her assertive power before swooping in

on those who challenged her. Margaret Thatcher caught public attention with her 'Milk Snatcher' persona – Scorpio has a reputation for making the ends justify the means. When she became Prime Minister, professionals increased her glamour and lowered her voice, transforming her ability to radiate authority. Another change stripped her of this identity, but this phoenix-like sign has a habit of rising from the ashes!

JACQUELINE KENNEDY

As First Lady of the United States, Jackie Kennedy projected a powerful mystique that had everyone trying to copy her image. However, Scorpio ascendants will never give the game away; they remain in control and essentially private. Jackie Kennedy, in her dark glasses, was always somehow out of reach. Precipitated into crisis, her outer role changed dramatically, but her presence remains both intriguing and secretive.

SAGITTARIUS ASCENDANT

People with Sagittarius rising usually look fit, healthy and energetic, the sort with colour in their cheeks even if they feel on death's door. There can be something outsize about them, either in the height or weight department, or just a general impression that they are somewhat larger than life. Their personal style is relaxed and this is reflected in their clothes which are designed for comfort and fun. When they do dress up, they tend to be flamboyant, and have the guts to wear the outrageous tie, the 'notice me' dress. The overall impression, however, is one of naturalness and ease. Sagittarius Ascendants are not false eyelashes and primped hair types.

They exude a friendly manner, and there is an adventurous streak that

makes itself felt. The image they project is good humoured and fun-loving and they have a natural ability to create a relaxed atmosphere and break down other people's defences.

Sagittarians have little sense of limitation and tend to overdo things. They frequently stretch themselves so far that the nervous system is ready to snap. It can be a case of too much, too soon, as eager Sagittarius rising types reach out for more. In their thirst for life the phrases that pop up with this placement are 'over-the-top' and 'out of hand'. For generous, read extravagant, and for spontaneous, read reckless, although Sagittarius Ascendants have a fortunate ability to land on their feet.

Those with this rising sign need a great deal of space, a free rein to charge ahead and a goal to fix upon. There must be somewhere for the archer to aim those arrows or he can achieve no sense of direction. They love to travel, explore and learn and have a great deal to teach others about simply enjoying life.

GEMINI DESCENDANT
Gemini on the point of partnership stops Sagittarius in its tracks. Where are you going, why and what for? The questioning nature of the partner forces Sagittarius rising to reason rather than rampage. Instead of taking on more, Gemini encourages the examination of what is already there. An astute and mentally alive partner can

help Sagittarius to feel excited by thinking rather than doing.

EXAMPLES OF SAGITTARIUS ASCENDANT

BORIS BECKER
Freckled-faced and natural, Boris Becker displays the boy-next-door version of Sagittarius rising. His physical prowess and athleticism form a major part of his image. Sagittarius on the Ascendant is basically an outdoor type, or looks like one at the very least. Becker constantly travels in pursuit of his goal – to be a world class tennis champion. He may fire balls instead of arrows over the net, but he is a typical archer.

PAUL HOGAN
Crocodile Dundee is the personification of the Sagittarian quest for adventure and reflects the gung-ho attitude that revels in challenge and has no concept of limitation. Although this character is permanently poised for the next task, he maintains the kind of relaxed perspective on life that is never ruffled or uptight. Both on and off screen, Paul Hogan embodies the larger than life persona that reaches across continents and opens doors. Those with Sagittarius rising also favour humour as an important opener.

CAPRICORN ASCENDANT

Capricorn Ascendants give an impression of being in control, well organized and hard-working. They can find it difficult to justify time off and are hard task masters to themselves. Their responsibilities require an enormous amount of self discipline. Usually Capricornians set themselves up with many people dependent on them.

The self-control that is the main principle in their lives is reflected in their outward manner. They give little away and set great store by physical and inner strength. Consequently they can appear to be tough and aloof. Maintaining a stoical attitude can come at the expense of allowing others to see their vulnerability. Often the bone structure is pronounced, with the back and teeth feeling the strain and grumbling with tension. Their presentation tends towards the conservative, yet weakness can show itself in label flashing, whether it be Armani or Gucci.

Capricorn rising people ripen with age. They come into their own later in life and, like Camembert, relax and soften up in time. It is important however, that these Ascendants acknowledge their ambitio᠎ to climb their own particul᠎ mountain. Capricorn rising enjoys the perseverance involved in achieving a goal over a long period of time.

CANCER DESCENDANT
Because Capricorn Ascendants give out that 'I'll take care of it' attitude; they tend to attract a partner who needs looking after. Cancer on the Descendant indicates a partner who is attuned to feelings and encourages Capricorn rising to come in from the cold, so to speak.

Parental issues are often revisited in the partnership, as Cancer and Capricorn represent the mother and father, that is, the old patterns from the past.

EXAMPLES OF CAPRICORN ASCENDANT

HM THE QUEEN
With a Capricorn Ascendant, the image of the Queen must be one of duty first. The seriousness of the role she

27

When the sign of Aquarius is on the Ascendant there is often a struggle for identity. It is of vital importance that Aquarius rising individuals make a fresh impression, aside from expectations, and this is why their outward image can suddenly change. Aquarians actually enjoy being a square peg in a round hole – it means they stand out from the crowd. Their approach to life is unusual; put into situations where behaviour is 99 percent predictable they seem to embody the 'there is always one who' philosophy.

Physically, they appear intelligent and have a far-seeing look in their eyes which can make them seem to be 'on another planet'. They switch in and out of the conversation. Often they appear to be on their own and separate from the crowd. They can be eccentric in their personal presentation – after all Aquarius is noted for being original and ahead of its time. Aquarius rising is noted for doing it 'my way', and they may dress deliberately inappropriately for an occasion just to please themselves.

There is often a conflict between acting as an individual or as part of a team or group. The sign of Aquarius is connected with

performs demands a professionalism with which Capricorn is uniquely equipped. The Queen has always maintained her public image of correctness and propriety, and her hard work has never been questioned – Capricorn rising is unswerving in dedication. An image is carefully built up and preserved over the years and the Queens's personal style is typically traditional and conservative. Quality rather than fashion is the priority, and her manner and posture appear to be 'upright'. It is rare to catch Capricorn rising off guard, and the features can seem to be frozen or immobile so that personal reaction does not slip out.

SEAN CONNERY

Another version of Capricorn rising is 'the tough man', personified by the inscrutable Sean Connery. Never allowing emotion to distract from the business in hand, his screen persona has attracted many roles as a professional hard nut, James Bond included. Capricorn on the Ascendant has the capacity to establish an identity that stands the test of time and one that yields financial reward to boot.

development on both these levels. Those with this Ascendant can either act as a powerful force for change in society or cut a swathe as a distinct figure. Either way, they can appear at times to be something of an outsider, and they need to create some kind of distance in order to see life from an objective stand-point.

LEO DESCENDANT
In the area of partnerships, Aquarius confronts human nature as it is, rather than as an abstract ideal. The sign of Leo on the partnership point creates a fire that draws attention to one-to-one relationships, and Aquarius rising types have to find a way of dealing with the heat if they want to relate closely to other people.

EXAMPLES OF AQUARIUS ASCENDANT

GERMAINE GREER
Germaine Greer has always carried the spirit of

controversy with a style that displays her Aquarian colours. Aquarius on the Ascendant is seen in the way she identifies with concepts and theories. Publicly she has come full circle from ardent women's libber to promoter of home and family, ever ready to shock and turn tail. Her appearance is also unhampered by convention – her look embodies the freedom of Aquarians to create themselves.

ERIC CLAPTON
As a member of a band, and then as a solo performer, Eric Clapton's image has embraced the team spirit and the individuality of Aquarius. Over the years he has also projected the wildness and originality of this sign, and today he still experiments with many types of music; his is an eclectic mix that refuses to be pigeon-holed. Dressing in Armani also makes a statement that he has created his own version of a rock-and-roll man.

PISCES ASCENDANT
There is something that is constantly shifting about those with Pisces rising. Just when you think you have their measure, they metamorphose into something else. It is not a shocking change, more a gradual dissolving of one image into another. Pisces rising people are, in fact, immensely impressionable and tend to reflect the influence of the current environment. The eyes look luminous, large and watery and the overall impression is one of softness. They do not have a distinct style of their own but, like a chameleon, adopt the image that blends in with their surroundings. However, they draw the line at looking 'ordinary'- some special effect has to be achieved, an illusion created.

Physically, they often carry an aura of romance, and an elusive quality makes them appear enigmatic. They can sometimes seem to be not quite of this world – people who need rooting firmly on the ground because they are in danger of floating off completely. Escapist behaviour can be a means for them to avoid reality although, in a sense, Pisces rising are born to experience life on another plane. Their sensitivity, compassion and creativity sweep away any starkness

and allow a little bit of magic into their lives.

They are subtle in their approach and there is a gentleness about them that elicits sympathy and can melt hearts. Pisces rising signs can appear waif-like and permanently in need of rescuing from a relationship, a trauma or from themselves. On the other hand, these Ascendants can dedicate themselves to the well-being of others. The artistic type of Pisces rising can raise awareness in others through presenting images that provoke an emotional response.

VIRGO DESCENDANT

Virgo is the sign of order and discrimination which challenges Pisces rising to exercise choice. The practical attitude of a partner helps to ground his or her idealistic nature and provides a place for reality to meet possibility. Clarity is important in these partnerships especially if the saviour/victim interplay emerges.

EXAMPLES OF PISCES ASCENDANT

PRINCESS CAROLINE OF MONACO

Princess Caroline of Monaco has embodied the spectrum of Pisces on the Ascendant. From a fairy-tale Princess, with a glamorous, jet set image, she then married Phillipe Junot, attempting to rescue him (unsuccessfully) in the process. After the tragic death of her mother and a second marriage, Caroline's image changed, revolving around charity work and dedication to others. Now in the face of the death of her husband, Caroline herself is a victim in need of rescue. Note the large eyes which convey the impression of emotion close to the surface.

ROBERT REDFORD

As a celluloid Romeo, Robert Redford has won many hearts, personifing the dream romance. Pisces on the Ascendant has a way of captivating a magical quality and projecting it outwards in a way that entrances others. It is possible to hide behind the illusion of Pisces on the Ascendant and, in Robert Redford's case, it is difficult to get to the man underneath. Millions of people have heard of him, millions have fantasized about him, but how many actually know anything about him other than the image he presents? The sign of Pisces is connected to film because it is a medium which blurs reality and makes it possible to view life through a series of images. Because Robert Redford has Pisces rising he is able to put aside his own identity and act as a channel for an image to be projected onto him.

DATES	FROM	TO	SIGN	DATES	FROM	TO	SIGN	DATES	FROM	TO	SIGN
1/1-3/1	00.00	02.12	LIB	10/1-12/1	00.00	01.40	LIB	19/1-21/1	OO.OO	01.05	LIB
	02.13	05.05	SCO		01.41	04.30	SCO		01.06	03.40	SCO
	05.06	07.34	SAG		04/31	07.00	SAG		03.41	06.21	SAG
	07.35	09.19	CAP		07.01	08.44	CAP		06.22	08.08	CAP
	09.20	10.28	AQU		08.45	09.52	AQU		08.09	09.16	AQU
	10.29	11.20	PIS		09.53	10.45	PIS		09.17	10.19	PIS
	11.21	12.13	ARI		10.46	11.38	ARI		10.20	11.02	ARI
	12.14	13.22	TAU		11.39	12.46	TAU		11.03	12.11	TAU
	13.23	15.09	GEM		12.47	14.34	GEM		12.12	13.56	GEM
	15.10	17.45	CAN		14.35	17.05	CAN		13.57	16.30	CAN
	17.46	20.05	LEO		17.06	19.54	LEO		16.31	19.18	LEO
	20.06	23.18	VIR		19.55	22.45	VIR		19.19	22.17	VIR
	23.19	00.00	LIB		22.46	00.00	LIB		22.18	00.00	LIB
4/1-6/1	00.00	02.00	LIB	13/1-15/1	00.00	O1.25	LIB	22/1-24/1	00.00	00.54	LIB
	02.01	04.44	SCO		01.26	04.18	SCO		00.55	03.42	SCO
	04.45	07.21	SAG		04.19	06.50	SAG		03.43	06.13	SAG
	07.22	09.08	CAP		06.51	08.33	CAP		06.14	07.57	CAP
	09.09	10.24	AQU		08.34	09.39	AQU		07.58	09.57	AQU
	10.25	11.08	PIS		09.40	10.33	PIS		09.58	10.51	ARI
	11.09	12.00	ARI		10.34	11.25	ARI		10.52	12.00	TAU
	12.01	13.09	TAU		11.26	12.33	TAU		12.01	13.50	GEM
	13.10	14.56	GEM		12.34	14.04	GEM		13.51	16.18	CAN
	14.57	17.35	CAN		14.05	16.54	CAN		16.19	19.06	LEO
	17.36	20.12	LEO		15.55	19.42	LEO		19.07	22.00	VIR
	20.12	23.06	VIR		19.43	22.30	VIR		22.01	00.00	LIB
	23.07	00.00	LIB		22.31	00.00	LIB				
7/1-9/1	00.00	01.40	LIB	16/1-18/1	00.00	01.15	LIB	25/1-27/1	00.00	00.40	LIB
	01.41	04.40	SCO		01.16	04.05	SCO		00.41	03.30	SCO
	04.41	07.09	SAG		04.06	06.34	SAG		03.31	06.00	SAG
	07.10	08.55	CAP		06.35	08.19	CAP		06.01	07.44	CAP
	08.56	10.04	AQU		08.20	09.28	AQU		07.45	08.52	AQU
	10.05	10.57	PIS		09.29	10.20	PIS		08.53	09.45	PIS
	10.58	11.49	ARI		10.21	11.14	ARI		09.46	10.38	ARI
	11.50	12.58	TAU		11.15	12.22	TAU		10.39	11.53	TAU
	12.59	14.45	GEM		12.23	14.09	GEM		11.54	13.34	GEM
	14.46	17.15	CAN		14.10	16.40	CAN		13.35	16.06	CAN
	17.16	20.06	LEO		16.41	19.30	LEO		16.07	18.54	LEO
	20.07	22.55	VIR		19.31	22.20	VIR		18.55	21.45	VIR
	22.56	00.00	LIB		22.21	00.00	LIB		21.46	00.00	LIB

15/2-17/2	00.00	02.06	SCO	24/2-26/2	00.00	01.30	SCO	4/3-6/3	00.00	00.55	SCO
	02.07	04.38	SAG		01.31	04.00	SAG		00.56	03.26	SAG
	04.39	06.22	CAP		04.01	05.46	CAP		03.27	05.11	CAP
	06.23	07.30	AQU		05.47	06.54	AQU		05.12	06.20	AQU
	07.31	08.23	PIS		06.55	07.47	PIS		06.21	07.12	PIS
	08.24	09.16	ARI		07.48	08.40	ARI		07.13	08.04	ARI
	09.17	10.25	TAU		08.41	09.49	TAU		08.05	09.14	TAU
	10.26	12.18	GEM		09.50	11.35	GEM		09.15	11.00	GEM
	12.19	14.42	CAN		11.36	14.06	CAN		11.01	13.30	CAN
	14.43	17.30	LEO		14.07	16.55	LEO		13.31	16.24	LEO
	17.31	20.24	VIR		16.56	19.48	VIR		16.25	19.12	VIR
	20.25	23.12	LIB		19.49	22.36	LIB		19.13	22.00	LIB
	23.13	00.00	SCO		22.37	00.00	SCO		22.01	00.00	SCO
18/2-20-2	00.00	01.55	SCO	27/2-29/2	00.00	01.20	SCO	7/3-9/3	00.00	00.45	SCO
	01.56	04.20	SAG		01.21	03.50	SAG		00.46	03.13	SAG
	04.21	06.12	CAP		03.51	05.35	CAP		03.14	05.00	CAP
	06.13	07.18	AQU		05.36	06.43	AQU		05.01	06.08	AQU
	07.19	08.12	PIS		06.44	07.35	PIS		06.09	07.00	PIS
	08.13	09.04	ARI		07.36	08.28	ARI		07.01	07.53	ARI
	09.03	10.14	TAU		08.29	09.38	TAU		07.54	09.03	TAU
	10.15	12.00	GEM		09.39	11.26	GEM		09.54	10.47	GEM
	12.01	14.30	CAN		11.27	13.55	CAN		10.48	13.20	CAN
	14.31	17.20	LEO		13.56	16.45	LEO		13.21	16.10	LEO
	17.21	20.12	VIR		16.46	19.36	VIR		16.11	19.00	VIR
	20.13	23.00	LIB		19.37	22.25	LIB		19.01	21.50	LIB
	23.01	00.00	SCO		22.26	00.00	SCO		21.51	00.00	SCO
21/2-23/2	00.00	01.42	SCO	1/3-3/3	00.00	01.06	SCO	10/3-12/3	00.00	00.30	SCO
	01.43	04.13	SAG		01.07	03.39	SAG		00.31	03.04	SAG
	04.14	06.00	CAP		03.40	05.25	CAP		03.05	04.48	CAP
	06.01	07.07	AQU		05.24	06.32	AQU		04.49	05.56	AQU
	07.08	08.00	PIS		06.33	07.23	PIS		05.57	06.49	PIS
	08.01	08.53	ARI		07.24	08.17	ARI		06.49	07.42	ARI
	08.54	10.00	TAU		08.18	09.25	TAU		07.43	08.52	TAU
	10.01	11.42	GEM		09.26	11.13	GEM		08.53	10.49	GEM
	11.48	14.18	CAN		11.14	13.42	CAN		10.50	13.06	CAN
	14.19	17.10	LEO		13.43	16.35	LEO		13.07	16.00	LEO
	17.11	20.00	VIR		16.36	19.24	VIR		16.01	18.18	VIR
	20.01	22.48	LIB		19.25	22.12	LIB		18.09	21.40	LIB
	22.49	00.00	SCO		22.13	00.00	SCO		21.41	00.00	SCO

Date	Start	End	Sign	Date	Start	End	Sign	Date	Start	End	Sign
19/1-21/1	00.00	01.05	LIB	28/1-30/1	00.00	00.30	LIB	6/2-8/2	00.00	00.04	LIB
	01.06	03.40	SCO		00.31	03.18	SCO		00.05	02.40	SCO
	03.41	06.21	SAG		03.19	05.45	SAG		02.41	05.13	SAG
	06.22	08.08	CAP		05.46	07.33	CAP		05.14	06.57	CAP
	08.09	09.16	AQU		07.34	08.41	AQU		06.58	08.07	AQU
	09.17	10.19	PIS		08.42	09.33	PIS		08.08	08.58	PIS
	10.20	11.02	ARI		09.34	10.26	ARI		08.59	09.31	ARI
	11.03	12.11	TAU		10.27	11.36	TAU		09.32	11.00	TAU
	12.12	13.56	GEM		11.37	13.21	GEM		11.01	12.47	GEM
	13.57	16.30	CAN		13.22	15.54	CAN		12.48	15.18	CAN
	16.31	19.18	LEO		15.55	18.42	LEO		15.19	18.06	LEO
	19.19	22.17	VIR		18.43	21.35	VIR		18.07	21.00	VIR
	22.18	00.00	LIB		21.36	00.00	LIB		21.01	23.53	LIB
									23.54	00.00	SCO
22/1-24/1	00.00	00.54	LIB	31/1-2/2	00.00	00.21	LIB	9/2-11/2	00.00	02.30	SCO
	00.55	03.42	SCO		00.22	03.06	SCO		02.31	05.00	SAG
	03.43	06.13	SAG		03.07	05.34	SAG		05.01	06.46	CAP
	06.14	07.57	CAP		05.35	07.21	CAP		06.47	07.52	AQU
	07.58	09.57	AQU		07.22	08.30	AQU		07.53	08.47	PIS
	09.58	10.51	ARI		08.31	09.22	PIS		08.48	09.40	ARI
	10.52	12.00	TAU		09.23	10.15	ARI		09.41	10.49	TAU
	12.01	13.50	GEM		10.06	11.25	TAU		10.50	12.34	GEM
	13.51	16.18	CAN		11.26	13.10	GEM		12.35	15.06	CAN
	16.19	19.06	LEO		13.11	15.42	CAN		15.07	17.55	LEO
	19.07	22.00	VIR		15.43	18.30	LEO		17.56	20.48	VIR
	22.01	00.00	LIB		18.31	21.20	VIR		20.49	23.32	LIB
					21.21	00.00	LIB		23.33	00.00	SCO
25/1-27/1	00.00	00.40	LIB	3/2-5/2	00.00	00.13	LIB	12/2-14/2	00.00	02.18	SCO
	00.41	03.30	SCO		00.14	02.54	SCO		02.19	04.47	SAG
	03.31	06.00	SAG		02.55	05.25	SAG		04.48	06.33	CAP
	06.01	07.44	CAP		05.26	07.08	CAP		06.34	07.41	AQU
	07.45	08.52	AQU		07.09	08.17	AQU		07.42	08.35	PIS
	08.53	09.45	PIS		08.18	09.10	PIS		08.36	09.26	ARI
	09.46	10.38	ARI		09.11	10.02	ARI		09.27	10.36	TAU
	10.39	11.53	TAU		10.03	11.12	TAU		10.37	12.21	GEM
	11.54	13.34	GEM		11.13	13.00	GEM		12.22	14.54	CAN
	13.35	16.06	CAN		13.01	15.30	CAN		14.55	17.45	LEO
	16.07	18.54	LEO		15.31	18.18	LEO		17.46	20.36	VIR
	18.55	21.45	VIR		18.19	21.10	VIR		20.37	23.24	LIB
	21.46	00.00	LIB		21.11	00.00	LIB		23.25	00.00	SCO

13/3-15/3	00.00	00.23	SCO	22/3-24/3	00.00	02.15	SAG	31/3-2/4	00.00	01.39	SAG
	00.24	02.51	SAG		02.16	04.00	CAP		01.40	03.25	CAP
	02.52	04.35	CAP		04.01	05.09	AQU		03.26	04.34	AQU
	04.35	05.44	AQU		05.10	06.02	PIS		04.35	05.26	PIS
	05.45	07.30	PIS		06.03	06.54	ARI		05.27	06.19	ARI
	07.31	08.39	TAU		06.55	08.53	TAU		06.20	07.28	TAU
	08.40	10.26	GEM		08.04	09.51	GEM		07.29	09.15	GEM
	10.27	12.55	CAN		09.52	12.20	CAN		09.16	11.45	CAN
	12.56	15.48	LEO		12.21	15.10	LEO		11.46	14.36	LEO
	15.49	18.36	VIR		15.11	18.00	VIR		14.37	17.25	VIR
	18.37	21.25	LIB		15.01	20.54	LIB		17.26	20.18	LIB
	21.26	00.00	SCO		20.55	23.42	SCO		20.19	23.06	SCO
					23.43	00.00	SAG		23.07	00.00	SAG
16/3-18/3	00.00	00.15	SCO	25/3-27/3	00.00	02.04	SAG	3/4-5/4	00.00	01.30	SAG
	00.16	02.39	SAG		02.05	03.49	CAP		01.31	03.14	CAP
	02.40	04.24	CAP		03.50	04.58	AQU		03.15	04.22	AQU
	04.25	05.32	AQU		04.59	05.50	PIS		04.21	06.06	PIS
	05.33	06.25	PIS		05.51	06.42	ARI		06.07	07.16	TAU
	06.26	07.18	ARI		06.43	07.52	TAU		07.17	09.04	GEM
	07.19	08.27	TAU		07.53	09.39	GEM		09.05	11.35	CAN
	08.28	10.13	GEM		09.40	12.10	CAN		11.36	14.24	LEO
	10.14	12.27	CAN		12.11	15.00	LEO		14.25	17.12	VIR
	12.28	15.36	LEO		15.01	17.48	VIR		17.13	20.06	LIB
	15.37	18.24	VIR		17.49	20.40	LIB		20.07	22.54	SCO
	18.25	21.15	LIB		20.41	23.30	SCO		22.55	00.00	SAG
	21.16	00.00	SCO		23.31	00.00	SAG				
19/3-21/3	00.00	00.08	SCO	28/3-30/3	00.00	01.51	SAG	5/4-8/4	00.00	01.17	SAG
	00.09	02.25	SAG		01.52	01.38	CAP		01.18	03.03	CAP
	02.26	04.11	CAP		03.39	04.45	AQU		03.04	04.09	AQU
	04,12	05.20	AQU		04.46	05.38	PIS		04.10	05.02	PIS
	05.21	06.13	PIS		05.39	06.30	ARI		05.03	05.55	ARI
	06.14	07.06	ARI		06.31	07.39	TAU		05.56	07.03	TAU
	07.07	08.15	TAU		07.40	09.26	GEM		07.04	08.51	GEM
	08.16	10.00	GEM		09.27	12.00	CAN		08.52	11.24	CAN
	10.01	12.30	CAN		12.01	14.48	LEO		11.25	14.12	LEO
	12.31	15.24	LEO		14.49	17.52	VIR		14.13	17.00	VIR
	15.25	18.12	VIR		17.53	12.30	LIB		17.01	19.54	LIB
	18.23	21.05	LIB		12.31	23.18	SCO		19.55	22.42	SCO
	21.06	23.54	SCO		23.19	00.00	SAG		22.03	00.00	SAG
	23.55	00.00	SAG								

9/4-11/4	00.00	02.49	SAG	18/4-20/4	00.00	00.30	SAG	27/4-29/4	00.00	00.03	SAG
	02.50	03.58	AQU		00.31	02.14	CAP		00.04	01.38	CAP
	03.59	04.50	PIS		02.15	03.22	AQU		01.39	02.17	AQU
	04.51	05.43	ARI		03.23	04.15	PIS		02.18	03.40	PIS
	05.44	06.42	TAU		04.16	05.08	ARI		03.41	04.32	ARI
	06.43	08.39	GEM		05.09	06.16	TAU		04.33	05.40	TAU
	08.40	11.10	CAN		06.17	08.04	GEM		05.41	07.30	GEM
	11.11	14.00	LEO		08.15	10.35	CAN		07.31	10.00	CAN
	14.01	16.50	VIR		10.36	13.24	LEO		10.01	12.48	LEO
	16.51	19.42	LIB		13.25	16.15	VIR		12.49	15.40	VIR
	19.43	22.30	SCO		16.16	19.06	LIB		15.41	18.30	LIB
	22.31	00.00	SAG		19.07	21.35	SCO		18.31	21.20	SCO
					21.36	00.00	SAG		21.21	23.54	SAG
									23.55	00.00	CAP

12/4-14/4	00.00	00.51	SAG	21/4-23/4	00.00	00.21	SAG	30/4-2/5	00.00	01.27	CAP
	00.52	02.38	CAP		00.22	02.03	CAP		01.28	02.36	AQU
	02.39	03.46	AQU		02.04	03.11	AQU		02.37	03.28	PIS
	03.47	04.38	PIS		03.12	04.03	PIS		03.29	04.21	ARI
	04.39	05.32	ARI		04.04	04.56	ARI		04.22	05.30	TAU
	05.33	06.41	TAU		04.57	06.06	TAU		05.31	07.17	GEM
	06.42	08.26	GEM		06.07	07.51	GEM		07.18	09.48	CAN
	08.27	11.00	CAN		07.52	10.24	CAN		09.49	12.36	LEO
	11.01	13.48	LEO		10.25	13.12	LEO		12.37	15.30	VIR
	13.49	16.40	VIR		13.13	16.05	VIR		15.31	18.18	LIB
	16.41	19.30	LIB		16.06	18.04	LIB		18.19	21.06	SCO
	19.31	22.18	SCO		18.45	21.42	SCO		21.07	23.40	SAG
	22.19	00.00	SAG		21.43	00.00	SAG		23.41	00.00	CAP

15/4-17/4	00.00	00.41	SAG	24/4-26/4	00.00	00.12	SAG	3/5-5/5	00.00	01.15	CAP
	00.42	02.27	CAP		00.13	01.51	CAP		01.16	02.12	AQU
	02.28	03.34	AQU		01.52	03.00	AQU		02.13	03.17	PIS
	03.35	04.27	PIS		03.01	03.52	PIS		03.18	04.09	ARI
	04.28	05.21	ARI		03.53	04.45	ARI		04.10	05.19	TAU
	05.22	06.28	TAU		04.46	05.55	TAU		05.20	07.04	GEM
	06.29	08.17	GEM		05.56	07.40	GEM		07.05	09.36	CAN
	08.18	10.48	CAN		07.41	10.12	CAN		09.37	12.25	LEO
	10.49	13.36	LEO		10.13	13.00	LEO		12.26	15.18	VIR
	13.37	16.25	VIR		13.01	15.54	VIR		15.19	18.06	LIB
	16.26	19.18	LIB		15.55	18.42	LIB		18.07	20.55	SCO
	19.19	22.06	SCO		18.43	21.30	SCO		20.56	23.24	SAG
	22.07	00.00	SAG		21.31	00.00	SAG		23.25	00.00	CAP

6/5-8/5	00.00	01.03	CAP	15/5-17/5	00.00	00.28	CAP	24/5-26/5	00.00	00.04	CAP
	01.04	02.11	AQU		00.29	01.36	AQU		00.05	01.02	AQU
	02.12	03.56	PIS		01.37	02.28	PIS		01.03	01.53	PIS
	03.57	05.06	TAU		02.29	03.23	ARI		01.54	02.44	ARI
	05.07	06.51	GEM		03.24	04.30	TAU		02.45	03.55	TAU
	06.52	09.24	CAN		04.31	06.17	GEM		03.56	05.43	GEM
	09.25	12.12	LEO		06.18	08.48	CAN		05.44	08.12	CAN
	12.13	15.05	VIR		08.49	11.40	LEO		08.13	11.05	LEO
	15.06	17.54	LIB		11.41	14.30	VIR		11.06	13.54	VIR
	17.55	20.45	SCO		14.31	17.18	LIB		13.55	16.42	LIB
	20.46	23.13	SAG		17.19	20.10	SCO		16.43	19.35	SCO
	23.14	00.00	CAP		20.11	22.39	SAG		19.36	22.04	SAG
					22.40	00.00	CAP		22.05	23.56	CAP
									23.57	00.00	AQU

9/5-11/5	00.00	00.52	CAP	18/5-20/5	00.00	00.20	CAP	27/5-29/5	00.00	00.49	AQU
	00.53	02.00	AQU		00.21	01.24	AQU		00.50	11.42	PIS
	02.01	02.53	PIS		01.25	02.17	PIS		11.43	02.34	ARI
	02.54	03.45	ARI		02.18	03.10	ARI		02.35	03.14	TAU
	03.46	04.55	TAU		13.11	04.19	TAU		03.15	05.30	GEM
	04.56	06.43	GEM		14.20	06.05	GEM		05.31	08.00	CAN
	06.44	09.12	CAN		06.06	08.36	CAN		08.01	10.54	LEO
	09.13	12.00	LEO		08.37	11.25	LEO		10.55	13.42	VIR
	12.01	14.54	VIR		11.26	14.18	VIR		13.43	16.30	LIB
	14.55	17.42	LIB		14.19	17.06	LIB		16.31	19.24	SCO
	17.43	20.35	SCO		17.07	20.00	SCO		19.25	21.51	SAG
	20.36	23.04	SAG		20.01	22.26	SAG		21.52	23.39	CAP
	23.05	00.00	CAP		22.27	00.00	CAP		23.40	00.00	AQU

12/5-14/5	00.00	00.40	CAP	21/5-23/5	00.00	00.11	CAP	30/5-2/6	00.00	00.38	AQU
	00.41	01.48	AQU		00.12	01.13	AQU		00.39	01.30	PIS
	01.48	02.41	PIS		01.14	02.05	PIS		01.31	02.23	ARI
	02.42	03.34	ARI		02.06	02.58	ARI		02.24	03.33	TAU
	03.35	04.44	TAU		02.59	04.08	TAU		03.34	05.17	GEM
	04.45	06.30	GEM		04.09	05.56	GEM		05.18	07.50	CAN
	06.31	09.00	CAN		05.57	08.25	CAN		07.51	10.42	LEO
	09.01	11.50	LEO		08.26	11.15	LEO		10.43	13.30	VIR
	11.51	14.42	VIR		11.16	14.06	VIR		13.31	16.20	LIB
	14.43	17.30	LIB		14.07	16.55	LIB		16.21	19.10	SCO
	17.31	20.20	SCO		16.56	19.45	SCO		19.11	21.39	SAG
	20.21	22.51	SAG		19.46	22.17	SAG		21.40	23.25	CAP
	22.52	00.00	CAP		22.18	00.00	CAP		23.26	00.00	AQU

Date	Start	End	Sign	Date	Start	End	Sign	Date	Start	End	Sign
3/6-5/6	00.00	00.25	AQU	12/6-14/6	00.00	00.38	PIS	21/6-23/6	00.00	00.11	PIS
	00.26	01.15	PIS		00.39	01.32	ARI		00.12	00.56	ARI
	01.16	02.08	ARI		01.33	02.41	TAU		00.57	02.06	TAU
	02.09	03.16	TAU		02.42	04.26	GEM		02.07	03.51	GEM
	02.17	05.04	GEM		04.27	07.00	CAN		03.52	06.24	CAN
	05.05	07.35	CAN		07.01	09.48	LEO		06.25	09.12	LEO
	07.36	10.24	LEO		09.49	12.40	VIR		09.13	12.05	VIR
	10.25	13.15	VIR		12.41	15.30	LIB		12.06	14.54	LIB
	13.16	16.06	LIB		15.31	18.18	SCO		14.55	17.42	SCO
	16.07	18.54	SCO		18.19	20.47	SAG		17.43	20.13	SAG
	18.55	21.25	SAG		20.48	22.35	CAP		20.14	22.00	CAP
	21.26	23.08	CAP		22.36	23.44	AQU		22.01	23.07	AQU
	23.09	00.00	AQU		23.45	00.00	PIS		23.08	00.00	PIS
6/6-8/6	00.00	00.15	AQU	15/6-17/6	00.00	00.28	PIS	24/6-26/6	00.00	00.03	PIS
	00.16	01.02	PIS		00.29	01.21	ARI		00.04	00.45	ARI
	01.03	01.55	ARI		01.22	02.30	TAU		00.46	01.55	TAU
	01.56	03.17	TAU		02.31	04.17	GEM		01.56	03.40	GEM
	03.18	04.51	GEM		04.18	06.38	CAN		03.41	06.12	CAN
	04.52	07.24	CAN		06.39	09.36	LEO		06.13	09.00	LEO
	07.25	10.12	LEO		09.37	12.25	VIR		09.01	11.54	VIR
	10.13	13.00	VIR		12.26	15.18	LIB		11.55	14.42	LIB
	13.01	15.54	LIB		15.19	18.06	SCO		14.43	17.30	SCO
	15.55	18.42	SCO		18.07	20.39	SAG		17.31	20.00	SAG
	18.43	21.13	SAG		20.40	22.16	CAP		20.01	21.46	CAP
	21.14	22.57	CAP		22.17	23.30	AQU		21.47	22.56	AQU
	22.58	00.00	AQU		23.31	00.00	PIS		22.57	23.51	PIS
									23.52	00.00	ARI
9/6-11/6	00.00	00.07	AQU	18/6-20/6	00.00	00.19	PIS	27/6-29/6	00.00	00.32	ARI
	00.08	00.50	PIS		00.20	01.08	ARI		00.33	01.42	TAU
	00.51	01.44	ARI		01.09	02.16	TAU		01.43	03.30	GEM
	01.45	02.50	TAU		02.17	04.04	GEM		03.31	06.00	CAN
	02.51	04.39	GEM		04.05	06.35	CAN		06.01	08.48	LEO
	04.40	07.10	CAN		06.36	09.24	LEO		08.49	11.40	VIR
	07.10	10.00	LEO		09.25	12.15	VIR		11.41	14.30	LIB
	10.01	12.50	VIR		12.16	15.06	LIB		14.31	17.20	SCO
	12.51	15.42	LIB		15.07	17.55	SCO		17.21	19.51	SAG
	15.43	18.30	SCO		17.56	20.26	SAG		19.52	21.35	CAP
	18.31	21.00	SAG		20.27	22.11	CAP		21.36	23.43	AQU
	21.01	22.46	CAP		22.12	23.19	AQU		23.44	23.38	PIS
	22.47	27.58	AQU		23.20	00.00	PIS		23.39	00.00	ARI
	23.59	00.00	PIS								

30/6-2/7	00.00	00.23	ARI	9/7-11/7	00.00	00.55	TAU	18/7-20/7	00.00	00.23	TAU
	00.24	01.30	TAU		00.56	02.43	GEM		00.24	02.05	GEM
	01,31	03.17	GEM		02.44	05.12	CAN		02.06	04.36	CAN
	03.18	05.48	CAN		05.13	08.00	LEO		04.37	07.25	LEO
	05.48	08.36	LEO		08.01	10.54	VIR		07.26	10.18	VIR
	08.37	11.30	VIR		10.55	13.42	LIB		10.19	13.06	LIB
	11.31	14.18	LIB		13.43	16.35	SCO		13.07	16.00	SCO
	14.19	17.10	SCO		16.36	19.04	SAG		16.01	18.26	SAG
	17.11	19.47	SAG		19.05	20.48	CAP		18.27	20.14	CAP
	19.48	21.24	CAP		20.49	21.56	AQU		20.15	21.21	AQU
	21.25	22.32	AQU		21.57	22.48	PIS		21.22	22.13	PIS
	22.33	23.23	PIS		22.49	23.44	ARI		22.14	23.12	ARI
	23.24	00.00	ARI		23.45	00.00	TAU		23.13	00.00	TAU
3/7-5/7	00.00	00.15	ARI	12/7-14/7	00.00	00.44	TAU	21/7-23/7	00.00	00.14	TAU
	00.16	01.19	TAU		00.45	02.30	GEM		00.15	01.56	GEM
	01.20	03.14	GEM		02.31	05.00	CAN		01.57	04.25	CAN
	03.05	05.36	CAN		05.01	07.50	LEO		04.26	07.15	LEO
	05.37	08.25	LEO		07.51	10.42	VIR		07.16	10.06	VIR
	08.26	11.18	VIR		10.43	13.30	LIB		10.17	22.55	LIB
	11.19	14.06	LIB		13.31	16.20	SCO		22.56	15.45	SCO
	14.47	16.55	SCO		16.21	18.51	SAG		15.46	18.17	SAG
	19.56	19.26	SAG		18.52	20.41	CAP		18.18	20.00	CAP
	19.27	21.11	CAP		20.42	21.44	AQU		20.01	21.09	AQU
	21.12	22.20	AQU		21.45	23.37	PIS		21.10	22.02	PIS
	22.21	23.12	PIS		23.38	23.30	ARI		22.03	22.54	ARI
	23.13	00.00	ARI		23.31	00.00	TAU		22.55	00.00	TAU
6/7-8/7	00.00	00.07	ARI	15/7-17/7	00.00	00.30	TAU	24/7-26/7	00.00	00.06	TAU
	00.08	01.06	TAU		00.31	02.17	GEM		00.07	01.43	GEM
	01.07	03.51	GEM		02.18	04.48	CAN		01.44	04.12	CAN
	03.52	05.24	CAN		04.49	07.40	LEO		04.13	07.05	LEO
	05.25	08.12	LEO		07.41	10.30	VIR		07.06	09.54	VIR
	08.13	11.05	BIR		10.31	13.18	LIB		09.55	12.42	LIB
	11.06	13.54	LIB		13.19	16.10	SCO		12.43	15.35	SCO
	13.55	16.45	SCO		16.11	18.39	SAG		15.36	18.04	SAG
	16.46	19.13	SAG		18.40	20.24	CAP		18.05	19.49	CAP
	19.14	21.00	CAP		20.25	21.33	AQU		19.50	20.58	AQU
	21.01	22.08	AQU		21.34	22.25	PIS		20.59	21.50	PIS
	22.09	23.00	PIS		22.26	23.19	ARI		21.51	22.43	ARI
	23.01	23.56	ARI		23.20	00.00	TAU		22.44	23.54	TAU
	23.57	00.00	TAU						23.55	00.00	GEM

27/7-29/7	00.00	01.30	GEM	5/8-7/8	00.00	00.36	GEM				
	01.31	04.00	CAN		00.37	03.25	CAN	14/8-16/8	00.00	00.24	GEM
	04.01	06.54	LEO		03.26	06.18	LEO		00.25	02.50	CAN
	06.55	09.42	VIR		06.19	09.06	VIR		02.51	05.42	LEO
	09.43	12.30	LIB		09.07	11.55	LIB		05.43	08.30	VIR
	12.31	15.24	SCO		11.56	14.48	SCO		08.31	11.24	LIB
	15.25	17.51	SAG		14.49	17.17	SAG		11.25	14.12	SCO
	17.52	19.38	CAP		17.18	19.03	CAP		14.13	16.43	SAG
	19.39	20.45	AQU		19.04	20.09	AQU		16.44	18.27	CAP
	20.46	21.38	PIS		20.10	21.03	PIS		18.28	19.35	AQU
	21.39	22.30	ARI		21.04	21.55	ARI		19.36	20.27	PIS
	22.31	23.40	TAU		21.56	23.03	TAU		20.28	21.21	ARI
	23.41	00.00	GEM		23.06	00.00	GEM		21.22	22.30	TAU
									22.31	00.00	GEM
30/7-1/8	00.00	01.17	GEM	8/8-10/8	00.00	00.43	GEM	17/8-19/8	00.00	00.15	GEM
	01.18	03.50	CAN		00.44	03.15	CAN		00.16	02.40	CAN
	03.51	06.40	LEO		03.16	06.06	LEO		02.41	05.30	LEO
	06.41	09.30	VIR		06.07	02.47	VIR		05.31	08.18	VIR
	09.31	12.20	LIB		02.48	11.45	LIB		08.19	11.10	LIB
	12.21	15.10	SCO		11.46	14.35	SCO		11.11	14.00	SCO
	15.11	17.29	SAG		14.36	17.04	SAG		14.01	16.30	SAG
	17.40	19.25	CAP		17.05	18.49	CAP		16.31	18.14	CAP
	19.26	20.34	AQU		18.50	18.58	AQU		18.15	19.23	AQU
	20.35	21.27	PIS		19.59	20.50	PIS		19.24	20.15	PIS
	21.28	22.19	ARI		20.51	21.44	ARI		20.16	21.08	ARI
	22.20	23.28	TAU		21.45	22.46	TAU		21.09	22.18	TAU
	23.29	00.00	GEM		22.47	00.00	GEM		22.19	00.00	GEM
2/8-4/8	00.00	01.09	GEM	11/8-13/8	00.00	00.30	GEM	20/8-22/8	00.00	00.02	GEM
	01.10	03.36	CAN		00.31	03.00	CAN		00.03	02.25	CAN
	03.37	06.30	LEO		03.01	05.54	LEO		02.26	05.18	LEO
	06.31	09.18	VIR		05.55	08.36	VIR		05.19	08.06	VIR
	09.19	12.10	LIB		08.37	11.35	LIB		08.07	11.00	LIB
	12.11	15.00	SCO		11.36	14.24	SCO		11.01	13.48	SCO
	15.01	17.30	SAG		14.25	16.51	SAG		13.49	16.17	SAG
	17.31	19.14	CAP		16.52	18.38	CAP		16.18	18.03	CAP
	19.15	20.22	AQU		18.39	19.46	AQU		18.04	19.11	AQU
	20.23	21.15	PIS		19.47	20.39	PIS		19.12	20.03	PIS
	21.16	22.08	ARI		20.40	21.32	ARI		20.04	20.56	ARI
	22.09	23.16	TAU		21.33	22.41	TAU		20.57	22.06	TAU
	23.17	00.00	GEM		22.42	00.00	GEM		22.07	23.55	GEM
									23.56	00.00	CAN

23/8-25/8	00.00	02.15	CAN	1/9-3\9	00.00	01.40	CAN	10/9-12/9	00.00	01.05	CAN
	02.16	05.06	LEO		01.41	04.30	LEO		01.06	03.54	LEO
	05.07	07.55	VIR		04.31	07.20	VIR		03.05	06.45	VIR
	07.56	10.48	LIB		07.21	10.12	LIB		06.46	09.36	LIB
	10.49	13.36	SCO		10.13	13.00	SCO		09.37	12.25	SCO
	13.37	16.04	SAG		13.01	15.30	SAG		12.26	14.56	SAG
	16.05	17.51	CAP		15.31	17.16	CAP		14.57	16.41	CAP
	17.52	19.00	AQU		17.17	18.24	AQU		16.42	17.48	AQU
	19.01	19.52	PIS		18.25	19.17	PIS		17.49	18.42	PIS
	19.53	20.45	ARI		19.18	20.10	ARI		18.43	19.34	ARI
	20.46	21.55	TAU		20.11	21.19	TAU		19.35	20.44	TAU
	21.56	23.40	GEM		21.20	23.04	GEM		20.45	22.30	GEM
	23.41	00.00	CAN		23.05	00.00	CAN		22.31	00.00	CAN
26/8-28/8	00.00	02.05	CAN	4/9-6/9	00.00	01.30	CAN	13/9-15/9	00.00	00.54	CAN
	02.06	04.54	LEO		01.31	04.18	LEO		00.55	03.42	LEO
	04.55	07.42	VIR		04.19	07.10	VIR		03.43	06.35	VIR
	07.43	10.36	LIB		07.11	10.00	LIB		06.36	09.20	LIB
	10.37	13.06	SCO		10.01	12.48	SCO		09.21	12.06	SCO
	13.07	15.55	SAG		12.49	15.17	SAG		12.07	14.43	SAG
	15.56	17.38	CAP		15.18	17.05	CAP		14.44	16.30	CAP
	17.39	18.47	AQU		17.06	18.11	AQU		16.31	17.37	AQU
	18.48	19.40	PIS		18.12	19.05	PIS		17.38	18.30	PIS
	19.41	20.32	ARI		19.06	19.58	ARI		18.31	19.23	ARI
	20.33	21.42	TAU		19.59	21.06	TAU		19.24	20.30	TAU
	21.43	23.30	GEM		21.07	22.51	GEM		20.31	22.17	GEM
	23.31	00.00	CAN		22.52	00.00	CAN		22.18	00.00	CAN
29/8-31/8	00.00	01.50	CAN	7/9-9/9	00.00	01.18	CAN	16/9-18/9	00.00	00.42	CAN
	01.51	04.42	LEO		01.19	04.06	LEO		00.43	03.30	LEO
	04.43	07.30	VIR		04.07	06.55	VIR		03.31	06.20	VIR
	07.31	10.24	LIB		06.56	09.48	LIB		06.21	09.12	LIB
	10.25	13.12	SCO		09.49	12.36	SCO		09.13	12.00	SCO
	13.13	15.43	SAG		12.37	15.08	SAG		12.01	14.30	SAG
	15.44	17.27	CAP		15.09	16.52	CAP		14.31	16.16	CAP
	17.28	19.28	AQU		16.53	18.00	AQU		16.17	17.24	AQU
	19.29	20.21	ARI		18.01	18.53	PIS		17.25	18.17	PIS
	20.22	21.30	TAU		18.54	19.46	ARI		18.18	19.10	ARI
	21.31	00.00	GEM		19.47	20.55	TAU		19.11	20.19	TAU
					20.56	22.43	GEM		20.20	22.05	GEM
					22.44	00.00	CAN		22.06	00.00	CAN

Date	Start	End	Sign	Date	Start	End	Sign	Date	Start	End	Sign
19/9-21/9	00.00	00.30	CAN	28/9-30/9	00.00	00.04	CAN	7/10-9/10	00.00	02.06	LEO
	00.31	03.18	LEO		00.05	02.42	LEO		02.07	05.00	VIR
	03.19	06.10	VIR		02.43	05.35	VIR		05.01	07.51	LIB
	06.11	09.00	LIB		05.36	08.24	LIB		07.52	10.40	SCO
	09.01	11.50	SCO		08.25	11.15	SCO		10.41	13.09	SAG
	11.51	14.20	SAG		11.16	13.43	SAG		13.10	14.54	CAP
	14.21	16.05	CAP		13.44	15.30	CAP		14.55	16.02	AQU
	16.06	17.13	AQU		15.31	16.38	AQU		16.03	16.55	PIS
	17.14	18.05	PIS		16.39	17.30	PIS		16.56	17.48	ARI
	18.06	18.58	ARI		17.31	18.23	ARI		17.49	18.57	TAU
	18.59	20.08	TAU		18.24	19.33	TAU		18.58	20.43	GEM
	20.09	21.56	GEM		19.34	21.17	GEM		20.44	23.15	CAN
	21.57	00.00	CAN		21.18	23.54	CAN		23.16	00.00	LEO
					23.55	00.00	LEO				
22/9-24/9	00.00	00.21	CAN	1/10-3/10	00.00	02.30	LEO	10/10-12/10	00.00	01.55	LEO
	00.22	03.06	LEO		02.31	05.24	VIR		01.56	04.48	VIR
	03.07	06.00	VIR		05.25	08.12	LIB		04.49	07.36	LIB
	06.01	08.48	LIB		08.13	11.00	SCO		07.37	10.30	SCO
	08.49	11.36	SCO		11.01	13.34	SAG		10.31	12.56	SAG
	11.37	14.09	SAG		13.35	15.18	CAP		12.57	14.41	CAP
	14.10	15.54	CAP		15.19	16.26	AQU		14.42	15.40	AQU
	15.55	17.02	AQU		16.27	17.18	PIS		15.41	16.43	PIS
	17.03	17.53	PIS		17.19	18.12	ARI		16.44	17.36	ARI
	17.54	18.47	ARI		18.13	19.22	TAU		17.37	18.45	TAU
	18.48	19.55	TAU		19.23	21.09	GEM		18.46	20.30	GEM
	19.56	21.43	GEM		21.10	23.38	CAN		20.31	23.00	CAN
	21.44	00.00	CAN		23.39	00.00	LEO		23.01	00.00	LEO
25/9-27/9	00.00	00.13	CAN	4/10-6/10	00.00	02.20	LEO	13/10-15/10	00.00	01.45	LEO
	00.14	02.54	LEO		02.21	05.12	VIR		01.46	04.36	VIR
	02.55	05.48	VIR		05.13	08.00	LIB		04.37	07.24	LIB
	05.49	08.36	LIB		08.01	10.50	SCO		07.25	10.15	SCO
	08.37	11.25	SCO		10.51	13.21	SAG		10.16	12.47	SAG
	11.26	13.56	SAG		13.22	15.05	CAP		12.48	14.30	CAP
	13.57	15.41	CAP		15.06	16.14	AQU		14.31	15.39	AQU
	15.42	16.50	AQU		16.15	17.07	PIS		15.40	16.32	PIS
	16.51	17.42	PIS		17.08	18.00	ARI		16.33	17.24	ARI
	17.43	18.34	ARI		18.01	19.09	TAU		17.25	18.33	TAU
	18.35	19.44	TAU		19.10	20.56	GEM		18.34	20.21	GEM
	19.45	21.30	GEM		20.57	23.25	CAN		20.22	22.50	CAN
	21.31	00.00	CAN		23.26	00.00	LEO		22.51	00.00	LEO

Date	Start	End	Sign	Date	Start	End	Sign	Date	Start	End	Sign
16/10-18/10	00.00	01.35	LEO	25/10-27/10	00.00	01.00	LEO	3/11-5/11	00.00	0.26	LEO
	01.36	04.24	VIR		01.01	03.48	VIR		00.27	03.12	VIR
	14.25	07.12	LIB		03.49	06.36	LIB		03.13	06.05	LIB
	07.13	10.05	SCO		06.37	09.30	SCO		06.06	08.54	SCO
	10.06	12.34	SAG		09.31	12.00	SAG		08.55	11.21	SAG
	12.35	14.19	CAP		12.01	13.43	CAP		11.22	13.08	CAP
	14.20	15.28	AQU		13.44	14.52	AQU		13.09	14.16	AQU
	15.29	16.20	PIS		14.53	15.44	PIS		14.17	15.08	PIS
	16.21	17.12	ARI		15.45	16.36	ARI		15.09	16.02	ARI
	17.13	18.22	TAU		16.37	17.46	TAU		16.03	17.11	TAU
	18.23	20.09	GEM		17.47	19.34	GEM		17.12	18.56	GEM
	20.10	22.40	CAN		19.35	22.05	CAN		18.57	21.30	CAN
	22.41	00.00	LEO		22.06	00.00	LEO		21.31	00.00	LEO
19/10-21/10	00.00	01.20	LEO	28/10-30/10	00.00	00.48	LEO	6/11-8/11	00.00	00.17	LEO
	01.21	04.12	VIR		00.49	03.36	VIR		00.18	03.00	VIR
	04.13	07.00	LIB		03.37	06.25	LIB		03.01	05.50	LIB
	07.01	09.54	SCO		06.26	09.18	SCO		05.51	08.42	SCO
	09.55	12.21	SAG		09.19	11.47	SAG		08.43	11.11	SAG
	12.22	14.08	CAP		11.48	13.32	CAP		11.12	12.57	CAP
	14.09	15.15	AQU		13.33	14.39	AQU		12.58	14.04	AQU
	15.16	16.08	PIS		14.40	15.32	PIS		14.05	14.57	PIS
	16.09	17.00	ARI		15.33	16.25	ARI		14.58	15.51	ARI
	17.01	18.09	TAU		16.26	17.33	TAU		15.52	16.58	TAU
	18.10	19.56	GEM		17.34	19.21	GEM		16.59	18.47	GEM
	19.57	22.30	CAN		19.22	21.54	CAN		18.48	21.18	CAN
	22.31	00.00	LEO		21.55	00.00	LEO		21.19	00.00	LEO
22/10-24/10	00.00	01.10	LEO	31/10-2/11	00.00	00.35	LEO	9/11-11/11	00.00	00.09	LEO
	01.11	04.00	VIR		00.36	03.24	VIR		00.10	02.48	VIR
	04.01	06.50	LIB		03.25	06.15	LIB		02.49	05.40	LIB
	06.51	09.40	SCO		06.16	09.05	SCO		05.41	08.30	SCO
	09.41	12.09	SAG		09.06	11.34	SAG		08.31	11.00	SAG
	12.10	13.55	CAP		11.35	13.19	CAP		11.01	12.44	CAP
	13.56	15.56	AQU		13.20	14.28	AQU		12.45	13.52	AQU
	15.57	16.49	ARI		14.29	15.20	PIS		13.53	14.45	PIS
	16.50	17.58	TAU		15.21	16.14	ARI		14.46	14.38	ARI
	17.59	19.45	GEM		16.15	17.22	TAU		15.39	16.46	TAU
	19.46	22.15	CAN		17.23	19.21	GEM		16.47	18.34	GEM
	22.16	00.00	LEO		19.22	21.40	CAN		18.35	21.05	CAN
					21.41	00.00	LEO		21.06	00.00	LEO

12/11-14/11	00.00	02.36	VIR	21/11-23/11	00.00	02.00	VIR	30/11-2/12	00.00	01.25	VIR
	02.37	05.30	LIB		02.01	04.54	LIB		01.26	04.18	LIB
	05.31	06.18	SCO		04.55	07.42	SCO		04.19	07.06	SCO
	06.19	10.47	SAG		07.43	10.13	SAG		07.07	09.38	SAG
	10.48	12.33	CAP		10.14	11.57	CAP		09.39	11.22	CAP
	12.34	13.41	AQU		11.58	13.06	AQU		11.23	12.30	AQU
	13.42	14.33	PIS		13.07	13.58	PIS		12.31	13.23	PIS
	14.34	15.26	ARI		13.59	14.51	ARI		13.24	14.15	ARI
	15.27	16.36	TAU		14.52	16.00	TAU		14.16	15.25	TAU
	16.37	18.21	GEM		16.01	17.47	GEM		15.26	17.13	GEM
	18.22	20.54	CAN		17.48	20.18	CAN		17.14	19.42	CAN
	20.55	23.45	LEO		20.19	23.06	LEO		19.43	22.30	LEO
	23.46	00.00	VIR		23.07	00.00	VIR		22.31	00.00	VIR
15/11-17/11	00.00	02.25	VIR	24/11-26/11	00.00	01.50	VIR	3/12-5/12	00.00	01.14	VIR
	02.26	05.18	LIB		01.51	04.42	LIB		01.16	04.06	LIB
	05.19	08.06	SCO		04.43	07.30	SCO		04.07	06.54	SCO
	08.07	10.34	SAG		07.31	10.00	SAG		06.55	09.26	SAG
	10.35	12.21	CAP		10.01	11.45	CAP		09.27	11.11	CAP
	12.22	13.30	AQU		11.46	12.54	AQU		11.12	12.18	AQU
	13.31	14.22	PIS		12.55	13.47	PIS		12.19	13.11	PIS
	14.23	15.15	ARI		13.48	14.39	ARI		13.12	14.04	ARI
	15.16	16.25	TAU		14.39	15.49	TAU		14.05	15.14	TAU
	16.26	18.10	GEM		15.50	17.34	GEM		15.15	17.00	GEM
	18.11	20.42	CAN		17.35	20.06	CAN		17.01	19.30	CAN
	20.43	23.30	LEO		20.07	22.55	LEO		19.31	22.20	LEO
	23.31	00.00	VIR		22.56	00.00	VIR		22.21	00.00	VIR
18/11-20/11	00.00	02.12	VIR	27/11-29/11	00.00	01.36	VIR	6/12-8/12	00.00	01.05	VIR
	02.13	05.05	LIB		01.37	04.30	LIB		01.06	03.54	LIB
	05.06	07.54	SCO		04.31	07.18	SCO		03.55	06.42	SCO
	07.55	10.25	SAG		07.19	09.47	SAG		06.43	09.13	SAG
	10.26	12.08	CAP		09.48	11.33	CAP		09.14	10.57	CAP
	12.09	13.11	AQU		11.34	12.41	AQU		10.58	17.07	AQU
	13.12	14.10	PIS		12.42	13.35	PIS		12.08	12.58	PIS
	14.11	15.02	ARI		13.36	14.26	ARI		12.59	13.53	ARI
	15.03	16.12	TAU		14.27	15.36	TAU		13.54	15.00	TAU
	16.13	18.00	GEM		15.37	17.21	GEM		15.01	16.47	GEM
	18.01	20.30	CAN		17.22	19.54	CAN		16.48	19.18	CAN
	20.31	23.18	LEO		19.55	22.42	LEO		19.19	22.10	LEO
	23.19	00.00	VIR		22.43	00.00	VIR		22.11	00.00	VIR

Date	Start	End	Sign	Date	Start	End	Sign	Date	Start	End	Sign
9/12-11/12	00.00	00.50	VIR	18/12-20/12	00.00	00.19	VIR	27/12-29/12	00.00	02.30	LIB
	00.51	03.42	LIB		00.20	03.06	LIB		02.31	05.20	SCO
	03.43	06.30	SCO		03.07	05.55	SCO		05.21	07.51	SAG
	06.31	09.00	SAG		05.56	08.26	SAG		07.52	09.35	CAP
	09.01	10.46	CAP		08.27	10.11	CAP		09.36	10.44	AQU
	10.47	11.54	AQU		10.12	11.19	AQU		10.45	11.37	PIS
	11.55	12.47	PIS		11.20	12.12	PIS		11.38	12.30	ARI
	12.48	13.40	ARI		12.13	13.04	ARI		12.31	13.39	TAU
	13.41	14.49	TAU		13.05	14.14	TAU		13.40	15.26	GEM
	14.50	16.35	GEM		14.15	16.00	GEM		15.27	17.55	CAN
	16.36	19.06	CAN		16.01	18.30	CAN		17.56	20.48	LEO
	19.07	21.55	LEO		18.31	21.24	LEO		20.49	23.38	VIR
	21.56	00.00	VIR		21.25	00.00	VIR		23.39	00.00	LIB
12/12-14/12	00.00	00.40	VIR	21/12-23/12	00.00	00.11	VIR	30/12-31/12	00.00	02.18	LIB
	00.41	03.30	LIB		00.12	02.54	LIB		02.19	05.10	SCO
	03.31	06.20	SCO		02.55	05.45	SCO		05.11	08.09	SAG
	06.21	08.50	SAG		05.46	08.13	SAG		08.10	09.24	CAP
	08.51	10.35	CAP		08.14	10.00	CAP		09.25	10.34	AQU
	10.36	11.43	AQU		10.01	11.08	AQU		10.35	11.25	PIS
	11.44	12.35	PIS		11.09	12.00	PIS		11.26	12.18	ARI
	12.36	13.28	ARI		12.01	12.13	ARI		12.19	13.27	TAU
	13.29	14.38	TAU		12.14	14.03	TAU		13.28	15.13	GEM
	14.39	16.26	GEM		14.04	15.47	GEM		15.14	17.45	CAN
	16.27	18.55	CAN		15.48	18.20	CAN		17.46	20.36	LEO
	18.56	21.45	LEO		18.21	21.10	LEO		20.37	23.24	VIR
	21.46	00.00	VIR		21.11	00.00	VIR		23.25	00.00	LIB
15/12-17/12	00.00	03.18	LIB	24/12-26/12	00.00	00.04	VIR				
	03.19	06.06	SCO		00.05	02.42	LIB				
	06.07	08.39	SAG		02.43	05.35	SCO				
	08.40	10.22	CAP		05.36	08.04	SAG				
	10.23	11.32	AQU		08.05	09.48	CAP				
	11.33	12.23	PIS		09.49	19.56	AQU				
	12.24	13.17	ARI		10.57	11.48	PIS				
	13.18	14.25	TAU		11.49	12.42	ARI				
	14.26	16.13	GEM		12.43	13.52	TAU				
	16.14	18.42	CAN		13.53	15.39	GEM				
	18.43	21.35	LEO		15.40	18.06	CAN				
	21.36	00.00	VIR		18.07	21.00	LEO				
					21.01	00.00	VIR				

CHAPTER TWO

The Sun:
Your potential self

What is central to your life? Where do you want to shine? What are your core qualities?

In a sense, the Sun is the fabric of our life and the sign it is in shows us what kind of material we are. The Sun sign at birth is a key factor in determining our essential self expression. It makes up our core personality and identity and forms a large part of the person we recognize ourselves to be. The Sun sign describes the seed of our individuality and so points the way to fulfilling our potential. We possess special gifts or natural talents that resonate with our Sun sign, and we want to make something of ourselves according to this sign. It shows us the main focus of our life-path, and what needs to be developed to fulfil a basic sense of who each of us is. To put it another way we are able to radiate our Sun sign out to others because it is our unique spark of light. The placement of the Sun describes our vitality and life force which can be diminished if we are not able to express our identity in a way that is fulfilling.

Because the Sun sign describes a person's ego or will, it indicates the male side of the character and also how individuals experience 'maleness'. For women, in particular, the placement of the Sun may describe the men in her life as well as the life in her men!

Just as the Sun casts a shadow where light is blocked, each Sun sign also carries a shadow or hidden side that operates as a blind spot, or a block in the personality. Every sign of the zodiac has a diametrically opposite sign. In behaviour, this counterpart embodies the other side, the other end of the scale, yet there is an undeniable link because both signs are joined to the same pole of experience. At times we can 'flip' into our opposite sign, although we may not be aware of it, showing the negative qualities associated with the opposing sign.

For example, those with the Sun in Cancer may hide their sensitivity to such an extent that other people are only aware of a calculating self-protection more usually exhibited by those with a Capricorn Sun sign. The Sun in Virgo may be caught in a fantasy world, pulled towards the escapism that characterizes its opposite sign of Pisces. If we are not feeling good about ourselves we can turn tail - agreeable Libra becomes aggressive, decisive Aries can't make up his mind and so on.

OPPOSING SIGNS

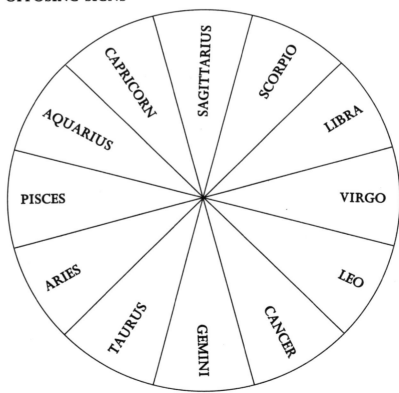

SUN IN ARIES

Drive, impatience, assertiveness, and ambition are quickly in evidence with those born under the symbol of the ram. Aries cannot help but exhibit a natural enthusiasm for getting things done. That means now, not next week or next month. There is no time to stand still when there is so much to be achieved in the results-oriented Aries world. Ariens are keen to move forward and quick to see and set a goal. They really need something (or someone) to pit themselves against, and an inborn courage, boldness and audacity pushes them forward.

Ariens are in their element fighting for something. They need a challenge, a test which engages their competitive instinct. Winning is important to them and those born under the Aries Sun sign are natural leaders, firing others with their zest for life. They are often unaware that they stir up a sense of competition in others through their automatic assumption that they will be first.

A pioneering spirit enables Ariens to dare to create new enterprises. Essentially alert and ready for action, they possess immense energy that is best channelled into a constructive outlet. Ariens must be able to burn off steam, and it is vital that they keep their energy flowing. After all, their idea of a relaxing end to the working day is to trounce an opponent on the squash court.

Staying still is imprisoning to Ariens who want to be on the go, at the forefront of the action. They are impatient with anything that takes up too much of their time and are always looking for the short-cut. Once a project has been established they cast around for another adventure. They simply cannot survive on routine and security, and need something to whip them up into a state of excitement, to feel the adrenalin coursing through their veins.

Aries is associated with the self, and those born under this sign are naturally aware of what they want. The me-first attitude of Aries is free to act without the restraints of long deliberation or excessive sensitivity to others. The impulse to assert is primarily healthy and self-expressive. It is exhilarating to behold an Aries in full battle pose - and every army needs a captain.

SUN IN TAURUS

Patient, stable, constant and practical, Taureans exhibit all the endurance and stamina of the bull that is their symbol. Like the bull, Taureans are capable of putting up with most things for a long time but, pushed too far, they will certainly rampage in the china shop. Then you had better beware, because although a tormented Taurean is at best as stubborn as the immovable object, at worst a thundering raging beast. So steady with the red rag!

Taureans are firmly attached to what they know. They like to build something solid with their lives and are basically grounded in reality. It is important for them to achieve tangible results and that is why they invest so much time and energy in the things in life that can be seen and touched. Material matters are never far from Taureans' minds and a naturally practical instinct helps to procure them the financial security they crave. However, Taureans also derive enormous satisfaction from anything that is solid and lasting. Taurus is the tortoise, not the hare. It is his or her perseverance and cautiousness that enables a Taurean to revel in the career or marriage built up over some 20 or 30 years.

Taureans are not comfortable with too much change or surprise in a lifetime. They thrive on the closeted brand of familiarity that breeds contempt in the fire and air signs.

Taureans possess a natural flair for the good life. They have an inborn taste for good food and comfortable surroundings. Like their earthy cousins, Virgoans and Capricorns, Taureans appreciate the physical body, although they may not wish to exert it in the energetic style of the fiery signs. Taureans know how to relax, how to slow down the pace of life. They enjoy revitalizing the body with a pampering massage or a beautiful walk in the countryside.

Those born under the sign of the bull are able to contain the uncertainties, doubts and confusion of others. They can be relied upon to provide comfort and security - the shoulder to cry on, the rock to cling to. When all else fails, their sense of routine and order keeps life on the straight and narrow. Let others shout from the rooftops or pin their hopes on dreams - Taureans know what makes their lives worth living. A special combination of pure obstinacy and gentle affection permeates their being and ensures their path is steady and companionable.

SUN IN GEMINI
Versatility, movement and communication characterize those born with the Sun in Gemini. As an air sign, Gemini identifies primarily with the mind, and therefore what matters to them is what they are thinking rather than feeling.

The 'doubleness' or duality that Geminis display is reflected in their symbol, the twins. It is easier for Geminis to think in plural terms because they are naturally able to think and do several things at once. They like to blend and mix experiences, believing that variety is the spice of life. Gemini are dazzling in their capacity to keep many things going simultaneously.

They are fascinated by the world of communication which usually proves to be the main arena for their self expression. They are great carriers of ideas and information and, like butterflies, can briefly alight on a particular topic and take it to another place.

It is their questioning attitude and enormous curiosity that makes them seem like a walking directory. However, probe beneath their surface opinion and you may find their knowledge is often superficial. They scan the headlines of life rather than getting bogged down in the small print.

The sign of Gemini is associated with movement of all kinds - a Gemini's mental and physical agility is often breathtaking. Gemini surpasses the other signs as salespeople; they have the gift of the gab and move in many circles with great ease.

Although the sociable nature of Gemini finds them many friends, they often run scared of commitment. Geminis like to keep their options open and their restless natures keeps them juggling all possibilities. It is not surprising that these people live on their nerves; their busy lifestyles demand a hectic pace. They also get bored easily; once something is known it no longer holds their interest so Geminis skip on to the next quest. They can exhibit all the qualities of a Peter Pan - enchanting and infuriating, mesmerising and childlike at once.

A clear, cool head enable Geminis to detach and observe without prejudice. They are skilled tacticians and thrive in an environment where they can use their highly developed logic and verbal skills, yet the duality is ever-present and they can change in the blink of an eye. Geminis will twist and turn to suit the moment. They think on their feet, respond in a split second and move on.

SUN IN CANCER
Nurturing, protecting and providing for others comes easily to those born with the Sun in Cancer. As a water

sign, Cancerians are in touch with the feeling side of life and it is the heart, not the head which dominates their existence. With so much sensitivity and empathy it is important that Cancerians find an outlet for their need to be needed. They seek security, and yet the power of their emotion can overwhelm them to such an extent that they feel they are afloat on dangerous seas. They view life subjectively and the mood of the moment colours everything and everyone.

The crab looks as though it is impervious to the environment with its tough outer shell protecting the soft tissue underneath. Like the crab, those born under the Cancer Sun sign can sometimes look as though nothing touches them; in fact, they never lose sight of their inner vulnerability. They also exhibit the sideways step of the crab, often approaching things in an obscure manner which is non-confrontational.

The personal issues of life are of paramount importance. Cancerians always remember their roots and their purpose is often to provide a sense of security and solid foundation for themselves and others. They need to belong, to feel at home in their environment, and they are capable of creating a sense of family amongst people with whom they feel close.

The actual home is often a true reflection of themselves and it is important for them to have a permanent place to call their own. Cancerians will often carry around with them the sentimental items that become like talismans protecting them from what is unfamiliar and therefore potentially frightening. They are great hoarders and collectors and love to reconnect with the past through objects like the businessman who carries his grandfather's pocket watch.

The sensitivity that enables Cancerians to tune into the feelings of others can create emotional chaos and make it difficult for them to stand back and see the larger perspective. When feelings take over they can become clinging, possessive and unable to let go enough to see others as individuals in their own right. However, the crab is a creature that is equally at home on land or in water, and Cancerians can find satisfaction and poise through balancing their activities in the outer world with their feelings.

SUN IN LEO

The lion is a proud and magnificent beast and Leo radiates the 'king of the jungle' attitude that is both awe-inspiring and impressive. At their best, Leos uplift others with their sunny, generous presence. They are aware of being special and therefore know just how to give out that self-expressive touch that makes others feel appreciated, unique and worthwhile. Leos are capable of making the sun appear to come out around the person, event or experience that they preside over.

Leos are performers at heart. Whatever their chosen work they are capable of producing a star turn to their audience and all they require is the applause and admiration that shows them they are loved. Without the recognition they so badly need, they are dejected souls, the light goes out and they become as unsure of themselves as the lion in the Wizard of Oz.

The dignity and style that is the hallmark of Leo is evident in every aspect of their lives. They won't make do or accept second best because everything must match the level of high standards and quality that drive them. Inevitably, Leo is usually to be found at the centre of things, the centre of attention, the vital nucleus of the team, the star of the show. Leo wants to be the best, and will never pass up an opportunity to bask in the limelight. As leaders, they can be autocratic and egotistical yet, being a fire sign in common with Aries and Sagittarius, they possess the life-giving energy that generates enthusiasm and motivates others to action.

When these lions play, they shine out their infectious warmth which carries a kind of heat and power that can heal others and bring them out of the shadows. They have an inborn sense of fun and sparkle that in its essence is a simple capacity to enjoy life spontaneously like a child.

There is a creative streak in Leo that needs to be expressed if they are to feel truly themselves. Leos need to feel proud of their achievements whether this is seen in his own offspring, or in the birth of an idea. The creative capacity of Leo is evident whether they are staging a children's tea party or Swan Lake.

SUN IN VIRGO
Virgo brings together two worlds - those of the realist and the idealist. In the search for perfection, Virgo sifts through all life's experiences and ultimately finds the best working solution. There is, too, a precise and puritanical streak in Virgo that manifests as parsimony, orderliness and an appreciation of all things useful. Virgo's idea of a good time is to ensure everything is in its place.

The earthy practicality that Virgo exhibits in common with Taurus and Capricorn is combined with a finely tuned capacity for mental analysis. And dotting the i's and crossing the t's comes naturally to Virgoans. They are sticklers for detail and will notice the minutiae that others gloss over.

Unlike Leo, Virgoans tend to hide their light under a bushel. There is a sense of modesty that reflects the Virgoan symbol of the pure maiden, yet often means that while the fire signs are pushing ahead for recognition, Virgo is quietly getting on with the job.

Virgoans cannot help casting their critical eye over everyone and everything. Nothing is taken at face value but analysed, and put through their own personal grading system. This critical faculty can serve a purpose and be constructively employed on the work front. However, Virgoans will not leave the critic behind in the office but bring it home for dinner, much to the chagrin of the family. On the other hand it is the Virgoan penchant for efficiency that keeps them performing all the jobs that keep the wheels of life turning at home.

In fact Virgoans do not stop at worrying, fussing over and analysing everybody else. They are also their own worst critics. It is as if there is a constant voice in their ears saying 'you could do better'. Virgoans can spare no one in their appraisals, least of all themselves, and they can end up their own worst enemies. It is important to Virgo signs to feel useful, to find a niche in life that allows them to do what they do best, and that is often found at the service of others. Virgoans can easily fall into the role of martyr, running around after everyone else, performing all the thankless tasks that are the routine duties of the day.

Virgo is essentially a gentle soul harbouring a mind that works on constant overtime and no-one appreciates like Virgo the ability to 'do your best' rather than coming first.

SUN IN LIBRA
Librans perform a great balancing act throughout life. As soon as someone starts to tip the scales one way or the other Librans begin to weigh up the situation and form a line of argument for the other point of view. Suddenly the scales start to tip back the other way. Yet Librans do want the scales to stop somewhere in the middle. The Libran sense of harmony depends on maintaining a balance. Yet the scales keep moving; Libra is constantly engaged

in working out the give and take in a relationship.

It is also true that Librans enjoy sitting on the fence. In this position they can measure up both options and actually see whether the grass is greener on the other side before making a choice. Librans cannot be forced into making that vital decision. They feel uncomfortable taking the initiative and are far happier biding their time until you have shown your hand so they can act accordingly. This is not to say that Librans are damp squibs; they usually get what they want.

In the popularity stakes, Librans score highly. They display the same pleasant manner whether you are Mother Theresa or the Yorkshire Ripper. Even as babies, Librans seem to know the power of a perfectly timed happy smile that defuses the tension between mother-in-law and mother. However the desire to please and always act the nice guy comes with its own price tag, and only Librans know the cost to their well-being when suppressed anger lurks behind their amiable manner. Librans often want to be true to themselves, and yet their own inner balance depends on them learning how to recognize their own feelings.

Because Librans have an innate appreciation of beauty, they are often drawn towards work that allows expression of their creativity and sense of style. As air signs, Librans often find the proportion and symmetry they seek through words rather than material objects. However, looks are of the utmost importance to them, too, and go right across the board from choice of partner to choice of kitchen kettle.

As negotiators or diplomats Librans have a whole box of tricks unrivalled anywhere else in the zodiac. They are able to charm the public, deflect criticism, and smooth over difficulties. They do their best to make sure everyone has a fair deal (or thinks they have). Librans always put their best foot forward, although they may have a reputation for being lazy. In fact, they have such a knack for packaging and presenting everything 'in the best possible taste' that they make it look effortless.

SUN IN SCORPIO
Those born with the powerful light of the Sun in the mysterious sign of Scorpio discover much about what is usually hidden from view in life. Scorpios are concerned not so much with what takes place on a day-to-day level as with understanding the meaning of what happens.

Scorpios believe that there is usually more to everything than initially meets the eye. They will delve right into the heart of the issue in pursuit of the absolute truth. However dazzling the outer image, Scorpios will dismiss it if it contains no inner substance - that goes for people, places and activities. They will penetrate through the surface to see if something is worth investigating and, if not it will be cast aside like a doughnut devoid of jam.

Scorpios will sting when threatened, and because they are so aware of their own vulnerability, they know just where to hurt you. Their intuition and instinctive feeling for people gives them access to the parts other signs cannot reach. Therefore they can become unusually close to others, sharing a communion with the inner person. Their insight into human nature poses them the ultimate choice of whether to use their knowledge as a vehicle to hurt or to heal. They are capable of letting people into their lives to the most extraordinary degree or locking them out and throwing away the key.

The intensity with which Scorpio approaches life can be disconcerting to those happy to skate on the surface. Yet Scorpios are driven by their passionate nature, and daily wrestle to keep their powerful emotions under control. You would not necessarily be aware of the turbulence that lies at the heart of Scorpio because they like to present themselves as being in control, even detached. Do not be fooled. Scorpios can put forward a barrage of light and frothy banter, or a stunningly convincing cool poise but both are deceptive. The inner world of Scorpio constantly churns.

No one is better in a crisis than Scorpio. With so much in reserve, they can summon up a hidden strength, as easily as switching on a hidden turbo charge. They are great survivors, which is just as well considering the life-path of Scorpio is often strewn with many emotional challenges. Even after coming to the end of one particular road, Scorpios can find a new journey and phoenix-like transform themselves on to a new level.

SUN IN SAGITTARIUS

The archer needs to aim his arrows at a particular goal. Sagittarians must have a vision of something, some potential to work at to keep their vitality and enthusiasm flowing. They are always on the way somewhere in their mind, if not in their bodies too, and although they can inspire others with their optimism, they often overlook the reality of the here and now.

For them there is always something bigger and better just over the horizon. Where Geminis cannot see the wood for the trees, their opposite number, Sagittarians, cannot see the trees for the wood. They are often lost in the larger perspective and unable to focus.

Sagittarians will not accept something purely at face value because they can usually see where it might lead. They are one step ahead. The problem is the natural Sagittarian tendency to run away with themselves. It must have been a Sagittarian who invented the line 'think of a number and double it'.

These individuals hate to be confined; they need space and freedom to express themselves. In a sense, they are larger than life and cannot be contained in a small environment. Fun and frolic is life-blood to this sign. Sagittarians need room to play and, the world can seem like one gigantic playroom to them as they lurch from one adventure to the next. As a fire sign they can seem boisterous, clumsily falling over themselves and riding roughshod over dangerous ground. They never mean to step on other people's toes; they are just over-eager, like puppy dogs.

It often seems as though the end of the rainbow has been magnetised into the lap of Sagittarians. They have a lucky touch and always seem to be able to pull something out of the hat. It is because Sagittarians are born optimists, always believing that things will turn up for them that they usually do. They are the chief exponents of positive thinking - it certainly works for them.

They can teach the other signs a thing or two about perspective - for them the bottle is always half full, never half empty. They will always advise you to take that risk, follow that hunch and keep an eye on the main chance.

SUN IN CAPRICORN

Those with the Sun in Capricorn share with Taurus and Virgo the over-riding need to find security, and likewise it is in visible earth-bound form that Capricorns tend to measure their sense of well-being. Capricorns are no shirkers, and they are always prepared to put in a great deal of effort to get what they want and never expect something for nothing. Like mountain goats, they are willing to make the climb to the top, but can be blind to anything other than proving their capacity to reach the goal. It can be hard for Capricorns to let go and enjoy the scenery. Self-control and self-discipline keep them on their chosen path, but often they put in more effort than is really required.

Although they can resemble Atlas, carrying the responsibility of the world on their shoulders (and chronic back pain is associated with this sign), Capricorns actually thrive on being in charge. Capricorns with no duties to attend to, no routine to organize, feel purposeless. They operate at their best when they are stretched to the limit and other people rely on them.

Capable Capricorns enjoy money and position - job title, status and recognition are important to them. They like to feel accepted by others and possessions are seen as an important communication of worldly standing. Their legendary patience and staying power in achieving their ambition ensures that they well and truly earn their rewards.

Suspicious by nature, Capricorns like to have proof that everything is present and correct, and they are not the type to try short cuts or trust to luck. In fact, when it comes to trust, Capricorns often feel at a loss. They are not equipped to follow their intuition or to allow themselves to be swept away on impulse. They are essentially realists and like their feet to be on solid ground.

The defensive nature of Capricorns can make them appear serious and stand-offish, when in fact they are shy and self-conscious. This lack of spontaneity often stems from a childhood that requires Capricorn to grow up quickly. In fact, they often feel as if they were never able to be children and feel denied the freedom to express themselves that comes so easily to Leos.

Capricorns value permanence above all else, and their loyalty and ability to endure setbacks keeps them true to their commitments. They like to be the mainstay, the structure holding the family or the business together. Capricorns invest their time wisely, knowing that their turn will come eventually and, when it does, they will be prepared..

SUN IN AQUARIUS

Aquarius holds an inherent contrast because it is the sign of both the individual and of the group. How to stay true to oneself whilst maintaining the best interests for other people is often a recurring theme in the life of an Aquarius.

Aquarius is frequently mistaken for a water sign, yet the water bearer pours forth ideas which are borne from his airy mentality rather than his feelings. Aquarius grapples with concepts and thoughts rather than emotions. They stand back from the mire of involvement and detach themselves from what they see. Only then can they get a clear picture of what is going on. They are concerned with the over-view, not the personal content. Their friendly interest may extend to discussing your opinions on the merits of natural childbirth, but they will be bored to tears by the tale of a baby cutting her first tooth. These rational souls attract so many friends largely because they will not allow subjective feelings to magnify petty differences and interfere with their capacity to relate to people.

Aquarians do like to live their lives unfettered by other people's expectations. They must be free to carve their own paths in their own style, otherwise their ability to come up with original ideas is severely debilitated. Craving excitement, they are at home in an environment that is constantly changing. they thrive on the unexpected, the sudden ups and downs that drive the earth signs to despair. For Aquarius any change, however disruptive, is essentially a breath of fresh air - the stuff of life that allows something new to emerge.

Aquarians are uncomfortable with the non-rational side of life. they like things that can be explained logically. Systems and theories are of infinite interest to them, whereas outbursts of feeling leave them cold.. And they do have a reputation for hovering several degrees below human temperature in the emotional stakes. It is not that Aquarians cannot feel, they just cannot *explain* how they feel. They are actually very caring and concerned, but the changing moods and screaming hab dabs of their more expressive watery and fiery cousins leave them perplexed. Why can't they just think things through?

Aquarians are idealists. Their vision of how things ought to be is an inspiration, yet often cannot be wholly translated into life. For all their team efforts they can still feel like outsiders and misunderstood by those who cannot soar into their universal perspective.

SUN IN PISCES

The highly sensitive fish swims with the current of life, flowing with whatever comes along. Pisceans, in common with Cancerians and Scorpios, can become caught up in their feelings. They do best when accepting natural rhythm and process of life.

Their impressionable natures respond immediately to change in the atmosphere and enable them to fit in exactly with their environment. The ability to adapt comes so easily to them that they may not even be aware of it, or even of themselves as separate individuals with their own preferences, wants and needs; Pisceans can be so busy responding to their partners, parents, clients or bosses that they lose sight of themselves. Somehow the fish gets swallowed up.

The romantic and creative spirit of Pisceans is unmistakable. Even when behind a dental drill, or in the guise of the local estate agent, Pisceans have a dream. There is something that fires their imaginations and, in their minds, 'takes them away from all this': Pisceans need to feed themselves with something uplifting; they need to escape from reality from time to time. Many Pisceans actually help others to soar above the real world, for instance, by capturing something magical on film, or on stage or by extending their compassionate healing to those in pain.

The unique capacity for selflessness enables Pisceans to give so much to others. The flip side of all this altruism is the Piscean capacity for avoidance - which can mean anything from avoiding confrontation to avoiding paying the bills!

Pisceans can often feel adrift in life. they can go through periods of emotional confusion where they cannot really be sure of what they want. Unlike Ariens, who are first to dive in, Pisceans stand around not really sure whether they should or shouldn't or, if they do, what the consequences might be. Strangely, it is because Pisceans know the state of unknowingness that they are able to connect with others. Pisceans see so many shades of grey in between the black and white that they have a special kind of vision to offer.

SUN SIGN TABLES

Aries	March 21 - April 20
Taurus	April 21 - May 21
Gemini	May 22 - June 21
Cancer	June 22 - July 23
Leo	July 24 - August 23
Virgo	August 24 - September 23
Libra	September 24 - October 23
Scorpio	October 24 - November 22
Sagittarius	November 23 - December 22
Capricorn	December 23 - January 20
Aquarius	January 21 - February 19
Pisces	February 20 - March 20

CHAPTER THREE

The Moon:
Your home life

What are you like in private? What type of home do you have?
How do you show your feelings? What makes you feel secure?

Discovering the sign that the Moon is in at birth adds a new dimension when interpreting a person's astrological profile. Whereas the Sun gives orientation in the outer life, the Moon relates to the inner, private world. Each of the twelve Moon signs describes the conditions that people need in order to feel secure at their roots. In other words the position of the Moon enables us to see what a person really needs in order to feel truly comfortable and 'at home.' Because the Moon is linked to the emotions, its position at birth will describe how a person responds emotionally. In this sense it is related to feminine rather than masculine themes in life. But whether people are male or female the Moon's placement will describe how they take care of others and will reveal how they were looked after in their early years. The Moon sign will give a picture of the type of mother and home a person had as a child.

What is nurturing to one person is suffocating to another and the level of closeness needed for optimum contentment will be shown by the sign of the Moon. In general, the fire signs Aries, Leo and Sagittarius, thrive on outbursts of feeling. Earthy Taurus, Virgo and Capricorn prefer constancy and stability and attach importance to material security. The emotional needs of the airy signs, Gemini, Libra and Aquarius, are fed by expressing their thoughts, and enjoying plenty of space. The water signs Cancer, Scorpio and Pisces perceive life through their feelings and value emotional connections between people above all else.

Comparing the Moon and Venus: security and romantic attraction

The Moon sign will reveal emotional patterns in both sexes. For a man, it will give clues as to the kind of woman with whom he feels comfortable. Although the Venus sign may reveal the type of lover he feels attracted to, a man will often marry someone resembling his Moon sign (and the Moon describes the mother so we can see how history repeats itself). For instance, if a man has Venus in Scorpio and the Moon in Capricorn he may lust after Lolita with the flashing eyes and the promise of passion, but when you meet his wife she is a formidably organized type of woman, dressed for success rather than sex.

A man with the Moon in a sign that expresses itself in a completely different mode to his Venus sign will act in one way during the wooing and another after marriage. Take a man with Venus in Leo and the Moon in Cancer. In the throes of romance, when Venus is at its height, he will shower a woman with expensive presents and treat her like a Leonine Princess. But, after their dressing gowns are hanging on the same door, his Moon in Cancer will require someone to mother him. So it is as well for a woman to check out a man's Moon and Venus sign so she can be prepared for any changes in temperature!

A woman's Moon sign will describe how she embodies an image of womanhood as a mother or partner. If the Moon and Venus are in the same element, she feels able to flow easily between her role as a wife, mother and lover. If, however, the Moon and Venus are in any other combination then there is more tension between the roles, which jar when shifting from one to the other. For example, to a woman with Moon in Taurus a comfortable family life means mountains of home cooking and a stable domestic routine. However, with Venus in Aquarius she will long for excitement and freedom and feel an attraction towards independence and lack of 'ties' in relationships. She also needs plenty of friends to provide mental stimulation. We have seen how important it is to consider both the

Comparing the Moon and Sun: how we are in private and public

Moon and Venus when looking at relationship patterns. It is also vital to see how the Sun and Moon signs of the individual work together to find out whether the outer and inner life are either integrated or disjointed.

If the Sun and Moon are both in signs of the same element then there is little conflict between the outer and inner life. Combinations of air and fire signs or water and earth enable people to establish a home life that supports them as individuals. However, if there is an air/water, air/earth, fire/earth or fire/water mix, then they have to work at keeping a balance in life as their emotional needs are at odds with how they want to develop in the world. For instance, the chatty Gemini salesman with Moon in Scorpio may withdraw into silence with his family. The ambitious Aries Sun is a powerhouse of drive at work but, with a Pisces Moon, will flop in front of the TV with a glass of wine at home.

THE ELEMENT OF FIRE
ARIES, LEO, SAGITTARIUS,

THE ELEMENT OF AIR
GEMINI, LIBRA, AQUARIUS

THE ELEMENT OF WATER
CANCER, SCORPIO, PISCES,

ELEMENT OF EARTH
TAURUS, VIRGO, CAPRICORN

MOON IN ARIES

The vibrancy of Moon in Aries makes itself felt like a laser beam. Whatever the level of activity of the Sun sign, the individual with the Moon in Aries is bursting with impulsive feelings. Moon in Aries reacts immediately to any situation, is quick to feel anger, love and sadness and is equally quick to recover.

As children, people with the Moon in Aries felt their mothers' desire to get things done quickly, so they learnt to be decisive because there were no second chances. Those with the Moon in Aries instinctively reach out to grab what they need to feel secure. Their lack of patience can mean that they are itching to tie the knot, buy the house, produce the family before they are truly ready. For Ariens, feeling something means doing it. If they wait then the feeling and the urge to do it may pass so they believe in striking while the iron is hot.

Ariens need passion and action around them and, because the Moon is related to domestic life, this can frequently lead to family fireworks. The home of someone with the Moon in Aries is alive with a constant buzz, with people coming and going, doing their own thing, sparring and making up. Peace and tranquillity are hard to come by in the Aries home as this is the place where he or she switches on rather than off.

This Moon sign carries a very strong image of femininity. For a man this can mean that he is used to women making the domestic decisions. He wants his partner to be capable and independent, to run things without turning to him for support on every detail. Women with Moon in Aries will need to feel independent and unfettered by the kitchen sink.

People with the Moon in Aries have a desire to get on with things. It is hard for them to slow down because relaxation comes from some form of activity. Emotionally, too, they are in a rush and tend to over-react because they do not allow themselves time to get the right end of the stick. Their hot-bloodedness and passion make their emotional life rather lively. They have the capacity to stir up feelings with their direct approach. They know how they feel and want to act on emotions immediately. Unfortunately, once the heat of the moment has gone Aries has usually long gone too. This sign always poses something of an emotional challenge.

The home is usually awash with time-saving gadgetry and meals are taken on the hoof, as people with the Moon in Aries are always in a hurry. Things around the home are done on the spur of the moment. They are not ones painstakingly to stencil the kitchen floor; for them decoration must be achieved with the minimum of fuss and delay. Pondering over paint palettes is not their scene; they want instant results even if their initial rapture with Sizzling Pink does wear a bit thin a week later.

MOON IN TAURUS

Those with the Taurus Moon are eminently comfortable where they are, digging in their heels when it comes to making any suggested change in their domestic life even though it might be the greatest idea since Newton cracked gravity. It is not that they cannot appreciate improvements - Taureans will always hanker after the good life - it is just that they cannot bear the unknown.

These types like their emotional life to be on an even keel and they are not prone to sudden ups and downs or changes of direction. Loyalty is important to them, and they enjoy protecting and providing for others. Holding the home and family together is a prime source of emotional security for both men and women with this Moon sign. Because Taurus is associated with money, a man with this sign will often feel that his role is to provide financial security, and he feels comfortable with the sort of partner who would not dream of making cheese sauce from a packet.

Because they are content with stability, people with the Moon in Taurus focus on what exists for them in the here and now, not what might be or could be just over the horizon. This eliminates much of the dreaming that takes place with some other Moon signs and allows them truly to enjoy the present.

Taurus Moons tend to idealize the image of the Earth Mother - the capable, all-sustaining archetype of motherhood who rests a child on one hip whilst baking the bread. Although his or her real mother may not embody this image exactly, she is usually resourceful and placid, and models the Taurean virtues of patience and constancy for the child. As a mother, Moon in Taurus may place higher value on sustaining the physical needs of the child before the emotional ones. In later life, good food remains a typical Taurean comfort and, in times of stress, Taurus Moon is likely to assuage angst via the stomach.

At home, Taurus Moon likes to do things 'properly', which usually means one thing at a time and at their own pace. They are great family organizers and believe in the traditional rituals of family life such as eating at the table. They are pulled towards preserving the status quo at home and fulfilling some kind of rosy family picture. Unconsciously, Taurus Moon believes that a log fire, crumpets for tea and a family game of Monopoly equals all that is secure in life.

Taurus Moons may not show their feelings in words, but they are able to demonstrate how much they care through the things they do for you. To them, giving you a perfectly timed cup of tea is the same as saying they love you. Being such a tactile sign, touch speaks louder than words - read the message in the massage. Although their stubbornness can aggravate those of more flighty nature, they are adept at providing a comforting form of stability which is a container for the passing whims of some of the other Moon signs.

MOON IN GEMINI

Geminian Moon people are at heart thinkers. Many things go round and round in their heads and they do not just feel; they tend to think about what they feel. They enjoy environments that feed their minds, and allow variety and knowledge to stimulate them. For this reason, they are uncomfortable with too much constancy, and like to be able to come and go as they please. Gemini Moon types feel happiest when on the move, so they are natural commuters between places. In many respects, having two homes is the ideal for these people, as they can flex their duality trying to have the best of both worlds.

The Geminian nature finds it hard to focus, and emotionally this makes for a lot of wear and tear on the nervous system. Those with Gemini Moon are like bloodhounds, sniffing the atmosphere for change. They juggle all the possibilities and eventualities. They can feel constantly distracted and on edge because, for them, something else is always about to happen.

The mother depicted by the Gemini Moon is one who may have her mind on both her baby and something completely different at the same time. Thus the infant responds by becoming aware of subtle changes in the environment. A busy background surrounds the Gemini Moon baby, who learns from the cradle how to adapt and be flexible.

Emotionally, Gemini Moon types feel threatened by soul-searching - surely there are other more interesting things to search for?

At the first sign of light-hearted banter turning more meaningful they will squirm uncomfortably and side-step the issue. Occasionally, you will catch sight of their feelings expressed in a look or a word that says it all, but you are only allowed a fleeting glimpse as this mercurial Moon wings on to the next subject. The male version of this Moon sign wants a home life which is undemanding, that is, emotionally undemanding. His partner must be prepared for sudden changes of plan without the bat of an eyelid.

Living with this Moon sign can mean that you are in constant competition with the telephone or newspaper for attention. Gemini Moon people like to be up on what's going on in the world. They hate to miss out on 'the latest'. That means both next door and in Outer Mongolia. A woman with Moon in Gemini is hard to pin down in the home, and is constantly flitting hither and thither leaving an endless trail of notes on the kitchen table: 'gone to the museum', 'gone shopping', sometimes 'gone away'!

Both sexes relate through the mind, so the secret to their hearts is to run down the convoluted corridors of their brains to catch their curiosity. After that, it is really just a matter of making sure that you are never short of an opinion. It does not matter if you change your mind the next day, it is your ability to play mental gymnastics that counts. If you stay supple enough to argue your way through a couple of double back flips and mid-air somersaults, they will be happy to stay at home just to spectate!

MOON IN CANCER

People born under the sign of Moon in Cancer are highly sensitive and emotionally aware; so much so that feelings tend to spill over into every aspect of life. Both men and women with this Moon sign relate to the image of mothering and looking after others. Infants with Moon in Cancer were on the receiving end of a kind of nurturing that was based on their having all their needs met, particularly the emotional needs. Later on, they look for this bond to be repeated with another person, expecting unconditional love and total emotional bonding. Of course, this kind of love is not always available from one adult to another, and Moon in Cancer adults can have a hard time making the adjustment to being with people who are insensitive to their needs. They are, however, exceptionally able to provide emotional support for others.

These Moon signs live with their emotional antennae permanently switched on, so they are usually aware of subtle shifts of mood in other people. They cannot help tuning into how other people are feeling and, if any form of 'looking after' is needed, they are first on the spot. A man with Moon in Cancer needs an exceptionally supportive domestic life, and loves to come home to roost, while a woman with Moon in Cancer views her personal life as the mainstay of her entire existence. And, if the vital emotional connection is missing in a relationship with another, both sexes are off-balance, guarded and defensive.

Cancer Moons are homely types, preferring familiar surroundings stashed with personal belongings. They are great hoarders, filling their homes with items of sentimental value. These Moon signs cannot live in the present without some reminders of the past. Therefore much emotional security is invested in Grandma's tea set, or the childhood teddy bear.

The family is of the utmost importance to these placements because they yearn for a sense of closeness and belonging. If this is missing in the family of origin, they will re-create it outside the blood-line with friends and colleagues - whoever said you can't choose your family had overlooked Moon in Cancer!

To live with Cancer Moon types means acknowledging an ever changing kaleidoscope of moods and feelings. Although this might rock the earth signs off balance, Cancer Moons actually get their stability through being in touch with their feelings. But sometimes they can be overwhelmed by emotions and their acute responsiveness can land them in emotional chaos; this is when they literally become 'crabby'. Other signs may cut off from emotions or shut out anything they do not wish to deal with. Those with Moon in Cancer have to find a way to accept that feelings are the linchpin of their existence. If you live with one, you will experience the kind of close communion that really makes it feel as though 'there's no-place like home!'

MOON IN LEO

What the lion needs most of all in order to feel secure and comfortable is affection and attention. Even if the Sun is in detached Aquarius, or practical Virgo, this Moon sign is a pussy cat at home, needing to bask in a sense of specialness and receive the kind of appreciation due to a king of the jungle!

The mother of the child born with Moon in Leo has usually developed a strong sense of who she is and therefore helps the child to form his own identity at a young age. Leo Moon types usually romp through their early years and carry with them a spontaneous playfulness which tends to last until they are 60.

Leo Moon places value on nurturing the self - for a woman with this placement going to the hairdresser to get the Leonine locks cut assumes the significance of an important rite that takes precedence over most other things. To feel truly comfortable in life, Moon Leo likes to lighten the load of daily responsibility with a little self-indulgence. A man with Moon in Leo does not want to come home to a woman knee-deep in domestic drudgery. His partner is his consort, not his caretaker. Moon in Leo gets more satisfaction from showing her off than from knowing his cupboards are clean.

As the proudest sign, Leo Moon signs need to be treated with respect, or their generous spirits can vanish in an instant. Wounding their feelings is taking the greatest risk. Any taste of humiliation incenses the lion - he really does need to be handled with care. So roll out the red carpet for the sign that likes to feel important.

Emotionally, Leos feel things on a grand scale. If they are in love it lights up their whole being. If they are unhappy they may attack in order to restore their self-confidence. They tend not to wallow in self-pity, and, as they are naturally active, they will usually find a way to redress the balance.

People with the Moon in Leo do like to be numero uno in their own home. They are not the type to save money by slipping into someone else's bathwater - although they will allow you to rub their backs! They will not skimp on furnishings and their homes often have grand touches. With a natural sense of theatre, they like to create an atmosphere that provides a perfect backdrop to their presence. Even their curtains seem to remind one of the stage, and of a performance about to begin.

Provided Leo Moon receive a certain amount of pampering, they radiate their warmth around their home and family. They are at their best on special occasions when their over-the-top style lifts an event out of the ordinary. However, living with Moon Leo types means not having to wait for high days and holidays because they live their lives at this level for much of the time.

MOON IN VIRGO

When the Moon is in the perfectionist sign of Virgo, it is not easy for the person to relax without feeling there is something else to be done. This Moon sign can feel constantly on the hop trying to keep personal life and home in order.

Virgo tends to worry over the details and this can create double work on the home-front. The military precision with which those born under this Moon sign co-ordinate their home lives is ingrained. These are the people who have to have the creases in their trousers just right and set great store by cleanliness and hygiene. I know of someone with this placement who once missed her holiday flight because she was so busy tidying up the house and ironing new sheets for her bed before she went away.

The Virgo Moons fuss over their loved ones like mother hens and usually their own mothers are more concerned with clean shoes and teeth than anything else. Their childhoods often revolve around practical matters so that they appear very well looked after. Yet often the emotional care, the simple spontaneous hug, is lacking in their backgrounds. Moon in Virgo children are often keenly aware of the critical eye of their mothers and embark on life with a slightly anxious feeling that they have to organize their lives to the highest standards.

When Virgo Moons are not preoccupied in analysing the 'E' additives in their groceries or the chalk level in their water, they are busy analysing YOU. Once their feelings are engaged, they begin the process of defining all the whys and wherefores of the relationship. All the little differences between them and their partners that would go unnoticed by any other sign are meticulously picked up and noted by Virgo Moon. It can be pretty disconcerting to have the way you peel potatoes, slice bread and take off your socks remarked upon, but people who live with a Moon in Virgo get used to it!

Virgo Moon placements are generally kind and concerned about those close to them. Both sexes are natural givers and feel comfortable with the concept of service. They enjoy the feeling of security it gives them to create order in life and, since this is their forte, they can usually organize you better than you can yourself!

When the Moon is in Virgo, there is a natural inclination to criticize. In fact the level of criticism is a good barometer of the feelings with this sign. The man with this Moon placement will gripe about small details when he is feeling insecure - if he is relaxed he will still comment on the fact that your roots are showing. Women with the Moon in Virgo would never let their roots show anyway!

MOON IN LIBRA

As an air sign, Libra is essentially cerebral, and it can appear that Moon in Libra placements are caught up in the thinking process when it comes to feelings. This has more to do with achieving something, some sort of inner balance, than actually expressing feelings aloud.

Everything in the carefully measured Libran world is snipped and tailored into a beautiful pattern, and feelings are adjusted to fit the situation. The Libran man will feel in a way that he considers is appropriate to the moment. That means he will readily tell you he loves you over a candlelit dinner, but not when you are wearing a face pack!

People born with Moon in Libra pick up their great appreciation of beauty from their mothers, and are usually encouraged to recognize what is attractive, pretty and desirable from a young age. Subsequently, they set great store by appearance and find it difficult to feel positively about anything or anyone who shows more clash than dash. A man with Moon in Libra wants to come home to a domestic set-up that is beautiful and unruffled, and this includes his partner. Women with Moon in Libra go to great lengths to keep everything smooth on the home front.

Moon in Libra children are the sort who never get chocolate round their mouth or have tantrums in the supermarket. From the outset they know that if they are good, they will be loved, and they grow up with their sense of survival based upon pleasing others. Later in life it can be hard for these people to learn to express their true feelings. It is ingrained in them to 'do the right thing', 'be the right way', and they can have very little idea as to what feels right for them as opposed to what others expect from them.

At home, Moon in Libra types like the atmosphere to be harmonious. Everything is tastefully arranged, and the ideal is for all family members to be nice to each other. They may bemoan their frequent position as 'the one in the middle' of the argument, but derive satisfaction from mediating and negotiating between sides. In this house, eating your spinach in return for a later bedtime is par for the course.

People with the Moon in Libra know how to make their partners feel appreciated. With the Moon in the sign of romance, partners might expect to find sentimental notes pinned to their satin sheets every night. Living with someone who has this Moon sign can come close to the proverbial bed of roses, but sometimes it can be hard to get comfortable with all those flowers in the way. Moon in Libra placements can use romance almost to obscure the need for real emotional contact. Ill at ease with strong feelings that threaten to upset the balance of their scales, they will charmingly deflect anything that looks as if it will spill over and spoil their beautiful picture. For them, emotional security depends on maintaining a peaceful equilibrium.

MOON IN SCORPIO
Feelings are exceptionally powerful with the Moon in this sign although they are not often on public view. Scorpio Moons like to keep their feelings hidden and under control. You may be amazed at the stillness of the glacier, but prepare for an avalanche.

Even as babies, those born with the Moon in Scorpio were able to discern all the undercurrents in the atmosphere. It is as if their nerve endings are directly linked into the feelings of others, often picking up messages that are not in conscious awareness. It is often said that Scorpio has a kind of x-ray vision, and when the Moon is in this sign, the individual can see straight through people's words to what they are actually feeling inside.

It can be difficult for Scorpio Moons to trust others because they are often on the receiving end of contradictory messages. It is as if they have access to a kind of double vision. How can they believe you when you say you love them if they feel you are holding something back? Men with Moon in Scorpio rather expect some kind of trial and tribulation on the home front. They feel more comfortable with a partner's tirades and tears, which at least means she is still connected, rather than absently grinning and bearing it. Women with Moon in Scorpio cannot live 'falsely' - acres of ruched curtains and handmade kitchen floor tiles will not make up for an acre of empty space in her personal relationships. She will not pretend for anyone, not even her mother-in-law. Even if all seems quiet on the home front, there is something that noisily rages inside her.

Both sexes with the Moon in Scorpio like to pull up the

drawbridge at home. They need time to recharge their emotional batteries and, anyway, they are not interested in carrying on an endless round of meaningless social banter. Their private lives are exactly that - private. The actual home is often hidden away, like a sanctuary and they are usually deeply attached to it. They will not invite you in unless they feel your vibration is basically in tune with theirs.

Moon Scorpio children often have to learn the lesson of survival, and, in anticipation of this, they are usually well-equipped to withstand crisis. They know what it is to 'come through', and this can often be linked right back to the struggle of birth itself.

The challenge for people with this Moon sign is to acknowledge their capacity for burying deep feelings and preventing those close to them from entering their private inner worlds. Once you have found the right password and gained access to their emotions, you could share in some of the most powerful feelings imaginable. The Scorpionic intensity transforms emotions into a tremendous richness, but it can prove too heavy for those that prefer a lighter diet. Scorpios are always moving between the poles. They are emotional

navigators and, whether they are plain sailing or battling the storm, their passion for life is immense.

MOON IN SAGITTARIUS

The Moon in fiery Sagittarius generates a lot of heat in the emotional sphere but, as Sagittarius is ever onwards and upwards, there is often little time to stay with the feelings.

This Moon sign is always in pursuit of the next emotional adventure, and a natural exuberance and friendliness ensures a seemingly never-ending supply of quests.

The mother of Moon in Sagittarius modelled the optimistic attitude that surfaces later in these signs in the form of an easy-going breeziness that allows them entry into most circles. Sagittarius travels light, therefore arriving on the scene with considerably less emotional baggage than other signs. This may seem an attractive prospect, but it is well to remember that Sagittarius Moons will not take kindly to very much personal clutter and responsibility. They are not cut out to handle emotional demands. They find commitment a big emotional pressure.

There is no pretence with Moon in Sagittarius. They are open and honest with people - which may be why they

are liked in the first place. Their child-like zest and good humour make them exhilarating playmates. They seem permanently at the fun fair, although they are smartly off the rollercoaster as soon as the game turns sour or the rules are changed.

Sagittarius Moons need a large amount of space at home. They are larger than life and it is hard to contain them in a small area - besides that, you need to make room for their exercise machines, skis, and, preferably, the indoor swimming pool. They are not traditionally homely types, and any idea of domestic routine is a complete anathema to them. The man with Moon in Sagittarius feels more secure with an outgoing, rather than stay-at-home partner. A woman with Moon in Sagittarius needs to feel there is more to life than the home. This Moon sign really cannot be bothered with such mundane concerns as cleaning the bath when there is so much going on in the world out there. Both sexes with the Moon in the sign of the archer will not sit still for long at home, unless, of course, they are expanding their minds by reading about, or watching on television, some fascinating subject.

They may be careless and

disorganized on the home-front, but they are never dull or down-in-the-dumps. You can rely on them to enthuse about your planned trip to Mozambique, but do not expect them to water the plants while you are away. Moon in Sagittarius types love to party and entertain at home. Emotionally they feel nourished as long as they are sure they are 'having a good time'.

These Moon signs are cheerleaders. If you can keep up with them then you are in for a piece of the action. They have no time for malingerers or moaners, so you will have to get used to dealing with your own problems as they arise, take a leaf out of their book and look on the bright side of life.

MOON IN CAPRICORN

The Moon in the serious sign of Capricorn suggests that affairs of the heart are not to be treated lightly. Since Capricorn is virtually synonymous with commitment, the Moon in this sign is looking for permanence and stability. Capricorn Moon requires you to sign on the dotted line, so beware if exchanging telephone numbers does not mean exchanging contracts for you.

Children born with this Moon sign experience the mother figure as being in control, highly organized and having a great deal of responsibility. Often the mother has had to take over responsibility for the family in some way and may not be able to meet the emotional requirements of the child as she is preoccupied with practical necessities. From a young age, Capricorn Moons learn to fend for themselves and to repress their emotional expression.

The barrier between themselves and others is already firmly established by the time adulthood arrives. What has been so carefully erected as a defence mechanism often turns out simply to get in the way of getting close to others. Although Moon in Capricorn adults feel safer with their walls around them, there are times when they realize it takes more effort to scale them then they had anticipated.

However, this safety structure has its compensations. For a start they are uniquely equipped to build stability and security in their personal lives. Because they take time to trust others, they may be slow starters, but, once they do trust someone, he or she is there for life. The man with the Moon in Capricorn actually needs to be needed. He will work long and hard to oil the wheels that hold the family together, and expects his partner to do the same. The family must all share his sense of priorities. A woman with Moon in Capricorn can lose sight of her feelings in the effort to keep up the appearance of being on top of her life.

People with Moon in Capricorn like to have routines that form the backbones of their lives. These are the types who feel they have to earn their relaxation and, so it is virtually impossible for them to throw caution to the winds when it comes to their daily schedule of tasks. A Capricorn Moon home always has the stamp of organization about it - things are generally 'under control' (usually their own).

Although Moon in Capricorn types are not ones to smother their loved ones with affection, if you live with one, you will know which side your bread is buttered. They are never short of solutions to a problem, in fact, they love to get to grips with sorting out a really knotty crisis. However, do not expect them to carry a handkerchief to mop up the tears - emotional aftermaths leave them at a loss. Whilst others fall by the wayside wallowing in self-pity, they are already back to work, building up their tower of strength.

MOON IN AQUARIUS

The sparkiness of Aquarius makes itself felt in this Moon placement by causing waves or currents of electricity to constantly ripple through the emotional life. These Moon signs thrive on excitement and can be in danger of overloading the voltage to such an extent that burn-out is inevitable. When this happens, it appears that the ability to make any form of emotional link with others is dead, and they retreat into a detached silence, until their curiosity kick-starts them into making a surprise visit into your emotional zone again.

With these Moon signs it is always best to leave the door open so that they are free to wander in and out as the mood takes them. Chances are, their penchant for being contrary will dictate that they will stay put as soon as the door is unbolted. Their capacity to surprise is endless. They love to appear unannounced, but may forget a date they made two weeks ago. A man with this Moon sign wants is partner to be independent because he feels trapped by the weight of responsibility.

Children with Moon in Aquarius usually have an unconventional upbringing. Because this placement could truly be seen as representing 'the mother of invention', the originality of Aquarius cannot be channelled easily into the confines of domestic bliss. Mothers are seen as highly individual people, so children can feel that a 'normal' family background is missing. Their environments are charged with a different quality.

Later in life, Moon in Aquarius tends to relate to others spontaneously and without any sense of inhibiting oughts and shoulds. These types carry a sparkle that can lift others out of their familiar pattern of being. This can be at once exhilarating and disturbing, depending on how well their companions can accommodate change.

People with the Moon in Aquarius feel comfortable literally taking each day as it comes. A form of claustrophobia makes them chomp at the bit if the scenery gets stale, and they love to get away to see something different. The sort of disruption that would throw a woman with an earthy Moon into complete panic, such as six people unexpectedly pitching up for dinner, is just a bit of fun for this Moon sign.

However, when people threaten to invade too much of these Moon signs time and space, they have to disentangle themselves and breathe in some fresh air. They make good friends, phoning to check you are all right and inviting you to share in their social lives, but the daily interweaving of family relationships require a constancy that is hard for them to find. They need time alone to replenish what has been lost in the whiz of their activity. They must shut down, and sometimes shut off, from others. If you can understand their need for independence and the habit they have of switching on and off, then you will be able to partner these Moon signs in their unique dance.

MOON IN PISCES

When the Moon is positioned in the sensitive sign of Pisces, the feeling side of the individual is permanently plugged into the undercurrents in the atmosphere. No one can match Pisceans in their ability to 'tune in' and respond accordingly. In a sense, this relieves others of having to account for themselves, as Pisces Moons would rather accept than challenge. They are the Manta ray fish of the emotional world, sweeping up everything in their paths, whether it nourishes or not.

In childhood, these Moon signs are unusually sensitive to the emotions of their mothers who can tend to swamp their children with their feelings. Often these Moon signs see their mothers as people who have had to make a lot of adjustments in life, perhaps sacrificing their own needs for others. Later in life, Moon in Pisces adults have to be careful not to allow these models of self-denial to destroy their capacity for personal happiness.

The symbol of the two fish signifies the duality of the emotional life of those with Moon in Pisces. On the one hand their compassion gives them the potential for offering tremendous empathy to others, on the other, they run the risk of becoming victims if they always allow the feelings of others to dictate their reaction. Because they receive so much vibration from others, these moon signs can become waterlogged at times, and unclear as to their own feelings. They are not ones · to call the shots emotionally, preferring to watch and see how the plot of the play is unfolding. Pisces Moons often feel the emotional side of their lives to be very loosely scripted, so they need to take in everything around them to ensure that they do not miss their cue.

A man with Moon in Pisces will always tune into his partner's emotional needs. He quite understands that she has to watch every episode of Neighbours, or has a desire to play Handel's Water Music when in the bath. He feels comfortable with soft, feminine women rather than those who want to prove themselves as hod-carriers. Women with Moon in Pisces need romance and escape from the humdrum world.

The earth signs especially may find the habit amongst Pisces Moons of 'floating' rather unnerving. It looks as if they dream up their lives as they go along, feet off the ground, heads in the clouds. Yet this ability they have to rise above reality enables them to see things from a wider perspective than others. These Moon signs are soul-searchers, and cannot find the answers they seek if they stay on street-level.

Pisces Moon signs love to lose themselves by getting totally absorbed in something that captures their imagination. Whether through film or fiction, they like to enter the fantasy of another realm, and, once there, it is not easy to bring them back to face the washing up!

People with Moon in Pisces are generally open to making emotional connections with others, they thirst for love and romance with a kind of longing that asks for them to be 'taken away from all this'. Living with this Moon sign can be a touch chaotic but their partner will never feel alone in this world again. Why worry about the state of the kitchen floor when music can carry them away and love conquers all.

USING THE MOON TABLES

These tables give the sign at midnight for every other day of each year. The key for the letters used as signs in the table is given at the foot of this page. Between every other midnight is a period of forty eight hours. If the sign given for two consecutive dates is the same, a person who was born in that forty-eight hour period bears that sign.

If the two signs are different you have to calculate the time at which the sign changed in order to decide which of them you were born under.

To do this follow the steps below. You will need a calculator.

1. Locate the dates either side of the point at which you were born.
2. Write down the two numbers given next to the two signs on each date. The first number shall be referred to as A and the second as B.
3. Deduct A from 30. This figure is C.
4. Add B to C. This is figure D.
5. Divide D by 48. Multiply the result by figure C.

This gives the number of hours after midnight on the first date that the sign changed from the first to the second. If this time is before your birthtime you were born under the first sign, if it is after your birthtime you were born under the second sign.

eg. For a birthtime and date of 3.14am, 18th October 1972.

step 1) 17th and 19th October 1972.
step 2) figure A is 10 and figure B is7.
step 3) 30 minus 10 (fig. A) equals 20. Hence, fig.C is 20.
step 4) 7 (fig.B) plus 20 (fig.C) equals 27. This is fig.D.
step 5) 27 (fig.D) divided by 48, multiplied by 20 (fig.C) equals 11.25.

Therefore, the sign changed 11.25 hours after midnight on the first date. Since the birthtime is over twenty-seven hours later, this person was born under the first sign, given at midnight on 17th October next to figure B.

If the sign actually changes in the hour that you were born, it is possible to calculate when in that hour the change took place by multiplying the decimal part of the final sum by sixty. This gives you the minute of the hour when the change took place.

eg. From the above example, the final figure was 11.25. Multiplying the decimal part (0.25) by sixty equals 15. Therefore, the sign changed at 11.15am, 17th October.

One additional note, these times are not in British Summer Time, the dates for which are given at the top of the table for each year. If you were born in BST you should deduct an hour from your birthtime.

Sign key for Moon table
V-Virgo, **L**-Libra, **S**-Scorpio, **G**-Sagittarius, **C**-Capricorn, **Q**-Aquarius, **P**-Pisces, **A**-Aries, **T**-Taurus, **I**-Gemini, **N**-Cancer, **O**-Leo.

1922 BST: 26/3-8/10

date	Jan		Feb		Mar		Apr		May		Jun		Jul		Aug		Sep		Oct		Nov		Dec	
1	10	Q	24	P	3	A	19	T	24	I	16	O	25	V	18	S	8	C	12	Q	26	P	28	A
3	4	P	18	A	27	A	14	I	21	N	14	V	23	L	15	G	2	Q	6	P	20	A	22	T
5	28	P	13	T	22	T	11	N	19	O	13	L	21	S	11	C	27	Q	29	P	14	T	18	I
7	22	A	9	I	18	I	9	O	18	V	11	S	18	G	6	Q	20	P	23	A	9	I	14	N
9	17	T	6	N	15	N	8	V	17	L	8	G	14	C	0	P	14	A	17	T	4	N	11	O
11	14	I	6	O	14	O	8	L	16	S	5	C	9	Q	24	P	8	T	12	I	1	O	9	V
13	13	N	7	V	14	V	7	S	14	G	1	Q	3	P	17	A	2	I	7	N	28	O	7	L
15	13	O	7	L	15	L	6	G	10	C	25	Q	27	P	11	T	28	I	4	O	26	V	5	S
17	13	V	5	S	14	S	2	C	5	Q	19	P	21	A	6	I	25	N	2	V	26	L	4	G
19	12	L	2	G	11	G	27	C	29	Q	13	A	15	T	3	N	24	O	2	L	25	S	2	C
21	9	S	27	G	6	C	21	Q	23	P	7	T	11	I	1	O	24	V	2	S	24	G	29	C
23	5	G	22	C	1	Q	15	P	17	A	3	I	8	N	1	V	24	L	2	G	21	C	24	Q
25	0	C	16	Q	25	Q	9	A	12	T	0	N	7	O	1	L	24	S	0	C	16	Q	18	P
27	25	C	9	P	18	P	3	T	7	I	28	N	7	V	0	S	21	G	26	C	11	P	12	A
29	19	Q			12	A	28	T	4	N	27	O	6	L	28	S	17	C	20	Q	4	A	6	T
31	13	P			6	T			2	O			4	S	25	G			14	P			1	I

1923 BST: 22/4-16/9

date	Jan		Feb		Mar		Apr		May		Jun		Jul		Aug		Sep		Oct		Nov		Dec	
1	13	I	2	O	10	O	2	L	11	S	3	C	9	Q	25	P	9	T	11	I	27	N	2	V
3	10	N	1	V	9	V	2	S	11	G	1	Q	5	P	19	A	3	I	6	N	23	O	29	V
5	7	O	0	L	9	L	2	G	9	C	27	Q	0	A	13	T	27	I	1	O	20	V	28	L
7	5	V	29	L	9	S	0	C	6	Q	22	P	23	A	7	I	23	N	28	O	20	L	28	S
9	4	L	27	S	7	G	27	C	1	P	15	A	17	T	2	N	20	O	27	V	20	S	29	G
11	2	S	24	G	4	C	22	Q	25	P	9	T	11	I	28	N	18	V	27	L	21	G	28	C
13	0	G	20	C	0	Q	16	P	19	A	3	I	7	N	26	O	18	L	27	S	19	C	25	Q
15	27	G	16	Q	25	Q	10	A	12	T	28	I	3	O	24	V	17	S	26	G	16	Q	20	P
17	24	C	10	P	19	P	3	T	6	I	23	N	0	V	23	L	16	G	24	C	12	P	14	A
19	20	Q	4	A	13	A	27	T	1	N	20	O	28	V	21	S	14	C	20	Q	6	A	8	T
21	14	P	28	A	6	T	22	I	26	N	17	V	26	L	19	G	10	Q	15	P	0	T	2	I
23	8	A	22	T	0	I	17	N	23	O	15	L	24	S	17	C	5	P	9	A	23	T	26	I
25	2	T	16	I	25	I	13	O	20	V	14	S	23	G	13	Q	0	A	3	T	17	I	21	N
27	26	T	12	N	20	N	11	V	19	L	13	G	21	C	9	P	24	A	26	T	11	N	16	O
29	21	I			18	O	10	L	19	S	12	C	17	Q	3	A	18	T	20	I	6	O	12	V
31	18	N			17	V			19	G			13	P	27	A			14	N			9	L

1924 BST: 13/4-21/9

date	Jan		Feb		Mar		Apr		May		Jun		Jul		Aug		Sep		Oct		Nov		Dec	
1	23	L	17	G	12	C	2	P	7	A	22	T	25	I	10	O	28	V	5	S	29	G	8	Q
3	22	S	16	C	9	Q	28	P	1	T	16	I	19	N	5	V	25	L	4	G	28	C	5	P
5	22	G	14	Q	6	P	22	A	25	T	10	N	13	O	2	L	24	S	3	C	25	Q	2	A
7	21	C	10	P	1	A	16	T	19	I	4	O	8	V	29	L	22	G	1	Q	22	P	27	A
9	19	Q	6	A	26	A	10	I	13	N	29	O	5	L	27	S	20	C	28	Q	17	A	21	T
11	16	P	0	T	20	T	4	N	7	O	25	V	2	S	26	G	18	Q	25	P	12	T	15	I
13	11	A	24	T	14	I	28	N	2	V	22	L	1	G	25	C	16	P	21	A	6	I	9	N
15	5	T	18	I	8	N	24	O	29	V	22	S	1	C	23	Q	12	A	16	T	0	N	2	O
17	28	T	13	N	3	O	21	V	28	L	22	G	1	Q	21	P	7	T	10	I	24	N	26	O
19	22	I	8	O	29	O	20	L	29	S	22	C	29	Q	17	A	2	I	4	N	18	O	21	V
21	17	N	5	V	27	V	20	S	29	G	21	Q	26	P	12	T	26	I	27	N	13	V	18	L
23	13	O	2	L	26	L	20	G	28	C	18	P	22	A	6	I	19	N	22	O	9	L	16	S
25	9	V	1	S	26	S	19	C	26	Q	13	A	16	T	0	N	14	O	18	V	8	S	16	G
27	6	L	29	S	24	G	16	Q	22	P	7	T	10	I	24	N	10	V	15	L	8	G	16	C
29	4	S	28	G	22	C	12	P	16	A	1	I	3	N	19	O	7	L	15	S	8	C	16	Q
31	3	G			19	Q			10	T			28	N	15	V			14	G			14	P

1925 BST: 19/4-4/10

date	Jan		Feb		Mar		Apr		May		Jun		Jul		Aug		Sep		Oct		Nov		Dec	
1	28	P	15	T	23	T	7	N	8	O	23	V	28	L	19	G	12	Q	20	P	11	T	15	I
3	24	A	9	I	17	I	0	O	2	V	19	L	25	S	18	C	12	P	19	A	7	I	10	N
5	18	T	2	N	11	N	24	O	28	V	17	S	25	G	19	Q	11	A	16	T	2	N	4	O
7	12	I	26	N	4	O	20	V	25	L	17	G	25	C	18	P	8	T	12	I	26	N	27	O
9	6	N	20	O	29	O	16	L	23	S	17	C	25	Q	16	A	4	I	6	N	20	O	21	V
11	29	N	15	V	24	V	14	S	22	G	16	Q	24	P	13	T	28	I	0	O	14	V	16	L
13	23	O	11	L	21	L	13	G	22	C	14	P	21	A	8	I	22	N	24	O	9	L	13	S
15	18	V	7	S	18	S	11	C	20	Q	11	A	16	T	2	N	16	O	18	V	5	S	11	G
17	14	L	5	G	16	G	9	Q	17	P	7	T	11	I	25	N	10	V	13	L	3	G	11	C
19	11	S	4	C	14	C	7	P	14	A	2	I	5	N	19	O	5	L	10	S	2	C	10	Q
21	9	G	3	Q	13	Q	4	A	10	T	26	I	28	N	13	V	0	S	7	G	0	Q	9	P
23	9	C	2	P	11	P	1	T	5	I	19	N	22	O	8	L	27	S	5	C	29	Q	7	A
25	9	Q	0	A	9	A	26	T	29	I	13	O	16	V	3	S	25	G	3	Q	26	P	4	T
27	9	P	27	A	5	T	21	I	23	N	7	V	11	L	0	G	23	C	2	P	24	A	29	T
29	6	A			0	I	14	N	16	O	1	L	7	S	28	G	21	Q	0	A	20	T	24	I
31	2	T			25	I			10	V			4	G	27	C			28	A			18	N

1926 BST: 18/4-3/10

date	Jan		Feb		Mar		Apr		May		Jun		Jul		Aug		Sep		Oct		Nov		Dec	
1	0	O	14	V	23	V	10	S	16	G	8	Q	17	P	10	T	29	I	2	O	16	V	18	L
3	24	O	9	L	18	L	6	G	14	C	7	P	16	A	6	I	23	N	26	O	10	L	13	S
5	18	V	3	S	13	S	3	C	11	Q	5	A	13	T	2	N	17	O	19	V	4	S	8	G
7	12	L	29	S	9	G	1	Q	10	P	3	T	9	I	26	N	11	V	13	L	0	G	5	C
9	7	S	27	G	6	C	29	Q	8	A	0	I	5	N	20	O	4	L	8	S	26	G	3	Q
11	5	G	27	C	5	Q	29	P	7	T	26	I	29	N	13	V	28	L	3	G	22	C	1	P
13	4	C	27	Q	5	P	28	A	4	I	21	N	23	O	7	L	23	S	29	G	20	Q	29	P
15	4	Q	27	P	5	A	26	T	0	N	15	O	17	V	1	S	19	G	25	C	18	P	28	A
17	4	P	26	A	4	T	22	I	25	N	8	V	11	L	26	S	16	C	24	Q	17	A	25	T
19	3	A	23	T	1	I	17	N	19	O	2	L	5	S	23	G	14	Q	23	P	16	T	23	I
21	0	T	18	I	27	I	11	O	12	V	27	L	1	G	21	C	15	P	23	A	14	I	19	N
23	26	T	12	N	21	N	4	V	7	L	23	S	29	G	21	Q	15	A	23	T	11	N	14	O
25	21	I	6	O	14	O	29	V	2	S	20	G	28	C	22	P	14	T	20	I	6	O	8	V
27	15	N	0	V	8	V	23	L	28	S	19	C	28	Q	21	A	12	I	16	N	0	V	2	L
29	9	O			2	L	19	S	26	G	18	Q	28	P	20	T	8	N	10	O	24	V	26	L
31	3	V			27	L			24	C			26	A	16	I			4	V			21	S

1927 BST: 10/4-2/10

date	Jan		Feb		Mar		Apr		May		Jun		Jul		Aug		Sep		Oct		Nov		Dec	
1	3	G	22	C	0	Q	23	P	2	T	24	I	29	N	15	V	29	L	2	G	18	C	24	Q
3	0	C	21	Q	29	Q	23	A	1	I	21	N	25	O	9	L	23	S	26	G	14	Q	21	P
5	28	C	21	P	0	A	23	T	0	N	17	O	19	V	3	S	17	G	21	C	11	P	20	A
7	27	Q	21	A	0	T	21	I	26	N	11	V	13	L	27	S	13	C	18	Q	11	A	19	T
9	26	P	19	T	29	T	17	N	21	O	5	L	7	S	22	G	10	Q	17	P	11	T	19	I
11	24	A	16	I	25	I	12	O	15	V	29	L	1	G	18	C	9	P	18	A	11	I	18	N
13	22	T	11	N	21	N	6	V	9	L	23	S	27	G	16	Q	9	A	18	T	10	N	15	O
15	19	I	6	O	15	O	0	L	3	S	18	G	23	C	15	P	9	T	17	I	7	O	10	V
17	15	N	0	V	9	V	24	L	27	S	14	C	21	Q	15	A	8	I	15	N	2	V	5	L
19	10	O	24	V	3	L	18	S	22	G	11	Q	20	P	14	T	5	N	11	O	26	V	28	L
21	4	V	18	L	27	L	12	G	18	C	9	P	19	A	11	I	1	O	5	V	20	L	22	S
23	28	V	12	S	21	S	8	C	15	Q	8	A	17	T	8	N	26	O	29	V	14	S	16	G
25	22	L	6	G	15	G	4	Q	12	P	6	T	15	I	4	O	20	V	23	L	8	G	11	C
27	16	S	2	C	11	C	2	P	11	A	5	I	11	N	29	O	14	L	17	S	2	C	7	Q
29	11	G			8	Q	2	A	11	T	2	N	8	O	23	V	8	S	11	G	27	C	4	P
31	8	C			8	P			10	I			3	V	17	L			5	C			2	A

1928 BST: 22/4-7/10

date	Jan		Feb		Mar		Apr		May		Jun		Jul		Aug		Sep		Oct		Nov		Dec	
1	16	A	9	I	3	N	23	O	28	V	12	S	15	G	0	Q	19	P	27	A	21	I	29	N
3	14	T	7	N	0	O	18	V	22	L	6	G	9	C	26	Q	18	A	26	T	19	N	27	O
5	13	I	4	O	26	O	13	L	15	S	0	C	4	Q	23	P	16	T	25	I	17	O	23	V
7	12	N	1	V	22	V	7	S	9	G	24	C	0	P	21	A	14	I	23	N	13	V	18	L
9	9	O	26	V	16	L	0	G	3	C	20	Q	27	P	19	T	12	N	20	O	8	L	12	S
11	5	V	20	L	10	S	24	G	27	C	16	P	24	A	18	I	10	O	16	V	3	S	5	G
13	0	L	14	S	4	G	18	C	23	Q	14	A	23	T	16	N	7	V	11	L	26	S	29	G
15	24	L	8	G	28	G	14	Q	20	P	13	T	22	I	14	O	3	L	6	S	20	G	23	C
17	18	S	2	C	23	C	12	P	19	A	13	I	21	N	11	V	27	L	0	G	14	C	17	Q
19	12	G	28	C	19	Q	11	A	19	T	13	N	19	O	7	L	21	S	23	G	8	Q	12	P
21	7	C	25	Q	18	P	11	T	20	I	11	O	16	V	2	S	15	G	17	C	3	P	9	A
23	3	Q	24	P	18	A	11	I	19	N	8	V	11	L	25	S	9	C	12	Q	0	A	7	T
25	0	P	23	A	17	T	10	N	16	O	3	L	6	S	19	G	4	Q	8	P	29	A	7	I
27	28	P	22	T	16	I	7	O	12	V	27	L	29	S	13	C	0	P	6	A	29	T	7	N
29	27	A	20	I	14	N	3	V	7	L	21	S	23	G	9	Q	28	P	6	T	29	I	7	O
31	25	T			10	O			1	S			18	C	5	P			6	I			5	V

1929 BST: 21/4-6/10

date	Jan		Feb		Mar		Apr		May		Jun		Jul		Aug		Sep		Oct		Nov		Dec	
1	19	V	5	S	12	S	26	G	28	C	13	P	18	A	10	I	4	O	12	V	2	S	6	G
3	14	L	29	S	6	G	20	C	22	Q	10	A	16	T	9	N	3	V	10	L	27	S	0	C
5	8	S	22	G	0	C	14	Q	18	P	7	T	15	I	9	O	1	L	6	S	22	G	24	C
7	2	G	16	C	24	C	10	P	15	A	7	I	16	N	9	V	28	L	1	G	15	C	17	Q
9	26	G	11	Q	19	Q	7	A	14	T	7	N	16	O	7	L	24	S	26	G	9	Q	11	P
11	20	C	6	P	15	P	5	T	14	I	7	O	15	V	3	S	18	G	19	C	3	P	6	A
13	14	Q	2	A	12	A	4	I	13	N	6	V	12	L	28	S	11	C	13	Q	29	P	3	T
15	9	P	29	A	10	T	3	N	12	O	2	L	7	S	21	G	5	Q	8	P	25	A	1	I
17	6	A	27	T	8	I	1	O	9	V	28	L	1	G	15	C	0	P	4	A	24	T	1	N
19	3	T	25	I	6	N	29	O	5	L	22	S	25	G	9	Q	25	P	1	T	23	I	2	O
21	1	I	24	N	5	O	26	V	1	S	16	G	18	C	4	P	22	A	29	T	22	N	1	V
23	0	N	23	O	2	V	21	L	25	S	9	C	12	Q	29	P	19	T	27	I	21	O	29	V
25	0	O	21	V	29	V	16	S	19	G	3	Q	7	P	25	A	17	I	26	N	19	V	25	L
27	29	O	17	L	25	L	10	G	13	C	27	Q	2	A	22	T	15	N	24	O	15	L	20	S
29	27	V			20	S	4	C	6	Q	22	P	28	A	20	I	14	O	22	V	11	S	15	G
31	22	L			14	G			1	P			26	T	19	N			19	L			8	C

1930 BST: 13/4-5/10

date	Jan		Feb		Mar		Apr		May		Jun		Jul		Aug		Sep		Oct		Nov		Dec	
1	20	C	5	P	14	P	1	T	7	I	0	O	10	V	1	S	19	G	22	C	6	P	8	A
3	14	Q	29	P	9	A	27	T	5	N	29	O	8	L	27	S	13	C	16	Q	0	A	2	T
5	8	P	24	A	4	T	25	I	4	O	27	V	4	S	22	G	7	Q	10	P	24	A	29	T
7	2	A	20	T	0	I	23	N	2	V	24	L	0	G	16	C	1	P	4	A	20	T	26	I
9	28	A	18	I	28	I	22	O	0	L	20	S	25	G	10	Q	25	P	28	A	17	I	25	N
11	25	T	18	N	27	N	20	V	28	L	16	G	19	C	4	P	19	A	24	T	14	N	24	O
13	24	I	18	O	26	O	19	L	24	S	11	C	13	Q	28	P	14	T	20	I	13	O	22	V
15	25	N	18	V	26	V	16	S	20	G	5	Q	7	P	22	A	10	I	18	N	11	V	20	L
17	25	O	17	L	24	L	12	G	14	C	28	Q	1	A	17	T	7	N	16	O	9	L	17	S
19	24	V	13	S	21	S	7	C	8	Q	22	P	25	A	14	I	6	O	15	V	7	S	13	G
21	22	L	8	G	16	G	1	Q	2	P	17	A	21	T	12	N	6	V	14	L	5	G	9	C
23	17	S	2	C	11	C	24	Q	26	P	13	T	19	I	12	O	6	L	13	S	1	C	4	Q
25	12	G	26	C	4	Q	19	P	22	A	11	I	19	N	13	V	5	S	10	G	26	C	28	Q
27	6	C	20	Q	28	Q	14	A	18	T	10	N	19	O	12	L	2	G	6	C	20	Q	21	P
29	29	C			23	P	10	T	17	I	10	O	19	V	10	S	28	G	0	Q	14	P	15	A
31	23	Q			18	A			16	N			18	L	6	G			24	Q			10	T

1931 BST: 19/4-4/10

date	Jan		Feb		Mar		Apr		May		Jun		Jul		Aug		Sep		Oct		Nov		Dec	
1	23	T	13	N	21	N	14	V	22	L	14	G	19	C	5	P	19	A	22	T	9	N	16	O
3	20	I	12	O	20	O	14	L	22	S	11	C	15	Q	29	P	13	T	16	I	5	O	13	V
5	19	N	13	V	21	V	14	S	20	G	7	Q	9	P	23	A	7	I	12	N	3	V	12	L
7	19	O	12	L	21	L	12	G	16	C	1	P	3	A	17	T	3	N	9	O	2	L	11	S
9	18	V	10	S	20	S	8	C	11	Q	25	P	26	A	12	I	1	O	8	V	2	S	10	G
11	17	L	7	G	16	G	3	Q	5	P	18	A	21	T	9	N	0	V	8	L	2	G	8	C
13	14	S	2	C	12	C	27	Q	29	P	13	T	17	I	7	O	0	L	9	S	0	C	5	Q
15	10	G	27	C	6	Q	20	P	22	A	9	I	14	N	7	V	0	S	8	G	27	C	0	P
17	5	C	21	Q	0	P	14	A	17	T	5	N	13	O	6	L	29	S	5	C	22	Q	24	P
19	0	Q	15	P	23	P	8	T	13	I	3	O	12	V	5	S	26	G	1	Q	16	P	18	A
21	24	Q	8	A	17	A	3	I	9	N	2	V	11	L	3	G	22	C	26	Q	10	A	12	T
23	18	P	2	T	11	T	29	I	7	O	0	L	9	S	0	C	17	Q	20	P	4	T	6	I
25	11	A	27	T	6	I	26	N	5	V	28	L	6	G	25	C	11	P	13	A	28	T	2	N
27	6	T	23	I	2	N	24	O	3	L	26	S	3	C	20	Q	4	A	7	T	23	I	29	N
29	1	I			0	O	23	V	2	S	23	G	28	C	14	P	28	A	1	I	19	N	26	O
31	28	I			29	O			0	G			23	Q	7	A			26	I			24	V

1932 BST: 17/4-2/10

date	Jan		Feb		Mar		Apr		May		Jun		Jul		Aug		Sep		Oct		Nov		Dec	
1	8	L	1	G	26	G	15	Q	18	P	2	T	5	I	21	N	10	V	18	L	12	G	20	C
3	6	S	29	G	22	C	9	P	12	A	26	T	29	I	17	O	9	L	18	S	11	C	17	Q
5	5	G	25	C	17	Q	3	A	6	T	21	I	25	N	15	V	8	S	17	G	8	Q	13	P
7	3	C	21	Q	12	P	27	A	29	T	16	N	21	O	13	L	7	G	15	C	4	P	8	A
9	0	Q	16	P	6	A	20	T	24	I	11	O	18	V	11	S	5	C	12	Q	29	P	2	T
11	25	Q	10	A	0	T	14	I	18	N	8	V	16	L	10	G	2	Q	7	P	23	A	25	T
13	20	P	3	T	24	T	9	N	14	O	6	L	15	S	8	C	28	Q	2	A	17	T	19	I
15	14	A	27	T	18	I	5	O	11	V	4	S	14	G	5	Q	23	P	26	A	10	I	13	N
17	7	T	22	I	13	N	2	V	10	L	4	G	12	C	2	P	17	A	20	T	4	N	8	O
19	2	I	18	N	10	O	1	L	10	S	3	C	10	Q	27	P	11	T	13	I	29	N	4	V
21	27	I	16	O	8	V	2	S	10	G	2	Q	6	P	21	A	5	I	7	N	24	O	0	L
23	24	N	15	V	8	L	2	G	10	C	28	Q	1	A	15	T	29	I	2	O	21	V	28	L
25	22	O	15	L	9	S	1	C	7	Q	23	P	25	A	9	I	24	N	28	O	19	L	28	S
27	20	V	14	S	8	G	28	C	3	P	17	A	19	T	3	N	20	O	26	V	19	S	28	G
29	19	L	12	G	6	C	24	Q	27	P	11	T	13	I	29	N	18	V	26	L	20	G	27	C
31	17	S			2	Q			21	A			8	N	26	O			27	S			25	Q

1933 BST: 9/4-8/10

date	Jan		Feb		Mar		Apr		May		Jun		Jul		Aug		Sep		Oct		Nov		Dec	
1	9	P	24	A	2	T	16	I	18	N	4	V	9	L	2	G	25	C	3	P	22	A	26	T
3	4	A	18	T	26	T	10	N	12	O	0	L	7	S	1	C	24	Q	0	A	17	T	20	I
5	28	A	12	I	20	I	4	O	8	V	28	L	7	G	1	Q	22	P	26	A	12	I	14	N
7	22	T	6	N	14	N	0	V	5	L	28	S	7	C	29	Q	18	A	21	T	5	N	7	O
9	16	I	1	O	9	O	27	V	4	S	29	G	7	Q	27	P	13	T	15	I	29	N	2	V
11	10	N	27	O	5	V	26	L	5	G	28	C	5	P	23	A	8	I	9	N	23	O	27	V
13	5	O	24	V	3	L	26	S	5	C	27	Q	2	A	18	T	1	N	3	O	18	V	23	L
15	1	V	21	L	2	S	25	G	4	Q	23	P	27	A	11	I	25	N	28	O	15	L	22	S
17	27	V	20	S	1	G	24	C	1	P	18	A	21	T	5	N	20	O	24	V	14	S	22	G
19	25	L	18	G	29	G	21	Q	27	P	12	T	15	I	29	N	16	V	21	L	14	G	23	C
21	23	S	16	C	27	C	17	P	21	A	6	I	9	N	24	O	13	L	20	S	14	C	22	Q
23	22	G	14	Q	24	Q	12	A	15	T	0	N	3	O	20	V	11	S	20	G	13	Q	20	P
25	21	C	11	P	20	P	6	T	9	I	24	N	28	O	17	L	9	G	18	C	10	P	16	A
27	19	Q	7	A	15	A	0	I	3	N	18	O	23	V	14	S	8	C	16	Q	6	A	11	T
29	16	P			10	T	24	I	27	N	13	V	20	L	12	G	6	Q	13	P	2	T	5	I
31	12	A			4	I			21	O			17	S	11	C			9	A			29	I

1934 BST: 22/4–7/10

date	Jan		Feb		Mar		Apr		May		Jun		Jul		Aug		Sep		Oct		Nov		Dec	
1	11	N	25	O	4	V	22	L	29	S	22	C	1	P	22	A	9	I	12	N	25	O	27	V
3	4	O	20	V	29	V	19	S	28	G	21	Q	29	P	18	T	4	N	6	O	19	V	22	L
5	28	O	16	L	26	L	17	G	26	C	19	P	26	A	13	I	27	N	29	O	14	L	19	S
7	23	V	12	S	23	S	16	C	25	Q	16	A	21	T	7	N	21	O	24	V	11	S	17	G
9	19	L	10	G	20	G	14	Q	22	P	12	T	16	I	0	O	15	V	19	L	8	G	16	C
11	16	S	9	C	19	C	12	P	19	A	7	I	10	N	24	O	10	L	15	S	7	C	15	Q
13	15	G	9	Q	18	Q	9	A	15	T	1	N	3	O	18	V	5	S	12	G	5	Q	14	P
15	16	C	8	P	17	P	6	T	10	I	25	N	27	O	13	L	2	G	10	C	3	P	12	A
17	16	Q	7	A	14	A	2	I	4	N	18	O	21	V	8	S	29	G	8	Q	1	A	8	T
19	15	P	3	T	11	T	26	I	28	N	12	V	16	L	5	G	28	C	7	P	28	A	4	I
21	12	A	28	T	6	I	20	N	22	O	7	L	12	S	3	C	27	Q	5	A	25	T	29	I
23	8	T	22	I	0	N	14	O	16	V	3	S	10	G	3	Q	26	P	3	T	21	I	24	N
25	2	I	16	N	24	N	8	V	12	L	1	G	9	C	3	P	25	A	0	I	16	N	17	O
27	26	I	10	O	18	O	4	L	9	S	1	C	10	Q	3	A	22	T	26	I	9	O	11	V
29	20	N			13	V	1	S	8	G	1	Q	10	P	1	T	18	I	20	N	3	V	5	L
31	13	O			8	L			7	C			8	A	27	T			13	O			0	S

1935 BST: 14/4–6/10

date	Jan		Feb		Mar		Apr		May		Jun		Jul		Aug		Sep		Oct		Nov		Dec	
1	13	S	3	C	12	C	5	P	14	A	5	I	10	N	25	O	9	L	13	S	0	C	7	Q
3	11	G	3	Q	11	Q	5	A	12	T	1	N	4	O	19	V	3	S	8	G	27	C	5	P
5	10	C	3	P	11	P	4	T	10	I	26	N	28	O	12	L	28	S	3	C	25	Q	4	A
7	10	Q	3	A	12	A	2	I	6	N	20	O	22	V	7	S	24	G	0	Q	23	P	2	T
9	10	P	2	T	10	T	28	I	1	O	14	V	16	L	2	G	21	C	29	Q	23	A	1	I
11	8	A	28	T	7	I	23	N	24	O	8	L	11	S	29	G	21	Q	29	P	22	T	28	I
13	5	T	23	I	2	N	16	O	18	V	3	S	7	G	27	C	21	P	0	T	21	I	25	N
15	1	I	17	N	26	N	10	V	12	L	29	S	5	C	27	C	21	A	29	T	17	N	20	O
17	26	I	11	O	20	O	4	L	8	S	26	G	4	Q	28	P	20	T	26	I	12	O	14	V
19	20	N	5	V	13	V	29	L	4	G	25	C	4	P	27	A	17	I	22	N	6	V	7	L
21	14	O	28	V	8	L	25	S	1	C	24	Q	3	A	25	T	13	N	16	O	0	L	2	S
23	8	V	23	L	2	S	21	G	29	C	22	P	1	T	21	I	7	O	9	V	24	L	26	S
25	2	L	18	S	28	S	18	C	27	Q	20	A	28	T	16	N	1	V	3	L	18	S	23	G
27	26	L	14	G	24	G	16	Q	25	P	18	T	24	I	10	O	25	V	27	L	14	G	20	C
29	22	S			21	C	15	P	24	A	14	I	19	N	4	V	18	L	22	S	10	C	18	Q
31	19	G			20	Q			21	T			13	O	27	V			17	G			16	P

1936 BST: 19/4–4/10

date	Jan		Feb		Mar		Apr		May		Jun		Jul		Aug		Sep		Oct		Nov		Dec	
1	1	A	23	T	17	I	5	O	8	V	22	L	25	S	11	C	1	P	9	A	3	I	10	N
3	29	A	20	I	13	N	29	O	2	L	16	S	20	G	8	Q	0	A	9	T	2	N	8	O
5	27	T	16	N	8	O	23	V	26	L	11	G	16	C	6	P	0	T	9	I	29	N	3	V
7	24	I	11	O	2	V	17	L	20	S	6	C	13	Q	5	A	29	T	7	N	25	O	28	V
9	20	N	6	V	26	V	11	S	14	G	3	Q	11	P	4	T	27	I	3	O	19	V	22	L
11	15	O	0	L	20	L	5	G	10	C	0	P	9	A	2	I	23	N	28	O	13	L	16	S
13	10	V	23	L	14	S	0	C	6	Q	28	P	7	T	0	N	18	O	22	V	7	S	9	G
15	3	L	17	S	8	G	26	C	3	P	27	A	6	I	26	N	13	V	16	L	1	G	4	C
17	27	L	12	G	3	C	23	Q	2	A	26	T	3	N	22	O	7	L	10	S	25	G	29	C
19	22	S	8	C	0	Q	22	P	1	T	24	I	0	O	17	V	1	S	4	G	19	C	25	Q
21	17	G	6	Q	29	Q	23	A	1	I	22	N	26	O	11	L	25	S	28	G	15	Q	22	P
23	14	C	6	P	29	P	23	T	0	N	18	O	21	V	5	S	19	G	23	C	12	P	20	A
25	13	Q	6	A	0	T	22	I	27	N	13	V	15	L	28	S	14	C	19	Q	11	A	19	T
27	12	P	6	T	29	T	19	N	22	O	7	L	8	S	23	G	10	Q	17	P	10	T	19	I
29	11	A	4	I	27	I	14	O	17	V	1	S	3	G	19	C	9	P	17	A	11	I	18	N
31	10	T			23	N			11	L			28	G	16	Q			18	T			15	O

1937 BST: 18/4-3/10

date	Jan		Feb		Mar		Apr		May		Jun		Jul		Aug		Sep		Oct		Nov		Dec	
1	29	O	14	L	22	L	6	G	8	C	25	Q	1	A	24	T	17	N	25	O	13	L	17	S
3	24	V	8	S	16	S	29	G	3	Q	21	P	29	A	23	I	15	O	21	V	8	S	10	G
5	18	L	1	G	9	G	24	C	28	Q	19	A	28	T	21	N	12	V	17	L	2	G	4	C
7	12	S	26	G	3	C	20	Q	26	P	19	T	28	I	20	O	8	L	11	S	25	G	28	C
9	6	G	21	C	29	C	18	P	25	A	19	I	27	N	17	V	3	S	5	G	19	C	22	Q
11	0	C	17	Q	26	Q	17	A	26	T	19	N	25	O	13	L	27	S	29	G	13	Q	17	P
13	25	C	15	P	24	P	17	T	26	I	17	O	22	V	7	S	21	G	23	C	9	P	14	A
15	22	Q	14	A	23	A	17	I	25	N	14	V	17	L	1	G	15	C	18	Q	6	A	13	T
17	19	P	12	T	23	T	15	N	22	O	9	L	11	S	25	G	10	Q	14	P	5	T	13	I
19	17	A	10	I	21	I	12	O	17	V	3	S	5	G	19	C	6	P	12	A	5	I	13	N
21	15	T	8	N	19	N	8	V	12	L	26	S	29	G	14	Q	4	A	12	T	5	N	13	O
23	14	I	5	O	15	O	3	L	6	S	20	G	23	C	11	P	3	T	11	I	4	O	11	V
25	12	N	2	V	11	V	27	L	29	S	14	C	18	Q	9	A	1	I	10	N	2	V	7	L
27	10	O	27	V	6	L	21	S	23	G	9	Q	15	P	7	T	0	N	8	O	28	V	2	S
29	6	V			0	S	14	G	17	C	5	P	12	A	5	I	28	N	5	V	23	L	25	S
31	2	L			24	S			12	Q			10	T	3	N			1	L			19	G

1938 BST: 10/4-2/10

date	Jan		Feb		Mar		Apr		May		Jun		Jul		Aug		Sep		Oct		Nov		Dec	
1	1	C	16	Q	25	Q	13	A	20	T	13	N	22	O	13	L	29	S	1	C	15	Q	17	P
3	25	C	11	P	21	P	11	T	19	I	13	O	20	V	9	S	23	G	25	C	9	P	12	A
5	19	Q	7	A	17	A	9	I	18	N	11	V	17	L	3	G	17	C	19	Q	5	A	9	T
7	14	P	4	T	15	T	8	N	17	O	7	L	12	S	27	G	11	Q	14	P	1	T	8	I
9	10	A	2	I	13	I	6	O	14	V	3	S	6	G	20	C	5	P	10	A	29	T	8	N
11	8	T	0	N	11	N	4	V	10	L	27	S	0	C	14	Q	1	A	6	T	28	I	7	O
13	6	I	0	O	9	O	1	L	6	S	21	G	24	C	9	P	27	A	4	I	27	N	6	V
15	6	N	29	O	8	V	27	L	0	G	15	C	17	Q	4	A	24	T	2	N	26	O	4	L
17	6	O	27	V	5	L	22	S	24	G	8	Q	12	P	0	T	21	I	0	O	23	V	0	S
19	5	V	23	L	1	S	16	G	18	C	3	P	7	A	27	T	20	N	29	O	20	L	25	S
21	3	L	18	S	26	S	10	C	12	Q	28	P	3	T	25	I	19	O	27	V	16	S	20	G
23	28	L	12	G	20	G	3	Q	6	P	24	A	1	I	24	N	18	V	24	L	11	G	14	C
25	22	S	6	C	14	C	28	Q	2	A	22	T	0	N	24	O	16	L	20	S	5	C	7	Q
27	16	G	0	Q	8	Q	24	P	29	A	22	I	0	O	23	V	12	S	15	G	29	C	1	P
29	9	C			3	P	21	A	28	T	22	N	1	V	21	L	7	G	9	C	23	Q	25	P
31	4	Q			29	P			28	I			29	V	17	S			3	Q			20	A

1939 BST: 16/4-19/11

date	Jan		Feb		Mar		Apr		May		Jun		Jul		Aug		Sep		Oct		Nov		Dec	
1	3	T	24	I	3	N	27	O	5	L	26	S	0	C	15	Q	0	A	3	T	22	I	0	O
3	1	I	24	N	2	O	26	V	3	S	21	G	25	C	9	P	24	A	29	T	19	N	28	O
5	1	N	24	O	2	V	25	L	0	G	16	C	18	Q	3	A	19	T	25	I	17	O	26	V
7	1	O	24	V	2	L	22	S	26	G	10	Q	12	P	27	A	15	I	22	N	16	V	24	L
9	1	V	23	L	1	S	18	G	20	C	4	P	6	A	22	T	12	N	21	O	14	L	22	S
11	0	L	19	S	27	S	12	C	14	Q	28	P	1	T	19	I	12	O	21	V	13	S	19	G
13	27	L	14	G	22	G	6	Q	8	P	23	A	27	T	18	N	12	V	20	L	10	G	15	C
15	22	S	8	C	16	C	0	P	2	A	19	T	25	I	18	O	12	L	19	S	7	C	9	Q
17	17	G	1	Q	10	Q	24	P	28	A	17	I	25	N	19	V	11	S	16	G	2	Q	3	P
19	11	C	25	Q	4	P	19	A	24	T	16	N	25	O	18	L	8	G	11	C	26	Q	27	P
21	4	Q	19	P	28	P	15	T	22	I	16	O	25	V	16	S	3	C	6	Q	19	P	21	A
23	28	Q	14	A	23	A	12	I	21	N	15	V	23	L	12	G	27	C	29	Q	13	A	16	T
25	22	P	9	T	19	T	10	N	19	O	12	L	19	S	6	C	21	Q	23	P	8	T	13	I
27	17	A	5	I	16	I	8	O	18	V	9	S	15	G	0	Q	15	P	18	A	4	I	11	N
29	12	T			13	N	7	V	16	L	5	G	9	C	24	Q	9	A	13	T	2	N	10	O
31	9	I			12	O			12	S			3	Q	18	P			9	I			9	V

1940 BST: 25/2-31/12

date	Jan	Feb	Mar	Apr	May	Jun	Jul	Aug	Sep	Oct	Nov	Dec
1	23 V	15 S	8 G	26 C	29 Q	12 A	14 T	1 N	22 O	0 L	23 S	0 C
3	21 L	12 G	4 C	20 Q	22 P	6 T	10 I	29 N	21 V	0 S	22 G	28 C
5	18 S	7 C	29 C	14 P	16 A	1 I	6 N	28 O	21 L	0 G	20 C	24 Q
7	15 G	2 Q	23 Q	7 A	10 T	27 I	4 O	27 V	20 S	28 G	15 Q	18 P
9	10 C	26 Q	17 P	1 T	5 I	24 N	3 V	26 L	18 G	24 C	10 P	12 A
11	5 Q	20 P	10 A	26 T	1 N	22 O	1 L	24 S	14 C	19 Q	3 A	5 T
13	29 Q	13 A	4 T	21 I	28 N	20 V	29 L	21 G	9 Q	13 P	27 A	29 T
15	23 P	7 T	29 T	17 N	25 O	19 L	27 S	17 C	4 P	6 A	21 T	25 I
17	17 A	2 I	24 I	15 O	24 V	17 S	24 G	13 Q	28 P	0 T	15 I	21 N
19	11 T	28 I	21 N	14 V	23 L	15 G	21 C	7 P	21 A	24 T	11 N	17 O
21	7 I	27 N	20 O	14 L	22 S	12 C	16 Q	1 A	15 T	18 I	7 O	15 V
23	4 N	27 O	20 V	.13 S	20 G	8 Q	11 P	24 A	9 I	14 N	4 V	13 L
25	4 O	27 V	20 L	12 G	17 C	3 P	4 A	18 T	4 N	10 O	2 L	11 S
27	4 V	27 L	20 S	9 C	12 Q	26 P	28 A	13 I	1 O	8 V	2 S	10 G
29	3 L	25 S	17 G	4 Q	7 P	20 A	22 T	9 N	0 V	8 L	1 G	8 C
31	2 S		13 C		0 A		18 I	7 O		8 S		6 Q

1941 BST: 4/5-10/8

date	Jan	Feb	Mar	Apr	May	Jun	Jul	Aug	Sep	Oct	Nov	Dec
1	19 Q	3 A	12 A	25 T	29 I	16 O	23 V	16 S	9 C	16 Q	4 A	7 T
3	14 P	27 A	5 T	19 I	23 N	13 V	21 L	14 G	6 Q	12 P	28 A	0 I
5	8 A	21 T	29 T	14 N	19 O	11 L	20 S	13 C	3 P	7 A	22 T	24 I
7	1 T	15 I	23 I	10 O	17 V	10 S	19 G	11 Q	28 P	1 T	15 I	18 N
9	25 T	11 N	19 N	8 V	16 L	10 G	18 C	7 P	23 A	25 T	9 N	13 O
11	20 I	8 O	16 O	8 L	16 S	10 C	16 Q	2 A	17 T	19 I	4 O	9 V
13	16 N	6 V	15 V	8 S	17 G	8 Q	12 P	27 A	10 I	13 N	29 O	5 L
15	13 O	5 L	15 L	8 G	16 C	4 P	7 A	21 T	5 N	8 O	26 V	4 S
17	11 V	4 S	14 S	7 C	13 Q	29 P	1 T	14 I	0 O	4 V	25 L	4 G
19	9 L	3 G	13 G	4 Q	8 P	23 A	24 T	9 N	26 O	3 L	26 S	4 C
21	8 S	0 C	11 C	29 Q	2 A	16 T	19 I	5 O	25 V	2 S	26 G	4 Q
23	6 G	27 C	7 Q	23 P	26 A	10 I	14 N	2 V	24 L	3 G	26 C	1 P
25	4 C	23 Q	2 P	17 A	19 T	5 N	9 O	0 L	23 S	2 C	23 Q	27 P
27	1 Q	17 P	26 P	11 T	13 I	0 O	6 V	28 L	22 G	0 Q	18 P	22 A
29	27 Q		20 A	4 I	8 N	26 O	4 L	27 S	20 C	26 Q	13 A	15 T
31	21 P		14 T		3 O		2 S	25 G		22 P		9 I

1942 BST: 5/4-9/8

date	Jan	Feb	Mar	Apr	May	Jun	Jul	Aug	Sep	Oct	Nov	Dec
1	21 I	7 O	15 O	3 L	11 S	5 C	13 Q	3 A	19 T	21 I	5 O	7 V
3	15 N	2 V	11 V	2 S	11 G	4 Q	11 P	29 A	13 I	15 N	29 O	2 L
5	10 O	29 V	9 L	1 G	10 C	2 P	7 A	23 T	7 N	9 O	24 V	29 L
7	6 V	26 L	7 S	0 C	9 Q	28 P	2 T	17 I	1 O	4 V	22 L	29 S
9	2 L	24 S	5 G	28 C	6 P	23 A	26 T	11 N	26 O	0 L	20 S	29 G
11	29 L	23 G	4 C	25 Q	1 A	17 T	20 I	5 O	21 V	27 L	20 G	29 C
13	28 S	21 C	2 Q	22 P	26 A	11 I	14 N	29 O	18 L	26 S	19 C	28 Q
15	28 G	20 Q	29 Q	17 A	20 T	5 N	8 O	25 V	15 S	25 G	18 Q	25 P
17	27 C	17 P	25 P	12 T	14 I	29 N	3 V	21 L	14 G	23 C	15 P	21 A
19	26 Q	13 A	21 A	6 I	8 N	23 O	28 V	19 S	12 C	21 Q	11 A	16 T
21	22 P	8 T	15 T	29 I	2 O	18 V	24 L	17 G	10 Q	18 P	7 T	10 I
23	18 A	2 I	9 I	23 N	26 O	15 L	22 S	16 C	8 P	15 A	1 I	4 N
25	12 T	25 I	3 N	18 O	22 V	13 S	22 G	15 Q	6 A	10 T	25 I	28 N
27	6 I	20 N	27 N	14 V	20 L	13 G	22 C	14 P	2 T	5 I	19 N	21 O
29	29 I		23 O	11 L	19 S	13 C	21 Q	11 A	27 T	29 I	13 O	16 V
31	24 N		19 V		19 G		19 P	7 T		23 N		11 L

1943 BST: 4/4-5/8

date	Jan		Feb		Mar		Apr		May		Jun		Jul		Aug		Sep		Oct		Nov		Dec	
1	24	L	15	G	25	G	19	Q	27	P	17	T	21	I	6	O	20	V	24	L	14	G	22	C
3	22	S	15	C	24	C	17	P	24	A	12	I	15	N	29	O	15	L	20	S	11	C	20	Q
5	22	G	15	Q	23	Q	15	A	20	T	6	N	9	O	23	V	10	S	17	G	9	Q	18	P
7	22	C	15	P	23	P	12	T	16	I	0	O	2	V	18	L	6	G	14	C	8	P	16	A
9	22	Q	13	A	21	A	8	I	10	N	24	O	26	V	13	S	4	C	13	Q	6	A	13	T
11	21	P	9	T	17	T	2	N	4	O	18	V	21	L	10	G	3	Q	12	P	4	T	10	I
13	18	A	4	I	12	I	26	N	27	O	13	L	18	S	9	C	3	P	11	A	1	I	5	N
15	13	T	28	I	6	N	19	O	22	V	9	S	16	G	9	Q	2	A	9	T	27	I	29	N
17	7	I	21	N	0	O	14	V	18	L	8	G	16	C	9	P	1	T	6	I	21	N	23	O
19	1	N	15	O	24	O	9	L	15	S	7	C	16	Q	9	A	28	T	1	N	15	O	17	V
21	25	N	10	V	18	V	6	S	14	G	7	Q	16	P	6	T	23	I	25	N	9	V	11	L
23	18	O	5	L	14	L	4	G	13	C	6	P	14	A	2	I	17	N	19	O	3	L	6	S
25	13	V	0	S	10	S	3	C	12	Q	4	A	10	T	27	I	11	O	13	V	28	L	3	G
27	7	L	27	S	8	G	1	Q	10	P	1	T	6	I	21	N	5	V	7	L	25	S	2	C
29	3	S			6	C	29	Q	7	A	26	T	0	N	14	O	29	V	3	S	23	G	1	Q
31	1	G			4	Q			4	T			24	N	8	V			0	G			1	P

1944 BST: 2/4-15/7

date	Jan		Feb		Mar		Apr		May		Jun		Jul		Aug		Sep		Oct		Nov		Dec	
1	15	P	7	T	29	T	16	N	18	O	2	L	4	S	21	G	12	Q	20	P	14	T	21	I
3	13	A	3	I	25	I	10	O	12	V	26	L	0	G	19	C	12	P	21	A	13	I	18	N
5	10	T	28	I	19	N	4	V	6	L	22	S	27	G	19	Q	12	A	21	T	10	N	13	O
7	6	I	22	N	13	O	27	V	0	S	18	G	25	C	19	P	12	T	18	I	5	O	7	V
9	1	N	16	O	7	V	22	L	26	S	16	C	24	Q	18	A	10	I	14	N	0	V	1	L
11	26	N	10	V	1	L	17	S	22	G	14	Q	23	P	16	T	5	N	9	O	23	V	25	L
13	19	O	4	L	25	L	12	G	20	C	13	P	22	A	13	I	0	O	3	V	17	L	20	S
15	13	V	28	L	20	S	9	C	17	Q	11	A	19	T	8	N	24	O	27	V	11	S	15	G
17	7	L	23	S	15	G	7	Q	16	P	9	T	16	I	3	O	18	V	20	L	6	G	12	C
19	1	S	19	G	13	C	5	P	14	A	6	I	11	N	27	O	11	L	15	S	2	C	9	Q
21	27	S	18	C	11	Q	5	A	13	T	2	N	6	O	21	V	5	S	9	G	29	C	7	P
23	25	G	17	Q	11	P	4	T	11	I	28	N	0	V	14	L	0	G	5	C	26	Q	5	A
25	24	C	18	P	11	A	2	I	7	N	22	O	24	V	8	S	25	G	2	Q	24	P	3	T
27	25	Q	18	A	10	T	29	I	2	O	16	V	18	L	3	G	22	C	0	P	23	A	2	I
29	24	P	16	T	8	I	24	N	26	O	10	L	12	S	29	G	20	Q	29	P	22	T	29	I
31	23	A			4	N			20	V			8	G	27	C			29	A			26	N

1945 BST: 2/4-15/7

date	Jan		Feb		Mar		Apr		May		Jun		Jul		Aug		Sep		Oct		Nov		Dec	
1	8	O	23	V	2	L	16	S	19	G	7	Q	15	P	9	T	1	N	8	O	24	V	27	L
3	3	V	17	L	5	L	10	G	14	C	4	P	13	A	7	I	28	N	3	V	18	L	21	S
5	27	V	11	S	9	S	5	C	10	Q	3	A	12	T	4	N	23	O	27	V	12	S	15	G
7	21	L	5	G	3	G	1	Q	8	P	2	T	11	I	1	O	18	V	21	L	6	G	9	C
9	15	S	1	C	9	C	29	Q	7	A	1	I	9	N	27	O	13	L	15	S	0	C	4	Q
11	10	G	28	C	6	Q	28	P	7	T	0	N	6	O	22	V	7	S	9	G	24	C	0	P
13	7	C	27	Q	5	P	29	A	7	I	28	N	2	V	16	L	0	G	3	C	20	Q	27	P
15	4	Q	27	P	6	A	29	T	6	N	24	O	26	V	10	S	24	G	28	C	17	P	26	A
17	3	P	26	A	6	T	28	I	3	O	18	V	20	L	4	G	19	C	25	Q	16	A	25	T
19	2	A	25	T	5	I	24	N	28	O	12	L	14	S	29	G	16	Q	23	P	17	T	25	I
21	0	T	22	I	2	N	19	O	22	V	6	S	8	G	25	C	15	P	23	A	17	I	24	N
23	28	T	18	N	28	N	14	V	16	L	0	G	4	C	22	Q	15	A	24	T	16	N	21	O
25	25	I	13	O	22	O	7	L	10	S	25	G	0	Q	21	P	15	T	23	I	13	O	17	V
27	21	N	7	V	16	V	1	S	4	G	21	C	27	Q	21	A	14	I	21	N	9	V	12	L
29	17	O			10	L	25	S	29	G	18	Q	26	P	20	T	12	N	17	O	3	L	6	S
31	11	V			4	S			24	C			24	A	18	I			12	V			29	S

1946 BST: 14/4-6/10

date	Jan		Feb		Mar		Apr		May		Jun		Jul		Aug		Sep		Oct		Nov		Dec	
1	11	S	27	C	5	Q	24	P	2	T	25	I	3	O	23	V	9	S	11	G	24	C	27	Q
3	6	C	23	Q	2	P	23	A	2	I	25	N	1	V	19	L	3	G	4	C	19	Q	23	P
5	1	Q	20	P	0	A	23	T	2	N	23	O	28	V	13	S	26	G	28	C	14	P	20	A
7	27	Q	18	A	29	A	22	I	0	O	19	V	23	L	7	G	20	C	23	Q	12	A	19	T
9	24	P	17	T	28	T	20	N	27	O	14	L	17	S	0	C	5	Q	20	P	11	T	19	I
11	2	A	15	I	26	I	17	O	22	V	8	S	10	G	25	C	12	P	18	A	11	I	20	N
13	20	T	13	N	23	N	13	V	17	L	2	G	4	C	20	Q	9	A	18	T	11	N	19	O
15	19	I	10	O	20	O	8	L	11	S	25	G	28	C	16	P	8	T	17	I	10	O	16	V
17	18	N	7	V	16	V	2	S	5	G	19	C	23	Q	13	A	6	I	15	N	7	V	12	L
19	16	O	3	L	11	L	26	S	28	G	14	Q	20	P	11	T	4	N	13	O	3	L	7	S
21	12	V	27	L	5	S	19	G	22	C	9	P	16	A	9	I	2	O	10	V	27	L	1	G
23	8	L	21	S	29	S	13	C	17	Q	6	A	14	T	8	N	0	V	6	L	22	S	24	G
25	2	S	15	G	23	G	8	Q	13	P	4	T	13	I	6	O	26	V	1	S	15	G	18	C
27	25	S	9	C	17	C	4	P	11	A	4	I	13	N	4	V	22	L	25	S	9	C	12	Q
29	19	G			12	Q	2	A	10	T	4	N	12	O	1	L	17	S	19	G	3	Q	6	P
31	14	C			10	P			10	I			10	V	27	L			12	C			2	A

1947 BST: 13/4-10/8

date	Jan		Feb		Mar		Apr		May		Jun		Jul		Aug		Sep		Oct		Nov		Dec	
1	15	A	7	I	17	I	10	O	19	V	8	S	11	G	26	C	11	P	15	A	5	I	13	N
3	13	T	6	N	16	N	9	V	15	L	2	G	5	C	20	Q	6	A	12	T	3	N	13	O
5	12	I	6	O	15	O	6	L	11	S	26	G	29	C	14	P	2	T	9	I	2	O	11	V
7	13	N	5	V	13	V	2	S	6	G	20	C	22	Q	9	A	28	T	7	N	0	V	8	L
9	13	O	3	L	11	L	27	S	0	C	14	Q	17	P	5	T	26	I	5	O	28	V	5	S
11	11	V	29	L	7	S	22	G	23	C	8	P	12	A	2	I	25	N	4	V	25	L	0	G
13	8	L	24	S	2	G	15	C	17	Q	3	A	8	T	0	N	24	O	2	L	21	S	25	G
15	3	S	18	G	26	G	9	Q	12	P	0	T	7	I	0	O	23	V	0	S	16	G	19	C
17	28	S	11	C	19	C	4	P	8	A	28	T	6	N	0	V	22	L	26	S	11	C	13	Q
19	21	G	15	Q	13	Q	0	A	5	T	28	I	7	O	29	V	18	S	21	G	5	Q	6	P
21	15	C	0	P	9	P	27	A	5	I	28	N	7	V	27	L	13	G	15	C	28	Q	1	A
23	9	Q	26	P	5	A	26	T	4	N	28	O	5	L	23	S	7	C	9	Q	23	P	26	A
25	3	P	22	A	2	T	24	I	4	O	26	V	1	S	17	G	1	Q	3	P	18	A	23	T
27	29	P	19	T	0	I	23	N	2	V	22	L	26	S	11	C	25	Q	28	P	15	T	22	I
29	25	A			28	I	21	O	29	V	17	S	20	G	4	Q	19	P	24	A	14	I	22	N
31	23	T			26	N			25	L			14	C	28	Q			21	T			22	O

1948 BST: 14/3-30/10

date	Jan		Feb		Mar		Apr		May		Jun		Jul		Aug		Sep		Oct		Nov		Dec	
1	7	V	28	L	20	S	6	C	8	Q	21	P	24	A	11	I	3	O	12	V	5	S	11	G
3	5	L	24	S	15	G	0	Q	2	P	16	A	20	T	10	N	3	V	12	L	3	G	8	C
5	2	S	19	G	10	C	24	Q	26	P	12	T	17	I	9	O	4	L	11	S	0	C	3	Q
7	27	S	13	C	3	Q	18	P	21	A	9	I	16	N	10	V	3	S	9	G	25	C	27	Q
9	22	G	6	Q	27	Q	12	A	16	T	7	N	16	O	10	L	0	G	5	C	19	Q	21	P
11	16	C	0	P	21	P	8	T	14	I	6	O	15	V	8	S	26	G	29	C	13	P	15	A
13	9	Q	24	P	16	A	4	I	11	N	5	V	14	L	4	G	20	C	23	Q	7	A	9	T
15	3	P	19	A	11	T	1	N	10	O	3	L	11	S	29	G	14	Q	17	P	1	T	5	I
17	27	P	14	T	7	I	29	N	8	V	1	S	7	G	23	C	8	P	11	A	27	T	2	N
19	22	A	10	I	4	N	27	O	6	L	27	S	2	C	17	Q	2	A	5	T	23	I	1	O
21	18	T	8	N	3	O	26	V	4	S	23	G	26	C	11	P	26	A	0	I	21	N	29	O
23	15	I	8	O	2	V	25	L	1	G	18	C	20	Q	5	A	21	T	27	I	18	O	28	V
25	15	N	9	V	2	L	23	S	27	G	12	Q	14	P	29	A	16	I	24	N	17	V	26	L
27	16	O	9	L	1	S	19	G	22	C	6	P	8	A	24	T	13	N	22	O	15	L	23	S
29	16	V	7	S	28	S	14	C	16	Q	0	A	2	T	20	I	12	O	21	V	13	S	20	G
31	15	L			24	G			10	P			28	T	18	N			20	L			16	C

1949 BST: 3/4-30/10

date	Jan	Feb	Mar	Apr	May	Jun	Jul	Aug	Sep	Oct	Nov	Dec
1	28 C	13 P	22 P	6 T	10 I	29 N	7 V	1 S	23 G	29 C	15 P	17 A
3	23 Q	7 A	15 A	1 I	6 N	27 O	6 L	29 S	19 C	24 Q	9 A	11 T
5	17 P	1 T	9 T	26 I	2 O	25 V	4 S	26 G	14 Q	18 P	2 T	5 I
7	11 A	25 T	4 I	22 N	0 V	23 L	2 G	22 C	9 P	12 A	26 T	0 N
9	5 T	21 I	29 I	20 O	29 V	22 S	29 G	18 Q	3 A	5 T	20 I	25 N
11	0 I	19 N	27 N	20 V	28 L	20 G	26 C	12 P	26 A	29 T	16 N	22 O
13	27 I	18 O	26 O	20 L	28 S	18 C	22 Q	6 A	20 T	23 I	12 O	19 V
15	25 N	18 V	27 V	20 S	26 G	14 Q	16 P	0 T	14 I	19 N	9 V	17 L
17	25 O	18 L	27 L	18 G	23 C	8 P	10 A	24 T	10 N	16 O	8 L	16 S
19	24 V	17 S	26 S	15 C	18 Q	2 A	4 T	19 I	7 O	14 V	7 S	16 G
21	23 L	13 G	23 G	10 Q	12 P	26 A	28 T	15 N	6 V	14 L	7 G	14 C
23	20 S	9 C	19 C	4 P	6 A	20 T	24 I	13 O	6 L	14 S	6 C	12 Q
25	16 G	4 Q	13 Q	28 P	0 T	15 I	21 N	13 V	6 S	14 G	4 Q	7 P
27	12 C	28 Q	7 P	21 A	24 T	12 N	19 O	12 L	5 G	12 C	29 Q	1 A
29	7 Q		1 A	15 T	19 I	9 O	18 V	11 S	3 C	8 Q	23 P	25 A
31	1 P		24 A		16 N		17 L	9 G		3 P		19 T

1950 BST:16/4-22/10

date	Jan	Feb	Mar	Apr	May	Jun	Jul	Aug	Sep	Oct	Nov	Dec
1	1 I	17 N	25 N	14 V	22 L	16 G	24 C	13 P	28 A	0 I	14 N	18 O
3	26 I	14 O	22 O	14 L	23 S	16 C	22 Q	8 A	22 T	24 I	9 O	14 V
5	22 N	12 V	21 V	14 S	23 G	14 Q	18 P	2 T	16 I	18 N	5 V	11 L
7	19 O	11 L	20 L	14 G	21 C	10 P	12 A	26 T	10 N	14 O	2 L	10 S
9	16 V	9 S	20 S	12 C	18 Q	4 A	6 T	20 I	6 O	10 V	2 S	10 G
11	14 L	7 G	18 G	9 Q	13 P	28 A	0 I	15 N	2 V	9 L	2 G	11 C
13	12 S	5 C	15 C	4 P	7 A	22 T	24 I	11 O	0 L	9 S	2 C	10 Q
15	11 G	2 Q	11 Q	28 P	1 T	15 I	19 N	7 V	29 L	8 G	1 Q	7 P
17	9 C	28 Q	7 P	22 A	25 T	10 N	15 O	5 L	28 S	7 C	28 Q	3 A
19	6 Q	23 P	1 A	16 T	18 I	5 O	11 V	3 S	27 G	5 Q	23 P	27 A
21	2 P	17 A	25 A	9 I	13 N	1 V	8 L	2 G	24 C	1 P	18 A	21 T
23	27 P	11 T	19 T	4 N	8 O	28 V	6 S	0 C	21 Q	26 P	12 T	14 I
25	21 A	4 I	13 I	28 N	4 V	26 L	5 G	28 C	17 P	21 A	6 I	8 N
27	15 T	29 I	7 N	25 O	2 L	25 S	4 C	25 Q	12 A	15 T	29 I	3 O
29	9 I		3 O	23 V	1 S	25 G	2 Q	21 P	6 T	9 I	23 N	28 O
31	4 N		0 V		1 G		0 P	16 A		2 N		23 V

1951 BST: 15/4-21/10

date	Jan	Feb	Mar	Apr	May	Jun	Jul	Aug	Sep	Oct	Nov	Dec
1	7 L	29 S	10 G	3 Q	10 P	28 A	2 I	16 N	1 V	6 L	26 S	5 C
3	4 S	28 G	8 C	0 P	6 A	22 T	25 I	10 O	27 V	3 S	25 G	5 Q
5	3 G	27 C	6 Q	27 P	1 T	16 I	19 N	5 V	23 L	1 G	24 C	3 P
7	4 C	26 Q	4 P	22 A	26 T	10 N	13 O	0 L	20 S	29 G	22 Q	0 A
9	3 Q	23 P	1 A	17 T	20 I	4 O	7 V	26 L	18 G	28 C	20 P	26 A
11	2 P	19 A	27 A	11 I	13 N	28 O	3 L	23 S	17 C	26 Q	16 A	21 T
13	28 P	13 T	21 T	5 N	17 O	23 V	29 L	22 G	16 Q	23 P	12 T	15 I
15	23 A	7 I	15 I	29 N	2 V	20 L	28 S	22 C	14 P	20 A	7 I	9 N
17	17 T	1 N	9 N	24 O	28 V	19 S	27 G	21 Q	12 A	16 T	1 N	3 O
19	11 I	25 N	3 O	20 V	26 L	19 G	28 C	20 P	8 T	11 I	24 N	27 O
21	5 N	21 O	29 O	18 L	25 S	19 C	27 Q	17 A	3 I	5 N	18 O	21 V
23	29 N	17 V	25 V	17 S	26 G	19 Q	25 P	12 T	27 I	28 N	13 V	16 L
25	24 O	14 L	23 L	16 G	25 C	17 P	22 A	7 I	20 N	22 O	8 L	14 S
27	20 V	11 S	22 S	16 C	24 Q	13 A	16 T	1 N	15 O	17 V	6 S	13 G
29	17 L		21 G	14 Q	20 P	8 T	10 I	24 N	9 V	14 L	5 G	13 C
31	15 S		19 C		16 A		4 N	19 O		12 S		14 Q

1952 BST: 20/4-26/10

date	Jan		Feb		Mar		Apr		May		Jun		Jul		Aug		Sep		Oct		Nov		Dec	
1	28	Q	19	A	10	T	26	I	27	N	11	V	14	L	2	G	24	C	3	P	25	A	2	I
3	26	P	15	T	5	I	20	N	21	O	6	L	10	S	0	C	24	Q	2	A	23	T	28	I
5	23	A	9	I	0	N	13	O	15	V	2	S	8	G	0	Q	24	P	1	T	20	I	23	N
7	18	T	3	N	23	N	7	V	10	L	29	S	7	C	1	P	23	A	29	T	15	N	17	O
9	12	I	27	N	17	O	2	L	7	S	28	G	7	Q	0	A	21	T	25	I	9	O	10	V
11	6	N	20	O	11	V	28	L	5	G	28	C	7	P	29	A	16	I	19	N	3	V	4	L
13	0	O	15	V	6	L	25	S	4	C	27	Q	5	A	25	T	11	N	13	O	26	V	29	L
15	24	O	9	L	2	S	23	G	2	Q	25	P	2	T	20	I	5	O	7	V	21	L	26	S
17	18	V	5	S	29	S	21	C	1	P	22	A	28	T	14	N	28	O	1	L	17	S	23	G
19	12	L	2	G	26	G	20	Q	28	P	18	T	23	I	8	O	22	V	26	L	15	G	22	C
21	9	S	0	C	25	C	18	P	25	A	14	I	17	N	1	V	17	L	22	S	13	C	21	Q
23	6	G	0	Q	24	Q	16	A	22	T	8	N	11	O	25	V	12	S	18	G	11	Q	20	P
25	6	C	29	Q	23	P	13	T	17	I	2	O	4	V	20	L	8	G	16	C	9	P	18	A
27	6	Q	29	P	21	A	9	I	12	N	26	O	28	V	15	S	5	C	14	Q	7	A	15	T
29	6	P	27	A	18	T	4	N	5	O	19	V	23	L	11	G	3	Q	12	P	5	T	11	I
31	5	A			13	I			29	O			18	S	9	C			11	A			6	N

1953 BST: 19/4-4/10

date	Jan		Feb		Mar		Apr		May		Jun		Jul		Aug		Sep		Oct		Nov		Dec	
1	19	N	3	V	12	V	27	L	1	G	21	C	29	Q	23	A	15	I	20	N	5	V	7	L
3	13	O	27	V	6	L	22	S	27	G	19	Q	28	P	21	T	10	N	14	O	29	V	1	S
5	7	V	21	L	0	S	17	G	24	C	17	P	26	A	18	I	5	O	8	V	22	L	25	S
7	0	L	15	S	25	S	14	C	22	Q	15	A	24	T	13	N	29	O	2	L	17	S	21	G
9	24	L	11	G	20	G	12	Q	21	P	14	T	21	I	8	O	23	V	26	L	11	G	17	C
11	20	S	9	C	18	C	11	P	20	A	11	I	17	N	2	V	17	L	20	S	7	C	14	Q
13	17	G	9	Q	17	Q	11	A	19	T	8	N	12	O	26	V	10	S	14	G	3	Q	11	P
15	16	C	9	P	17	P	10	T	17	I	3	O	6	V	20	L	5	G	10	C	1	P	10	A
17	16	Q	9	A	17	A	8	I	13	N	28	O	29	V	14	S	0	C	7	Q	29	P	8	T
19	15	P	8	T	16	T	5	N	8	O	21	V	23	L	9	G	27	C	5	P	29	A	7	I
21	14	A	5	I	14	I	0	O	2	V	15	L	18	S	5	C	26	Q	5	A	28	T	5	N
23	12	T	0	N	9	N	24	O	25	V	10	S	14	G	3	Q	27	P	5	T	27	I	1	O
25	8	I	24	N	3	O	17	V	19	L	6	G	11	C	3	P	27	A	5	I	24	N	27	O
27	3	N	18	O	27	O	11	L	14	S	3	C	10	Q	3	A	27	T	3	N	19	O	21	V
29	27	N			21	V	6	S	10	G	1	Q	9	P	3	T	24	I	29	N	13	V	15	L
31	21	O			15	L			7	C			9	A	1	I			23	O			9	S

1954 BST: 11/4-3/10

date	Jan		Feb		Mar		Apr		May		Jun		Jul		Aug		Sep		Oct		Nov		Dec	
1	21	S	7	C	15	C	5	P	13	A	7	I	14	N	3	V	18	L	20	S	5	C	9	Q
3	16	G	4	Q	12	Q	5	A	14	T	6	N	12	O	28	V	12	S	14	G	29	C	5	P
5	12	C	3	P	12	P	5	T	14	I	4	O	7	V	22	L	6	G	8	C	25	Q	2	A
7	10	Q	2	A	12	A	5	I	12	N	29	O	2	L	16	S	0	C	3	Q	23	P	1	T
9	8	P	1	T	11	T	3	N	8	O	24	V	26	L	10	G	25	C	1	P	23	A	1	I
11	6	A	0	I	10	I	29	N	3	V	18	L	20	S	5	C	22	Q	0	A	23	T	11	N
13	5	T	27	I	7	N	24	O	27	V	12	S	14	G	1	Q	21	P	0	T	23	I	0	O
15	3	I	23	N	3	O	19	V	21	L	6	G	9	C	28	Q	21	A	0	I	22	N	27	O
17	0	N	18	O	27	O	12	L	15	S	1	C	5	Q	27	P	21	T	29	I	19	O	23	V
19	27	N	13	V	22	V	6	S	9	G	26	C	3	P	26	A	19	I	26	N	14	V	17	L
21	22	O	7	L	15	L	0	G	4	C	22	Q	1	A	24	T	16	N	22	O	9	L	11	S
23	17	V	1	S	9	S	24	G	29	C	20	P	29	A	22	I	12	O	17	V	2	S	5	G
25	11	L	24	S	3	G	19	C	25	Q	18	A	27	T	19	N	8	V	11	L	26	S	29	G
27	4	S	19	G	27	G	16	Q	23	P	17	T	26	I	16	O	2	L	5	S	20	G	23	C
29	29	S			23	C	14	P	22	A	16	I	23	N	11	V	27	L	29	S	14	C	19	Q
31	24	G			20	Q			22	T			20	O	6	L			23	G			15	P

1955 BST: 17/4-2/10

date	Jan		Feb		Mar		Apr		May		Jun		Jul		Aug		Sep		Oct		Nov		Dec	
1	28	P	21	T	2	I	25	N	2	V	19	L	22	S	6	C	21	Q	26	P	18	T	26	I
3	26	A	20	I	0	N	22	O	27	V	13	S	15	G	0	Q	17	P	24	A	17	I	26	N
5	25	T	18	N	28	N	18	V	22	L	7	G	9	C	25	Q	15	A	23	T	16	N	24	O
7	25	I	16	O	25	O	13	L	16	S	0	C	3	Q	21	P	13	T	22	I	14	O	21	V
9	24	N	13	V	21	V	7	S	10	G	24	C	28	Q	18	A	11	I	20	N	11	V	17	L
11	22	O	9	L	17	L	1	G	3	C	19	Q	24	P	16	T	9	N	17	O	7	L	12	S
13	18	V	3	S	11	S	25	G	27	C	14	P	21	A	14	I	7	O	15	V	2	S	6	G
15	13	L	27	S	5	G	19	C	22	Q	11	A	19	T	13	N	5	V	11	L	27	S	29	G
17	7	S	21	G	28	G	13	Q	18	P	10	T	19	I	12	O	2	L	6	S	21	G	23	C
19	1	G	15	C	23	C	10	P	17	A	10	I	18	N	10	V	28	L	0	G	14	C	17	Q
21	25	G	11	Q	18	Q	8	A	16	T	10	N	18	O	7	L	22	S	24	G	8	Q	11	P
23	20	C	7	P	16	P	8	T	17	I	9	O	16	V	2	S	16	G	18	C	3	P	7	A
25	15	Q	5	A	15	A	8	I	16	N	7	V	12	L	27	S	10	C	12	Q	29	P	4	T
27	12	P	4	T	14	T	7	N	15	O	3	L	6	S	20	G	4	Q	7	P	26	A	3	I
29	9	A			13	I	5	O	11	V	28	L	0	G	14	C	29	Q	4	A	26	T	4	N
31	7	T			11	N			7	L			24	G	9	Q			3	T			4	O

1956 BST: 22/4-7/10

date	Jan		Feb		Mar		Apr		May		Jun		Jul		Aug		Sep		Oct		Nov		Dec	
1	19	O	9	L	0	S	15	G	17	C	1	P	4	A	23	T	1	N	24	O	17	L	23	S
3	17	V	5	S	25	S	9	C	11	Q	26	P	0	T	21	I	1	O	23	V	14	S	18	G
5	14	L	29	S	19	G	3	Q	5	P	22	A	28	T	21	N	1	V	22	L	10	G	12	C
7	9	S	23	G	13	C	27	Q	1	A	20	T	27	I	21	O	1	L	19	S	4	C	6	Q
9	3	G	17	C	7	Q	23	P	28	A	19	I	28	N	21	V	11	S	14	G	28	C	0	P
11	26	G	11	Q	1	P	19	A	26	T	19	N	28	O	19	L	6	G	9	C	22	Q	24	P
13	20	C	5	P	27	P	17	T	25	I	19	O	27	V	15	S	1	C	2	Q	16	P	19	A
15	14	Q	1	A	24	A	15	I	24	N	17	V	24	L	10	G	24	C	26	Q	11	A	16	T
17	8	P	27	A	21	T	14	N	23	O	14	L	19	S	4	C	18	Q	21	P	8	T	14	I
19	4	A	24	T	19	I	12	O	20	V	9	S	13	G	28	C	12	P	16	A	6	I	13	N
21	0	T	22	I	17	N	10	V	17	L	4	G	7	C	22	Q	8	A	13	T	4	N	13	O
23	28	T	21	N	15	O	7	L	13	S	28	G	1	Q	16	P	3	T	10	I	3	O	12	V
25	27	I	20	O	14	V	3	S	7	G	22	C	25	Q	11	A	0	I	8	N	2	V	10	L
27	27	N	19	V	12	L	29	S	1	C	16	Q	19	P	6	T	27	I	6	O	29	V	6	S
29	27	O	17	L	8	S	23	G	25	C	10	P	14	A	3	I	25	N	5	V	26	L	2	G
31	26	V			3	G			19	Q			10	T	1	N			3	L			27	G

1957 BST: 14/4-6/10

date	Jan		Feb		Mar		Apr		May		Jun		Jul		Aug		Sep		Oct		Nov		Dec	
1	9	C	23	Q	2	P	17	A	22	T	12	N	21	O	15	L	5	G	10	C	25	Q	27	P
3	3	Q	17	P	26	P	13	T	19	I	11	O	20	V	13	S	1	C	5	Q	19	P	20	A
5	27	Q	11	A	21	A	9	I	16	N	10	V	19	L	9	G	26	C	28	Q	12	A	15	T
7	20	P	6	T	16	T	5	N	14	O	8	L	16	S	4	C	20	Q	22	P	7	I	11	I
9	15	A	2	I	12	I	3	O	13	V	5	S	12	G	28	C	13	P	16	A	2	I	8	N
11	10	T	0	N	9	N	2	V	11	L	2	G	7	C	23	Q	7	A	10	T	28	I	6	O
13	7	I	29	N	8	O	2	L	9	S	28	G	2	Q	16	P	1	T	5	I	25	N	4	V
15	6	N	0	V	8	V	1	S	7	G	23	C	26	Q	10	A	26	T	1	N	23	O	2	L
17	7	O	0	L	8	L	29	S	3	C	17	Q	20	P	4	T	21	I	28	N	21	V	0	S
19	7	V	29	L	7	S	25	G	27	C	11	P	13	A	29	T	19	N	27	O	20	L	28	S
21	6	L	26	S	4	G	20	C	21	Q	5	A	8	T	26	I	18	O	26	V	19	S	25	G
23	3	S	21	G	29	G	13	Q	15	P	0	T	4	I	24	N	18	V	26	L	17	G	21	C
25	29	S	15	C	23	C	7	P	9	A	26	T	1	N	24	O	18	L	25	S	13	C	16	Q
27	24	G	9	Q	17	Q	1	A	4	T	23	I	1	O	25	V	17	S	23	G	9	Q	11	P
29	18	C			11	P	26	A	1	I	22	A	1	V	24	L	14	G	18	C	3	P	4	A
31	12	Q			5	A			28	I			1	L	22	S			13	Q			28	A

1958 BST: 20/4-5/10

date	Jan		Feb		Mar		Apr		May		Jun		Jul		Aug		Sep		Oct		Nov		Dec	
1	10	T	27	I	5	N	26	O	4	L	28	S	5	C	23	Q	8	A	10	T	25	I	0	O
3	6	I	25	N	3	O	26	V	4	S	26	G	2	Q	18	P	2	T	4	I	20	N	27	O
5	3	N	24	O	2	V	26	L	4	G	24	C	27	Q	12	A	25	T	28	I	17	O	24	V
7	1	O	24	V	3	L	26	S	2	C	19	Q	22	P	5	T	20	I	24	N	14	V	23	L
9	0	V	24	L	3	S	24	G	29	C	14	P	16	A	29	T	16	N	21	O	14	L	22	S
11	29	V	21	S	1	G	20	C	24	Q	8	A	9	T	24	I	13	O	20	V	14	S	22	G
13	27	L	18	G	28	G	15	Q	18	P	1	T	4	I	21	N	12	V	21	L	14	G	20	C
15	25	S	14	C	24	C	9	P	11	A	26	T	29	I	19	O	12	L	21	S	13	C	18	Q
17	21	G	9	Q	18	Q	3	A	5	T	21	I	26	N	18	V	12	S	20	G	9	Q	13	P
19	17	C	3	P	12	P	26	A	29	T	17	N	24	O	18	L	11	G	17	C	5	P	7	A
21	12	Q	27	P	6	A	20	T	24	I	14	O	23	V	16	S	8	C	13	Q	29	P	1	T
23	7	P	21	A	29	A	15	I	20	N	12	V	21	L	14	G	4	Q	8	P	22	A	24	T
25	0	A	14	T	23	T	10	N	17	O	10	L	19	S	11	C	29	Q	2	A	16	T	19	I
27	24	A	9	I	18	I	7	O	15	V	9	S	17	G	7	Q	23	P	26	A	10	I	14	N
29	18	T			14	N	5	V	14	L	7	G	14	C	2	P	17	A	19	T	5	N	10	O
31	14	I			11	O			13	S			10	Q	26	P			13	I			7	V

1959 BST: 19/4-4/10

date	Jan		Feb		Mar		Apr		May		Jun		Jul		Aug		Sep		Oct		Nov		Dec	
1	21	V	14	S	24	S	17	C	23	Q	9	A	12	T	26	I	12	O	17	V	8	S	17	G
3	18	L	12	G	23	G	13	Q	18	P	3	T	5	I	20	N	8	V	15	L	8	G	17	C
5	17	S	10	C	20	C	9	P	12	A	27	T	29	I	16	O	6	L	14	S	8	C	16	Q
7	16	G	7	Q	16	Q	3	A	6	T	21	I	24	N	13	V	4	S	14	G	6	Q	13	P
9	14	C	3	P	12	P	27	A	0	I	15	N	20	O	10	L	3	G	12	C	3	P	8	A
11	12	Q	29	P	7	A	21	T	24	I	10	O	16	V	8	S	1	C	10	Q	28	P	2	T
13	8	P	23	A	1	T	15	I	18	N	6	V	13	L	6	G	29	C	6	P	23	A	26	T
15	3	A	16	T	24	T	9	N	13	O	3	L	11	S	5	C	26	Q	1	A	17	T	20	I
17	27	A	10	I	18	I	4	O	9	V	1	S	10	G	3	Q	22	P	26	A	11	I	13	N
19	20	T	5	N	13	N	0	V	7	L	1	G	9	C	1	P	18	A	20	T	4	N	8	O
21	15	I	1	O	9	O	29	V	7	S	1	C	8	Q	27	P	12	T	14	I	28	N	2	V
23	10	N	28	O	6	V	29	L	7	G	0	Q	6	P	22	A	6	I	8	N	23	O	28	V
25	6	O	27	V	5	L	29	S	7	C	28	Q	2	A	16	T	0	N	2	O	19	V	25	L
27	3	V	26	L	5	S	29	G	6	Q	24	P	26	A	10	I	24	N	27	O	17	L	24	S
29	1	L			5	G	27	C	2	P	18	A	20	T	4	N	20	O	24	V	16	S	25	G
31	29	L			3	C			27	P			14	I	29	N			23	L			25	C

1960 BST: 10/4-2/10

date	Jan		Feb		Mar		Apr		May		Jun		Jul		Aug		Sep		Oct		Nov		Dec	
1	10	Q	29	P	20	A	5	I	7	N	21	O	25	V	14	S	7	C	16	Q	8	A	13	T
3	8	P	25	A	15	T	29	I	1	O	16	V	21	L	13	G	6	Q	15	P	4	T	8	I
5	4	A	19	T	9	I	22	N	25	O	12	L	19	S	12	C	6	P	12	A	0	I	3	N
7	29	A	13	I	3	N	17	O	20	V	10	S	18	G	12	Q	4	A	9	T	24	I	26	N
9	23	T	7	N	27	N	12	V	18	L	10	G	19	C	12	P	1	T	4	I	18	N	20	O
11	16	I	1	O	22	O	9	L	17	S	10	C	19	Q	10	A	26	T	28	I	12	O	14	V
13	10	N	26	O	18	V	8	S	16	G	10	Q	18	P	6	T	20	I	22	N	6	V	9	L
15	5	O	22	V	15	L	7	G	16	C	9	P	14	A	0	I	14	N	16	O	1	L	6	S
17	29	O	19	L	13	S	6	C	15	Q	5	A	9	T	24	I	8	O	11	V	28	L	4	G
19	25	V	16	S	11	G	4	Q	12	P	0	T	4	I	18	N	3	V	6	L	26	S	4	C
21	22	L	14	G	9	C	2	P	8	A	25	T	27	I	12	O	28	V	3	S	26	G	5	Q
23	19	S	13	C	8	Q	28	P	3	T	19	I	21	N	6	V	24	L	2	G	25	C	4	P
25	18	G	12	Q	5	P	24	A	28	T	12	N	15	O	2	L	22	S	0	C	24	Q	1	A
27	18	C	10	P	2	A	19	T	22	I	6	O	9	V	28	L	20	G	29	C	21	P	28	A
29	18	Q	7	A	28	A	13	I	15	N	0	V	5	L	25	S	18	C	27	Q	18	A	23	T
31	16	P			23	T			9	O			1	S	23	G			24	P			17	I

1961 BST:26/3-29/10

date	Jan	Feb	Mar	Apr	May	Jun	Jul	Aug	Sep	Oct	Nov	Dec
1	29 I	14 O	22 O	8 L	13 S	4 C	13 Q	6 A	26 T	0 N	15 O	16 V
3	23 N	8 V	17 V	4 S	10 G	3 Q	12 P	4 T	22 I	25 N	8 V	10 L
5	17 O	2 L	11 L	0 G	9 C	2 P	10 A	0 I	16 N	18 O	2 L	5 S
7	11 V	27 L	7 S	28 G	7 Q	0 A	7 T	25 I	10 O	12 V	27 L	2 G
9	5 L	23 S	3 G	26 C	5 P	27 A	3 I	19 N	3 V	6 L	23 S	29 G
11	1 S	21 G	1 C	24 Q	3 A	23 T	28 I	13 O	27 V	1 S	20 G	28 C
13	28 S	21 C	0 Q	23 P	0 T	19 I	22 N	6 V	22 L	27 S	17 C	26 Q
15	27 G	21 Q	29 Q	21 A	27 T	13 N	16 O	0 L	17 S	23 G	15 Q	24 P
17	28 C	21 P	29 P	19 T	23 I	7 O	9 V	24 L	13 G	20 C	13 P	22 A
19	28 Q	19 A	27 A	15 I	17 N	1 V	3 L	20 S	10 C	19 Q	12 A	20 T
21	27 P	16 T	24 T	9 N	11 O	25 V	28 L	17 G	9 Q	18 P	10 T	16 I
23	24 A	11 I	19 I	3 O	5 V	19 L	24 S	15 C	8 P	17 A	7 I	12 N
25	20 T	5 N	13 N	27 O	29 V	16 S	22 G	15 Q	8 A	15 T	4 N	6 O
27	14 I	29 N	7 O	21 V	24 L	14 G	22 C	15 P	7 T	13 I	28 N	0 V
29	8 N		1 V	16 L	21 S	13 C	22 Q	15 A	5 I	8 N	22 O	24 V
31	2 O		25 V		20 G		22 P	13 T		3 O		18 L

1962 BST: 25/3-28/10

date	Jan	Feb	Mar	Apr	May	Jun	Jul	Aug	Sep	Oct	Nov	Dec
1	0 S	17 G	26 G	17 Q	26 P	19 T	26 I	13 O	28 V	1 S	16 G	22 C
3	26 S	15 C	24 C	16 P	25 A	17 I	22 N	8 V	22 L	25 S	12 C	18 Q
5	23 G	15 Q	23 Q	17 A	25 T	14 N	17 O	1 L	16 S	19 G	8 Q	16 P
7	22 C	15 P	23 P	16 T	23 I	9 O	11 V	25 L	10 G	15 C	5 P	14 A
9	22 Q	15 A	24 A	14 I	19 N	3 V	5 L	19 S	6 C	12 Q	5 A	14 T
11	21 P	13 T	22 T	11 N	13 O	27 V	29 L	14 G	3 Q	11 P	5 T	13 I
13	19 A	10 I	19 I	5 O	7 V	21 L	24 S	11 C	3 P	11 A	5 I	11 N
15	16 T	5 N	14 N	29 O	1 L	16 S	20 G	10 Q	3 A	12 T	3 N	7 O
17	13 I	29 N	9 O	23 V	25 L	11 G	17 C	9 P	3 T	11 I	0 O	3 V
19	8 N	23 O	2 V	17 L	20 S	8 C	16 Q	9 A	2 I	8 N	25 O	27 V
21	3 O	17 V	26 V	11 S	16 G	6 Q	15 P	8 T	29 I	4 O	19 V	20 L
23	27 O	11 L	20 L	6 G	12 C	4 P	14 A	6 I	25 N	28 O	12 L	14 S
25	20 V	5 S	14 S	2 C	10 Q	3 A	12 T	2 N	19 O	22 V	6 S	9 G
27	14 L	0 G	9 G	29 C	7 P	1 T	9 I	28 N	13 V	16 L	1 G	5 C
29	8 S		5 C	27 Q	6 A	29 T	5 N	22 O	7 L	10 S	26 G	1 Q
31	4 G		3 Q		5 T		1 O	16 V		4 G		29 Q

1963 BST: 31/3-27/10

date	Jan	Feb	Mar	Apr	May	Jun	Jul	Aug	Sep	Oct	Nov	Dec
!	13 P	6 T	17 T	8 N	14 O	29 V	2 S	16 G	1 Q	7 P	29 A	8 I
3	11 A	4 I	15 I	4 O	9 V	23 L	25 S	10 C	29 Q	6 A	0 I	8 N
5	9 T	1 N	12 N	29 O	3 L	17 S	20 G	6 Q	27 P	6 T	29 I	6 O
7	8 I	28 N	7 O	24 V	26 L	11 G	15 C	4 P	26 A	6 I	28 N	3 V
9	5 N	23 O	2 V	18 L	20 S	6 C	11 Q	2 A	25 T	4 N	24 O	28 V
11	2 O	18 V	27 V	11 S	14 G	1 Q	7 P	0 T	24 I	1 O	19 V	23 L
13	28 O	12 L	21 L	5 G	9 C	27 Q	5 A	29 T	21 N	27 O	14 L	16 S
15	22 V	6 S	14 S	29 G	4 Q	24 P	4 T	27 I	17 O	22 V	7 S	10 G
17	16 L	0 G	8 G	24 C	0 P	23 A	2 I	24 N	13 V	17 L	1 G	4 C
19	10 S	25 G	3 C	21 Q	28 P	22 T	1 N	21 O	8 L	11 S	25 G	28 Q
21	4 G	21 C	29 C	19 P	28 A	22 I	29 N	17 V	2 S	4 G	19 C	23 Q
23	0 C	19 Q	26 Q	19 A	28 T	20 N	26 O	12 L	26 S	28 G	14 Q	20 P
25	27 C	18 P	26 P	20 T	28 I	18 O	21 V	6 S	19 G	22 C	10 P	17 A
27	24 Q	17 A	26 A	20 I	26 N	13 V	16 L	29 S	14 C	17 Q	8 A	16 T
29	23 P		26 T	18 N	22 O	8 L	10 S	23 G	9 Q	15 P	7 T	16 I
31	22 A		25 I		17 V		3 G	18 C		14 A		15 N

1964 BST: 22/3-25/10

date	Jan		Feb		Mar		Apr		May		Jun		Jul		Aug		Sep		Oct		Nov		Dec	
1	0	O	19	V	10	L	25	S	27	G	11	Q	16	P	6	T	29	I	8	O	29	V	4	S
3	28	O	15	L	5	S	18	G	20	C	6	P	12	A	5	I	28	N	6	V	25	L	29	S
5	24	V	9	S	29	S	12	C	15	Q	3	A	10	T	4	N	26	O	3	L	20	S	23	G
7	19	L	3	G	22	G	7	Q	11	P	1	T	10	I	3	O	24	V	29	L	14	G	16	C
9	13	S	26	G	16	C	2	P	8	A	1	I	10	N	2	V	21	L	24	S	8	C	10	Q
11	6	G	21	C	11	Q	0	A	7	T	1	N	9	O	0	L	16	S	18	G	1	Q	4	P
13	0	C	16	Q	8	P	29	A	8	I	1	O	8	V	26	L	10	G	12	C	26	Q	29	P
15	25	C	13	P	6	A	29	T	8	N	29	O	5	L	20	S	4	C	5	Q	21	P	26	A
17	20	Q	10	A	5	T	28	I	6	O	26	V	0	S	14	G	28	C	0	P	18	A	25	T
19	17	P	8	T	3	I	26	N	3	V	21	L	24	S	8	C	22	Q	27	P	17	T	25	I
21	14	A	7	I	2	N	23	O	29	V	15	S	17	G	2	Q	18	P	24	A	17	I	25	N
23	12	T	5	N	29	N	19	V	24	L	9	G	11	C	27	Q	16	A	23	T	17	N	25	O
25	10	I	3	O	26	O	15	L	18	S	2	C	5	Q	23	P	14	T	23	I	16	O	23	V
27	9	N	0	V	23	V	9	S	12	G	26	C	0	P	20	A	12	I	21	N	13	V	19	L
29	8	O	27	V	18	L	3	G	5	C	21	Q	26	P	17	T	10	N	19	O	9	L	14	S
31	6	V			13	S			29	C			23	A	15	I			16	V			8	G

1965 BST: 21/3-24/10

date	Jan		Feb		Mar		Apr		May		Jun		Jul		Aug		Sep		Oct		Nov		Dec	
1	20	G	4	Q	12	Q	28	P	3	T	25	I	4	O	27	V	17	S	20	G	4	Q	6	P
3	13	C	28	Q	7	P	25	A	2	I	25	N	4	V	25	L	12	G	14	C	28	Q	0	A
5	7	Q	23	P	2	A	22	T	0	N	24	O	2	L	21	S	6	C	8	Q	22	P	25	A
7	1	P	18	A	28	A	20	I	29	N	22	V	29	L	15	G	0	Q	2	P	17	A	22	T
9	26	P	15	T	25	T	18	N	27	O	19	L	24	S	9	C	24	Q	26	P	14	T	20	I
11	22	A	13	I	23	I	16	O	25	V	14	S	18	G	3	Q	18	P	22	A	11	I	19	N
13	19	T	12	N	21	N	15	V	22	L	9	G	12	C	27	Q	13	A	18	T	9	N	18	O
15	18	I	11	O	20	O	12	L	18	S	3	C	6	Q	21	P	8	T	15	I	8	O	17	V
17	18	N	11	V	19	V	9	S	13	G	27	C	0	P	16	A	4	I	13	N	6	V	15	L
19	18	O	10	L	17	L	4	G	7	C	21	Q	24	P	11	T	2	N	11	O	4	L	11	S
21	18	V	6	S	14	S	29	G	1	Q	15	P	19	A	8	I	0	O	10	V	1	S	7	G
23	15	L	1	G	9	G	23	C	24	Q	10	A	15	T	6	N	0	V	8	L	28	S	2	C
25	10	S	25	G	3	C	16	Q	19	P	6	T	13	I	6	O	29	V	6	S	23	G	26	C
27	5	G	19	C	27	C	11	P	14	A	4	I	12	N	6	V	28	L	3	G	18	C	20	Q
29	28	G			21	Q	6	A	12	T	4	N	12	O	6	L	25	S	28	G	12	Q	14	P
31	22	C			15	P			10	I			13	V	4	S			22	C			8	A

1966 BST: 20/3-23/10

date	Jan		Feb		Mar		Apr		May		Jun		Jul		Aug		Sep		Oct		Nov		Dec	
1	20	A	8	I	17	I	8	O	18	V	10	S	17	G	4	Q	18	P	21	A	7	I	13	N
3	16	T	6	N	14	N	8	V	17	L	8	G	12	C	28	Q	12	A	15	T	3	N	10	O
5	13	I	6	O	14	O	8	L	15	S	4	C	7	Q	21	P	6	T	10	I	0	O	8	V
7	13	N	6	V	14	V	7	S	12	G	29	C	1	P	15	A	1	I	6	N	28	O	7	L
9	13	O	6	L	15	L	5	G	8	C	23	Q	25	P	9	T	26	I	3	O	27	V	5	S
11	13	V	4	S	13	S	1	C	3	Q	17	P	19	A	5	I	24	N	2	V	26	L	3	G
13	11	L	1	G	10	G	25	C	27	Q	11	A	13	T	1	N	24	O	2	L	25	S	1	C
15	8	S	26	G	5	C	19	Q	21	P	6	T	10	I	0	O	24	V	2	S	23	G	27	C
17	4	G	20	C	29	C	13	P	15	A	1	I	7	N	0	V	24	L	1	G	19	C	22	Q
19	29	G	14	Q	22	Q	7	A	10	T	29	I	7	O	1	L	23	S	28	G	14	Q	16	P
21	23	C	7	P	16	P	2	T	6	I	27	N	6	V	0	S	20	G	24	C	9	P	10	A
23	17	Q	1	A	10	A	27	T	4	N	26	O	6	L	27	S	15	C	18	Q	2	A	4	T
25	10	P	25	A	5	T	23	I	1	O	25	V	4	S	23	G	10	Q	12	P	26	A	29	T
27	4	A	20	T	0	I	21	N	0	V	23	L	1	G	18	C	4	P	6	A	21	T	25	I
29	29	A			26	I	19	O	28	V	20	S	26	G	13	Q	27	P	0	T	16	I	23	N
31	24	T			24	N			26	L			21	C	7	P			25	T			21	O

1967 BST: 19/3–29/10

date	Jan		Feb		Mar		Apr		May		Jun		Jul		Aug		Sep		Oct		Nov		Dec	
1	5	V	28	L	8	S	29	G	4	Q	20	P	21	A	5	I	22	N	27	O	20	L	28	S
3	4	L	26	S	6	G	25	C	29	Q	13	A	15	T	0	N	19	O	27	V	20	S	28	G
5	2	S	23	G	3	C	20	Q	23	P	7	T	9	I	27	N	18	V	27	L	20	G	27	C
7	29	S	19	C	28	C	14	P	17	A	1	I	5	N	25	O	18	L	27	S	18	C	23	Q
9	26	G	14	Q	23	Q	8	A	10	T	26	I	2	O	24	V	17	S	25	G	15	Q	19	P
11	22	C	8	P	17	P	2	T	5	I	22	N	29	O	23	L	15	G	23	C	10	P	13	A
13	18	Q	2	A	11	A	25	T	29	I	19	O	28	V	21	S	12	C	18	Q	4	A	6	T
15	12	P	26	A	4	T	20	I	25	N	17	V	26	L	19	G	9	Q	13	P	28	A	0	I
17	6	A	20	T	28	T	15	N	22	O	15	L	24	S	16	C	4	P	7	A	21	T	24	I
19	0	T	14	I	23	I	12	O	20	V	14	S	22	G	12	Q	28	P	1	T	15	I	19	N
21	24	T	11	N	19	N	11	V	19	L	12	G	19	C	7	P	22	A	24	T	10	N	15	O
23	20	I	9	O	17	O	10	L	19	S	11	C	16	Q	2	A	16	T	18	I	5	O	12	V
25	17	N	9	V	17	V	11	S	18	G	8	Q	11	P	25	A	9	I	13	N	1	V	9	L
27	16	O	9	L	17	L	10	G	16	C	3	P	5	A	19	T	4	N	8	O	29	V	8	S
29	15	V			17	S	8	C	13	Q	28	P	29	A	13	I	0	O	6	V	28	L	7	G
31	14	L			16	G			8	P			23	T	8	N			5	L			6	C

1968

date	Jan		Feb		Mar		Apr		May		Jun		Jul		Aug		Sep		Oct		Nov		Dec	
1	20	C	9	P	0	A	14	T	17	I	2	O	7	V	28	L	22	G	1	Q	21	P	25	A
3	18	Q	4	A	24	A	8	I	11	N	27	O	4	L	26	S	20	C	28	Q	16	A	19	T
5	14	P	28	A	18	T	2	N	5	O	24	V	2	S	25	G	18	Q	24	P	10	T	13	I
7	9	A	22	T	12	I	27	N	1	V	22	L	1	G	24	C	15	P	19	A	4	I	7	N
9	2	T	16	I	6	N	23	O	29	V	21	S	0	C	23	Q	11	A	14	T	28	I	0	O
11	26	T	11	N	1	O	20	V	28	L	22	G	0	Q	20	P	6	T	8	I	22	N	25	O
13	20	I	7	O	28	O	20	L	28	S	22	C	28	Q	15	A	0	I	1	N	16	O	20	V
15	15	N	4	V	27	V	20	S	29	G	20	Q	25	P	10	T	23	I	25	N	11	V	17	L
17	12	O	2	L	26	L	20	G	28	C	17	P	20	A	4	I	17	N	20	O	8	L	16	S
19	8	V	1	S	25	S	18	C	25	Q	11	A	14	T	27	I	12	O	17	V	7	S	16	G
21	6	L	29	S	24	G	15	Q	20	P	5	T	7	I	22	N	9	V	15	L	8	G	16	C
23	4	S	27	G	22	C	11	P	14	A	29	T	1	N	17	O	7	L	14	S	8	C	16	Q
25	2	G	25	C	18	Q	5	A	8	T	23	I	26	N	14	V	5	S	14	G	7	Q	14	P
27	1	C	21	Q	14	P	29	A	2	I	17	N	21	O	11	L	4	G	13	C	5	P	10	A
29	29	C	17	P	8	A	23	T	26	I	12	O	17	V	9	S	3	C	11	Q	0	A	4	T
31	26	Q			3	T			20	N			14	L	7	G			8	P			28	T

1969

date	Jan		Feb		Mar		Apr		May		Jun		Jul		Aug		Sep		Oct		Nov		Dec	
1	10	I	24	N	2	O	18	V	24	L	16	G	25	C	18	P	7	T	10	I	24	N	25	O
3	4	N	19	O	27	O	15	L	23	S	16	C	25	Q	15	A	2	I	4	N	18	O	20	V
5	28	N	14	V	23	V	13	S	22	G	16	Q	23	P	11	T	26	I	28	N	12	V	15	L
7	22	O	10	L	20	L	12	G	21	C	14	P	20	A	6	I	20	N	22	O	7	L	12	S
9	17	V	7	S	17	S	11	C	20	Q	10	A	15	T	0	N	14	O	16	V	4	S	11	G
11	13	L	5	G	15	G	9	Q	17	P	5	T	9	I	23	N	8	V	12	L	2	G	11	C
13	10	S	3	C	14	C	6	P	13	A	0	I	3	N	17	O	3	L	9	S	1	C	10	Q
15	9	G	3	Q	12	Q	3	A	8	T	24	I	26	N	11	V	29	L	7	G	0	Q	9	P
17	9	C	2	P	10	P	29	A	3	I	17	N	20	O	6	L	26	S	5	C	28	Q	6	A
19	9	Q	0	A	8	A	24	T	27	I	11	O	14	V	2	S	24	G	3	Q	26	P	2	T
21	8	P	26	A	4	T	18	I	21	N	5	V	9	L	29	S	23	C	2	P	22	A	28	T
23	5	A	21	T	28	T	12	N	14	O	0	L	6	S	28	G	21	Q	29	P	18	T	22	I
25	0	T	15	I	22	I	6	O	9	V	26	L	4	G	27	C	20	P	26	A	14	I	16	N
27	25	T	8	N	16	N	1	V	4	L	25	S	3	C	27	Q	18	A	23	T	8	N	10	O
29	18	I			10	O	26	V	2	S	25	G	4	Q	26	P	15	T	18	I	2	O	4	V
31	12	N			5	V			1	G			3	P	24	A			12	N			28	V

1970

date	Jan		Feb		Mar		Apr		May		Jun		Jul		Aug		Sep		Oct		Nov		Dec	
1	10	L	28	S	8	G	1	Q	10	P	2	T	8	I	24	N	9	V	11	L	28	S	5	C
3	6	S	27	G	6	C	29	Q	8	A	28	T	3	N	18	O	2	L	6	S	25	G	3	Q
5	4	G	27	C	5	Q	29	P	6	T	24	I	27	N	11	V	26	L	1	G	22	C	1	P
7	4	C	27	Q	5	P	27	A	3	I	19	N	21	O	5	L	21	S	28	G	20	Q	29	P
9	4	Q	27	P	5	A	25	T	28	I	13	O	15	V	0	S	18	G	25	C	18	P	27	A
11	4	P	25	A	3	T	20	I	23	N	6	V	9	L	25	S	15	C	24	Q	17	A	25	T
13	3	A	21	T	0	I	15	N	17	O	0	L	3	S	22	G	15	Q	23	P	16	T	22	I
15	29	A	16	I	25	I	9	O	10	V	25	L	0	G	21	C	15	P	23	A	13	I	17	N
17	25	T	10	N	19	N	2	V	5	L	22	S	28	G	21	Q	15	A	22	T	9	N	12	O
19	19	I	4	O	12	O	27	V	0	S	20	G	28	C	22	P	13	T	19	I	4	O	6	V
21	13	N	28	O	6	V	22	L	27	S	19	C	28	Q	21	A	11	I	14	N	28	O	29	V
23	7	O	22	V	1	L	18	S	25	G	18	Q	27	P	18	T	6	N	8	O	22	V	24	L
25	1	V	16	L	26	L	15	G	24	C	17	P	25	A	14	I	0	O	2	V	16	L	19	S
27	25	V	12	S	22	S	13	C	22	Q	15	A	22	T	9	N	24	O	26	V	11	S	16	G
29	19	L			19	G	11	Q	21	P	12	T	18	I	3	O	17	V	20	L	7	G	14	C
31	15	S			16	C			18	A			12	N	27	O			15	S			13	Q

1971

date	Jan		Feb		Mar		Apr		May		Jun		Jul		Aug		Sep		Oct		Nov		Dec	
1	27	Q	20	A	0	T	20	I	25	N	9	V	11	L	25	S	12	C	18	Q	11	A	19	T
3	26	P	18	T	28	T	16	N	19	O	3	L	5	S	20	G	10	Q	17	P	11	T	19	I
5	24	A	14	IO	24	I	11	O	13	V	27	L	0	G	17	C	9	P	18	A	11	I	17	N
7	21	T	10	N	19	N	4	V	6	L	21	S	26	G	16	Q	9	A	18	T	9	N	13	O
9	18	I	5	O	14	O	28	V	0	S	17	G	23	C	15	P	9	T	17	I	5	O	8	V
11	13	N	29	O	7	V	22	L	25	S	14	C	21	Q	14	A	7	I	14	N	0	V	2	L
13	8	O	22	V	1	L	16	S	21	G	11	Q	20	P	13	T	4	N	9	O	24	V	26	L
15	2	V	16	L	25	L	11	G	17	C	9	P	18	A	11	I	0	O	3	V	18	L	20	S
17	26	V	10	S	19	S	7	C	14	Q	7	A	16	T	7	N	24	O	27	V	12	S	15	G
19	19	L	5	G	14	G	4	Q	12	P	6	T	14	I	3	O	18	V	21	L	6	G	10	C
21	14	S	1	C	10	C	2	P	11	A	4	I	11	N	27	O	12	L	15	S	1	C	6	Q
23	10	G	0	Q	8	Q	1	A	10	T	1	N	6	O	21	V	6	S	9	G	26	Q	3	P
25	7	C	29	Q	8	P	1	T	9	I	28	N	1	V	15	L	0	G	4	C	23	Q	1	A
27	7	Q	0	A	8	A	1	I	7	N	23	O	25	V	9	S	24	G	29	C	21	P	0	T
29	6	P			8	T	29	I	3	O	17	V	9	L	3	G	20	C	27	Q	20	A	29	T
31	6	A			7	I			27	O			3	S	28	G			26	P			27	I

1972   BST: 19/3-29/10

date	Jan		Feb		Mar		Apr		May		Jun		Jul		Aug		Sep		Oct		Nov		Dec	
1	11	N	29	O	20	V	5	S	7	G	23	C	29	Q	21	A	14	I	23	N	12	V	16	L
3	8	O	24	V	14	L	28	S	1	C	19	Q	26	P	19	T	12	N	19	O	6	L	10	S
5	4	V	18	L	8	S	22	G	26	C	15	P	24	A	18	I	9	O	15	V	1	S	3	G
7	28	V	12	S	2	G	17	C	22	Q	14	A	23	T	16	N	5	V	10	L	24	S	27	G
9	22	L	6	G	26	G	13	Q	20	P	13	T	22	I	13	O	1	L	4	S	18	G	21	C
11	16	S	1	C	21	C	11	P	19	A	13	I	21	N	10	V	25	L	28	S	12	C	16	Q
13	10	G	27	C	18	Q	10	A	19	T	12	N	18	O	5	L	19	S	21	G	6	Q	11	P
15	6	C	25	Q	17	P	11	T	20	I	10	O	14	V	29	L	13	G	15	C	2	P	8	A
17	2	Q	24	P	17	A	11	I	18	N	6	V	9	L	23	S	7	C	10	Q	29	P	7	T
19	0	P	23	A	17	T	9	N	15	O	1	L	3	S	17	G	2	Q	7	P	28	A	7	I
21	28	P	22	T	16	I	6	O	10	V	25	L	27	S	12	C	29	Q	5	A	29	T	7	N
23	26	A	19	I	13	N	1	V	5	L	19	S	21	G	7	Q	27	P	5	T	29	I	6	O
25	25	T	16	N	9	O	26	V	29	L	13	G	16	C	4	P	27	A	6	I	28	N	4	V
27	23	I	12	O	4	V	20	L	22	S	7	C	12	Q	3	A	26	T	5	N	25	O	0	L
29	20	N	7	V	29	V	13	S	16	G	3	Q	9	P	1	T	25	I	3	O	21	V	24	L
31	16	O			23	L			11	C			7	A	0	I			29	O			18	S

1973 BST: 18/3-28/10

date	Jan	Feb	Mar	Apr	May	Jun	Jul	Aug	Sep	Oct	Nov	Dec
1	0 G	14 C	22 C	8 P	14 A	7 I	16 N	8 V	27 L	0 G	13 C	15 Q
3	24 G	9 Q	17 Q	6 A	14 T	7 N	15 O	6 L	22 S	24 G	7 Q	9 P
5	18 C	5 P	14 P	5 T	14 I	7 O	14 V	1 S	16 G	17 C	1 P	5 A
7	13 Q	1 A	11 A	4 I	13 N	5 V	10 L	26 S	9 C	11 Q	27 P	2 T
9	8 P	29 A	10 T	3 N	11 O	1 L	5 S	19 G	3 Q	6 P	25 A	1 I
11	5 A	27 T	8 I	1 O	8 V	26 L	29 S	13 C	28 Q	3 A	23 T	1 N
13	2 T	25 I	6 N	28 O	4 L	20 S	23 G	7 Q	24 P	0 T	23 I	2 O
15	1 I	24 N	4 O	24 V	29 L	14 G	16 C	2 P	21 A	29 T	22 N	0 V
17	0 N	22 O	1 V	20 L	23 S	8 C	10 Q	28 P	19 T	27 I	20 O	28 V
19	0 O	20 V	28 V	14 S	17 G	1 Q	5 P	24 A	17 I	26 N	18 V	24 L
21	28 O	16 L	24 L	8 G	11 C	26 Q	1 A	22 T	15 N	24 O	14 L	19 S
23	25 V	10 S	18 S	2 C	4 Q	21 P	27 A	20 I	13 O	21 V	9 S	13 G
25	20 L	4 G	12 G	26 C	29 Q	18 A	25 T	19 N	11 V	17 L	2 G	7 C
27	15 S	28 G	6 C	20 Q	25 P	16 T	24 I	18 O	9 L	13 S	28 G	0 Q
29	8 G		0 Q	16 P	23 A	16 I	24 N	16 V	5 S	8 G	22 C	24 Q
31	2 C		25 Q		22 T		24 O	14 L		1 C		18 P

1974 BST: 17/3-7/10

date	Jan	Feb	Mar	Apr	May	Jun	Jul	Aug	Sep	Oct	Nov	Dec
1	1 A	20 T	0 I	23 N	2 V	23 L	29 S	14 C	29 Q	2 A	19 T	26 I
3	27 A	18 I	28 I	21 O	0 L	19 S	23 G	8 Q	23 P	27 A	16 I	24 N
5	25 T	17 N	27 N	20 V	27 L	14 G	17 C	2 P	18 A	23 T	14 N	23 O
7	24 I	18 O	26 O	18 L	23 S	9 C	11 Q	26 P	13 T	20 I	12 O	22 V
9	25 N	17 V	25 V	15 S	18 G	2 Q	5 P	20 A	9 I	17 N	11 V	19 L
11	25 O	16 L	23 L	10 G	12 C	26 Q	29 P	16 T	7 N	16 O	9 L	16 S
13	24 V	12 S	20 S	5 C	6 Q	20 P	24 A	13 I	6 O	15 V	7 S	12 G
15	20 L	7 G	15 G	28 C	0 P	15 A	20 T	12 N	6 V	14 L	4 G	7 C
17	16 S	0 C	9 C	22 Q	25 P	12 T	19 I	12 O	5 L	12 S	29 G	2 Q
19	10 G	24 C	2 Q	17 P	20 A	10 I	18 N	12 V	4 S	9 G	24 C	25 Q
21	4 C	18 Q	26 Q	12 A	18 T	10 N	19 O	12 L	1 G	4 C	18 Q	19 P
23	27 C	12 P	21 P	9 T	16 I	10 O	19 V	9 S	26 G	28 C	11 P	13 A
25	21 Q	7 A	17 A	7 I	15 N	9 V	17 L	5 G	20 C	22 Q	6 A	9 T
27	15 P	3 T	13 T	5 N	14 O	7 L	13 S	29 G	13 Q	16 P	1 T	6 I
29	10 A		11 I	4 O	13 V	3 S	8 G	23 C	7 P	10 A	28 T	4 N
31	6 T		8 N		10 L		2 C	17 Q		6 T		4 O

1975 BST: 16/3-24/10

date	Jan	Feb	Mar	Apr	May	Jun	Jul	Aug	Sep	Oct	Nov	Dec
1	19 O	12 L	21 L	11 G	14 C	29 Q	0 A	15 T	2 N	9 O	2 L	11 S
3	18 V	10 S	19 S	6 C	9 Q	23 P	24 A	10 I	0 O	8 V	2 S	9 G
5	16 L	6 G	15 G	1 Q	3 P	17 A	19 T	7 N	0 V	9 L	1 G	7 C
7	13 S	1 C	10 C	24 Q	26 P	11 T	16 I	6 O	0 L	9 S	29 G	3 Q
9	9 G	25 C	4 Q	18 P	21 A	7 I	13 N	6 V	0 S	7 G	25 C	28 Q
11	4 C	19 Q	28 Q	12 A	16 T	4 N	12 O	6 L	29 S	4 C	20 Q	22 P
13	28 C	12 P	21 P	7 T	12 I	3 O	12 V	5 S	25 G	29 C	14 P	16 A
15	22 Q	6 A	15 A	2 I	8 N	1 V	11 L	2 G	20 C	24 Q	8 A	10 T
17	16 P	0 T	10 T	28 I	6 O	0 L	8 S	28 G	15 Q	17 P	2 T	5 I
19	9 A	25 T	5 I	25 N	4 V	28 L	5 G	23 C	9 P	11 A	26 T	1 N
21	4 T	22 I	1 N	24 O	3 L	25 S	1 C	18 Q	2 A	5 T	22 I	28 N
23	0 I	20 N	29 N	23 V	2 S	22 G	26 C	12 P	26 A	0 I	18 N	26 O
25	28 I	20 O	29 O	22 L	0 G	18 C	21 Q	5 A	20 T	25 I	15 O	24 V
27	27 N	21 V	29 V	21 S	26 G	13 Q	15 P	29 A	15 I	21 N	13 V	22 L
29	27 O		29 L	19 G	22 C	7 P	9 A	23 T	11 N	18 O	12 L	20 S
31	28 V		27 S		17 Q		3 T	19 I		17 V		18 G

1976 BST: 21/3-24/10

date	Jan		Feb		Mar		Apr		May		Jun		Jul		Aug		Sep		Oct		Nov		Dec	
1	2	C	19	Q	10	P	25	A	27	T	14	N	20	O	13	L	6	G	14	C	3	P	6	A
3	28	C	14	P	4	A	18	T	22	I	10	O	18	V	11	S	4	C	10	Q	27	P	0	T
5	24	Q	8	A	28	A	12	I	17	N	7	V	16	L	9	G	0	Q	6	P	21	A	23	T
7	18	P	1	T	22	T	7	N	13	O	5	L	15	S	7	C	26	Q	0	A	15	T	17	I
9	12	A	25	T	16	I	4	O	11	V	4	S	13	G	4	Q	21	P	24	A	8	I	12	N
11	5	T	20	I	11	N	2	V	10	L	4	G	11	C	0	P	15	A	18	T	2	N	7	O
13	0	I	17	N	9	O	1	L	10	S	3	C	9	Q	25	P	9	T	11	I	27	N	3	V
15	26	I	15	O	8	V	2	S	10	G	0	Q	4	P	19	A	3	I	5	N	23	O	0	L
17	23	N	15	V	9	L	2	G	9	C	26	Q	29	P	13	T	27	I	1	O	20	V	28	L
19	21	O	15	L	9	S	0	C	5	Q	21	P	23	A	7	I	22	N	28	O	19	L	28	S
21	20	V	14	S	7	G	27	C	1	P	15	A	17	T	1	N	19	O	26	V	19	S	28	G
23	19	L	11	G	5	C	22	Q	25	P	9	T	11	I	28	N	18	V	26	L	20	G	27	C
25	17	S	8	C	0	Q	16	P	19	A	3	I	6	N	25	O	18	L	26	S	19	C	24	Q
27	14	G	3	Q	25	Q	10	A	12	T	28	I	3	O	24	V	18	S	26	G	16	Q	20	P
29	11	C	28	Q	19	P	4	T	6	I	24	N	0	V	23	L	17	G	24	C	12	P	14	A
31	7	Q			13	A			1	N			29	V	22	S			20	Q			8	T

1977 BST: 20/3-23/10

date	Jan		Feb		Mar		Apr		May		Jun		Jul		Aug		Sep		Oct		Nov		Dec	
1	20	T	4	N	12	N	29	O	5	L	28	S	7	C	29	Q	17	A	19	T	3	N	6	O
3	14	I	29	N	7	O	27	V	4	S	28	G	6	Q	26	P	11	T	13	I	27	N	0	V
5	8	N	26	O	4	V	26	L	5	G	28	C	4	P	21	A	5	I	7	N	21	O	25	V
7	4	O	23	V	3	L	26	S	4	C	26	Q	1	A	15	T	29	I	1	O	17	V	23	L
9	0	V	21	L	2	S	25	G	3	Q	22	P	25	A	9	I	23	N	26	O	15	L	22	S
11	27	V	19	S	0	G	23	C	0	P	17	A	19	T	3	N	18	O	23	V	14	S	22	G
13	24	L	18	G	29	G	20	Q	25	P	10	T	13	I	27	N	15	V	21	L	14	G	23	C
15	23	S	16	C	26	C	16	P	19	A	4	I	7	N	23	O	12	L	20	S	14	C	22	Q
17	22	G	13	Q	23	Q	10	A	13	T	28	I	1	O	19	V	10	S	19	G	12	Q	19	P
19	20	C	10	P	19	P	4	T	7	I	22	N	26	O	16	L	9	G	18	C	9	P	15	A
21	19	Q	6	A	14	A	28	T	1	N	17	O	22	V	14	S	7	C	16	Q	5	A	9	T
23	15	P	0	T	8	T	22	I	25	N	12	V	19	L	12	G	5	Q	12	P	0	T	3	I
25	10	A	24	T	2	I	16	N	20	O	9	L	17	S	11	C	3	P	8	A	24	T	27	I
27	4	T	17	I	25	I	11	O	16	V	7	S	16	G	9	Q	29	P	3	T	18	I	21	N
29	28	T			20	N	7	V	13	L	6	G	15	C	7	P	25	A	27	T	12	N	15	O
31	22	I			15	O			13	S			15	Q	4	A			21	I			9	V

1978 BST: 19/3-29/10

date	Jan		Feb		Mar		Apr		May		Jun		Jul		Aug		Sep		Oct		Nov		Dec	
1	22	V	11	S	22	S	15	C	24	Q	15	A	20	T	5	N	19	O	22	V	10	S	17	G
3	18	L	9	G	20	G	14	Q	22	P	10	T	14	I	28	N	13	V	18	L	8	G	16	C
5	16	S	9	C	19	C	11	P	18	A	5	I	8	N	22	O	8	L	14	S	6	C	15	Q
7	15	G	9	Q	18	Q	9	A	13	T	29	I	1	O	16	V	4	S	12	G	5	Q	14	P
9	15	C	8	P	16	P	5	T	8	I	23	N	25	O	11	L	1	G	10	C	3	P	11	A
11	16	Q	6	A	14	A	0	I	2	N	16	O	19	V	7	S	29	G	8	Q	1	A	7	T
13	14	P	2	T	9	T	24	I	26	N	10	V	14	L	4	G	28	C	6	P	28	A	3	I
15	11	A	26	T	4	I	18	N	20	O	5	L	11	S	3	C	27	Q	5	A	24	T	28	I
17	6	T	20	I	28	I	12	O	14	V	2	S	9	G	3	Q	26	P	2	T	19	I	22	N
19	0	I	24	N	22	N	6	V	10	L	1	G	9	C	3	P	24	A	28	T	14	N	15	O
21	24	I	8	O	16	O	2	L	8	S	1	C	10	Q	2	A	21	T	23	I	7	O	9	V
23	17	N	3	V	11	V	0	S	7	G	1	Q	10	P	29	A	16	I	18	N	1	V	3	L
25	12	O	28	V	7	L	28	S	7	C	1	P	8	A	25	T	10	N	11	O	25	V	29	L
27	6	V	25	L	5	S	27	G	7	Q	28	P	4	T	20	I	3	O	5	V	21	L	26	S
29	2	L			3	G	26	C	5	P	25	A	29	T	13	N	27	O	0	L	18	S	25	G
31	28	L			1	C			2	A			23	I	7	O			26	L			25	C

1979 BST: 18/3-28/10

date	Jan		Feb		Mar		Apr		May		Jun		Jul		Aug		Sep		Oct		Nov		Dec	
1	10	Q	3	A	11	A	1	I	4	N	18	O	20	V	5	S	23	G	0	Q	23	P	2	T
3	10	P	1	T	9	T	26	I	29	N	12	V	14	L	1	G	21	C	29	Q	23	A	0	I
5	8	A	27	T	5	I	21	N	22	O	6	L	9	S	28	G	21	Q	29	P	22	T	27	I
7	4	T	21	I	0	N	14	O	16	V	1	S	6	G	27	C	21	P	29	A	19	I	23	N
9	0	I	15	N	24	N	8	V	10	L	28	S	4	C	28	Q	21	A	28	T	15	N	18	O
11	24	I	9	O	18	O	2	L	6	S	26	G	4	Q	28	P	19	T	25	I	10	O	12	V
13	18	N	3	V	12	V	27	L	3	G	25	C	4	P	26	A	16	I	20	N	4	V	5	L
15	12	O	27	V	6	L	23	S	0	C	24	Q	2	A	24	T	11	N	14	O	27	V	29	L
17	6	V	21	L	1	S	20	G	29	C	22	P	0	T	19	I	5	O	7	V	22	L	25	S
19	0	L	16	S	26	S	18	C	27	Q	20	A	27	T	14	N	29	O	1	L	17	S	22	G
21	24	L	13	G	23	G	16	Q	25	P	17	T	22	I	8	O	22	V	25	L	13	G	19	C
23	20	S	12	C	21	C	15	P	23	A	13	I	17	N	2	V	16	L	20	S	10	C	18	Q
25	18	G	11	Q	20	Q	13	A	20	T	8	N	11	O	25	V	11	S	16	G	7	Q	16	P
27	18	C	12	P	20	P	11	T	17	I	3	O	5	V	19	L	6	G	13	C	5	P	14	A
29	18	Q			19	A	8	I	12	N	26	O	28	V	14	S	2	C	10	Q	3	A	12	T
31	18	P			17	T			6	O			22	L	9	G			9	P			9	I

1980 BST: 16/3-24/10

date	Jan		Feb		Mar		Apr		May		Jun		Jul		Aug		Sep		Oct		Nov		Dec	
1	23	I	10	O	1	V	15	L	18	S	5	C	12	Q	5	A	28	T	6	N	23	O	26	V
3	19	N	4	V	24	V	9	S	13	G	2	Q	10	P	4	T	26	I	2	O	17	V	20	L
5	13	O	28	V	18	L	3	G	9	C	29	Q	9	A	2	I	22	N	26	O	11	L	13	S
7	8	V	21	L	12	S	29	G	5	Q	27	P	7	T	29	I	17	O	20	V	5	S	8	G
9	1	L	15	S	6	G	25	C	3	P	26	A	5	I	25	N	11	V	14	L	29	S	3	C
11	25	L	11	G	2	C	23	Q	1	A	25	T	2	N	20	O	5	L	8	S	23	G	28	C
13	20	S	7	C	0	Q	22	P	1	T	23	I	29	N	15	V	29	L	2	G	18	C	24	Q
15	16	G	6	Q	29	Q	22	A	1	I	21	N	24	O	9	L	23	S	26	G	14	Q	22	P
17	14	C	6	P	29	P	22	T	29	I	16	O	19	V	2	S	17	G	21	C	11	P	20	A
19	13	Q	6	A	29	A	21	I	26	N	11	V	12	L	26	S	13	C	18	Q	10	A	19	T
21	12	P	5	T	28	T	17	N	21	O	4	L	6	S	21	G	10	Q	17	P	10	T	19	I
23	11	A	3	I	26	I	12	O	15	V	28	L	1	G	18	C	8	P	17	A	10	I	17	N
25	9	T	29	I	21	N	6	V	8	L	23	S	26	G	16	Q	9	A	17	T	9	N	14	O
27	6	I	24	N	16	O	0	L	2	S	18	G	23	C	15	P	9	T	17	I	6	O	10	V
29	2	N	19	O	9	V	24	L	27	S	15	C	22	Q	15	A	8	I	15	N	2	V	4	L
31	27	N			3	L			22	G			21	P	14	T			11	O			28	L

1981 BST: 29/3-25/10

date	Jan		Feb		Mar		Apr		May		Jun		Jul		Aug		Sep		Oct		Nov		Dec	
1	10	S	24	G	2	C	19	Q	25	P	19	T	28	I	19	O	6	L	9	S	23	G	26	C
3	4	G	20	C	27	C	17	P	25	A	19	I	27	N	15	V	1	S	3	G	17	C	20	Q
5	29	G	17	Q	25	Q	17	A	26	T	19	N	24	O	11	L	25	S	27	G	11	Q	16	P
7	24	C	15	P	23	P	17	T	26	I	16	O	20	V	5	S	19	G	21	C	7	P	14	A
9	21	Q	13	A	23	A	17	I	24	N	12	V	15	L	29	S	13	C	16	Q	5	A	13	T
11	19	P	12	T	22	T	15	N	21	O	2	L	9	S	23	G	8	Q	13	P	5	T	13	I
13	17	A	10	I	21	I	11	O	16	V	1	S	3	G	17	C	5	P	12	A	5	I	13	N
15	15	T	8	N	18	N	6	V	10	L	24	S	27	G	13	Q	3	A	12	T	5	N	12	O
17	14	I	4	O	14	O	1	L	4	S	18	G	22	C	10	P	2	T	11	I	4	O	10	V
19	12	N	0	V	9	V	25	L	27	S	13	C	17	Q	8	A	1	I	10	N	1	V	5	L
21	9	O	25	V	4	L	19	S	21	G	8	Q	14	P	6	T	0	N	8	O	26	V	0	S
23	5	V	20	L	28	L	12	G	16	C	3	P	11	A	5	I	27	N	4	V	21	L	23	S
25	0	L	13	S	22	S	6	C	11	Q	0	A	9	T	3	N	24	O	29	V	15	S	17	G
27	24	L	7	G	15	G	1	Q	7	P	29	A	8	I	1	O	20	V	24	L	8	G	11	C
29	17	S			10	C	27	Q	4	A	28	T	7	N	28	O	15	L	18	S	2	C	5	Q
31	12	G			5	Q			4	T			5	O	24	V			11	G			0	P

1982 BST: 28/3-24/10

date	Jan		Feb		Mar		Apr		May		Jun		Jul		Aug		Sep		Oct		Nov		Dec	
1	13	P	4	T	14	T	8	N	16	O	6	L	10	S	25	G	9	Q	12	P	1	T	8	I
3	9	A	2	I	13	I	5	O	13	V	1	S	4	G	18	C	4	P	8	A	29	T	8	N
5	7	T	1	N	11	N	3	V	9	L	25	S	28	G	12	Q	29	P	6	T	28	I	7	O
7	6	I	0	O	9	O	29	V	4	S	19	G	22	C	7	P	26	A	4	I	27	N	6	V
9	6	N	28	O	7	V	25	L	28	S	13	C	15	Q	3	A	23	T	2	N	25	O	3	L
11	6	O	26	V	4	L	20	S	22	G	6	Q	10	P	29	A	21	I	0	O	22	V	29	L
13	4	V	22	L	29	L	14	G	16	C	1	P	6	A	26	T	19	N	28	O	19	L	24	S
15	1	L	16	S	24	S	8	C	10	Q	26	P	2	T	25	I	18	O	26	V	15	S	18	G
17	26	L	10	G	18	G	1	Q	4	P	23	A	1	I	24	N	17	V	23	L	9	G	12	C
19	20	S	4	C	11	C	26	Q	1	A	22	T	0	N	24	O	14	L	19	S	3	C	5	Q
21	14	G	28	C	6	Q	22	P	29	A	22	I	0	O	22	V	11	S	13	G	27	C	29	Q
23	8	C	23	Q	1	P	20	A	28	T	22	N	0	V	20	L	5	G	7	C	21	Q	23	P
25	2	Q	19	P	28	P	20	T	28	I	21	O	28	V	15	S	29	G	1	Q	15	P	19	A
27	27	Q	16	A	26	A	19	I	28	N	19	V	24	L	9	G	23	C	25	Q	11	A	16	T
29	23	P			25	T	18	N	26	O	15	L	19	S	3	C	17	Q	20	P	9	T	16	I
31	20	A			23	I			23	V			13	G	27	C			17	A			16	N

1983 BST: 27/3-23/10

date	Jan		Feb		Mar		Apr		May		Jun		Jul		Aug		Sep		Oct		Nov		Dec	
1	1	O	24	V	2	L	21	S	24	G	8	Q	10	P	26	A	14	I	22	N	15	V	24	L
3	1	V	21	L	0	S	16	G	18	C	2	P	4	A	21	T	12	N	21	O	14	L	21	S
5	29	V	17	S	26	S	10	C	12	Q	26	P	29	A	19	I	11	O	20	V	12	S	18	G
7	26	L	12	G	20	G	4	Q	6	P	21	A	26	T	18	N	12	V	20	L	9	G	13	C
9	21	S	6	C	14	C	28	Q	0	A	18	T	25	I	18	O	12	L	18	S	5	C	7	Q
11	15	G	29	C	8	Q	22	P	26	A	16	I	25	N	18	V	10	S	15	G	29	C	1	P
13	9	C	23	Q	2	P	18	A	24	T	16	N	25	O	18	L	6	G	9	C	23	Q	25	P
15	2	Q	17	P	26	P	15	T	22	I	15	O	24	V	15	S	1	C	3	Q	17	P	19	A
17	26	Q	12	A	22	A	12	I	21	N	14	V	22	L	10	G	25	C	27	Q	12	A	15	T
19	20	P	8	T	18	T	10	N	19	O	12	L	18	S	5	C	19	Q	21	P	7	T	12	I
21	15	A	5	I	15	I	8	O	17	V	8	S	13	G	28	C	13	P	16	A	4	I	10	N
23	11	T	3	N	13	N	6	V	15	L	4	G	7	C	22	Q	7	A	11	T	1	N	9	O
25	9	I	2	O	12	O	5	L	11	S	28	G	1	Q	16	P	2	T	8	I	29	N	9	V
27	9	N	2	V	11	V	2	S	7	G	23	C	25	Q	10	A	28	T	5	N	28	O	7	L
29	9	O			10	L	29	S	2	C	16	Q	19	P	5	T	24	I	3	O	26	V	4	S
31	9	V			7	S			26	C			13	A	1	I			1	V			1	G

1984 BST: 25/3-28/10

date	Jan		Feb		Mar		Apr		May		Jun		Jul		Aug		Sep		Oct		Nov		Dec	
1	14	G	0	Q	21	Q	5	A	9	T	26	I	3	O	27	V	20	S	27	G	13	Q	16	P
3	9	C	24	Q	15	P	0	T	4	I	24	N	2	V	26	L	17	G	22	C	8	P	10	A
5	3	Q	18	P	8	A	24	T	0	N	22	O	1	L	24	S	13	C	17	Q	1	A	3	T
7	27	Q	11	A	2	T	20	I	27	N	20	V	29	L	20	G	8	Q	11	P	25	A	28	T
9	21	P	6	T	27	T	16	N	25	O	18	L	27	S	16	C	2	P	5	A	19	T	23	I
11	15	A	1	I	23	I	14	O	23	V	17	S	23	G	11	Q	26	P	28	A	14	I	19	N
13	10	T	28	I	20	N	14	V	23	L	14	G	19	C	5	P	19	A	22	T	9	N	16	O
15	6	I	26	N	20	O	14	L	21	S	11	C	14	Q	29	P	13	T	17	I	6	O	14	V
17	4	N	27	O	20	V	13	S	19	G	6	Q	8	P	22	A	7	I	12	N	4	V	13	L
19	3	O	27	V	20	L	11	G	15	C	0	P	2	A	16	T	3	N	9	O	2	L	11	S
21	4	V	27	L	19	S	7	C	10	Q	24	P	26	A	11	I	0	O	8	V	2	S	10	G
23	3	L	24	S	16	G	2	Q	4	P	18	A	20	T	8	N	29	O	8	L	1	G	7	C
25	1	S	21	G	12	C	26	Q	28	P	13	T	16	I	6	O	0	V	8	S	29	G	4	Q
27	28	S	15	C	6	Q	20	P	22	A	8	I	14	N	6	V	0	L	7	G	26	C	29	Q
29	23	G	9	Q	0	P	14	A	17	T	5	N	13	O	6	L	29	S	5	C	22	Q	24	P
31	18	C			23	P			13	I			12	V	6	S			1	Q			17	A

1985 BST: 31/3-27/10

date	Jan		Feb		Mar		Apr		May		Jun		Jul		Aug		Sep		Oct		Nov		Dec	
1	29	A	13	I	21	I	9	O	16	V	10	S	18	G	9	Q	27	P	29	A	13	I	17	N
3	23	T	9	N	17	N	8	V	16	L	10	G	17	C	6	P	21	A	23	T	7	N	12	O
5	18	I	7	O	15	O	8	L	16	S	9	C	14	Q	1	A	15	T	16	I	2	O	8	V
7	15	N	6	V	15	V	8	S	16	G	6	Q	10	P	25	A	8	I	11	N	28	O	5	L
9	13	O	5	L	15	L	8	G	15	C	2	P	5	A	18	T	3	N	6	O	26	V	4	S
11	11	V	4	S	14	S	6	C	11	Q	27	P	29	A	12	I	28	N	3	V	25	L	4	G
13	9	L	2	G	13	G	2	Q	6	P	21	A	22	T	7	N	25	O	2	L	26	S	4	C
15	8	S	29	G	9	C	27	Q	0	A	14	T	17	I	3	O	24	V	3	S	26	G	3	Q
17	5	G	25	C	5	Q	21	P	24	A	8	I	12	N	1	V	24	L	3	G	25	C	0	P
19	3	C	21	Q	0	P	15	A	18	T	3	N	8	O	0	L	23	S	2	C	22	Q	26	P
21	29	C	16	P	24	P	9	T	12	I	29	N	6	V	28	L	22	G	29	C	17	P	20	A
23	25	Q	10	A	18	A	2	I	6	N	25	O	3	L	27	S	19	C	25	Q	11	A	13	T
25	19	P	3	T	12	T	27	I	2	O	23	V	2	S	25	G	15	Q	20	P	5	T	7	I
27	13	A	27	T	5	I	22	N	28	O	21	L	0	G	22	C	11	P	14	A	28	T	1	N
29	7	T			0	N	18	O	26	V	20	S	28	G	18	Q	5	A	8	T	22	I	26	N
31	1	I			26	N			25	L			26	C	14	P			1	I			22	O

1986 BST: 30/3-26/10

date	Jan		Feb		Mar		Apr		May		Jun		Jul		Aug		Sep		Oct		Nov		Dec	
1	5	V	26	L	7	S	0	C	8	Q	27	P	1	T	15	I	29	N	2	V	21	L	28	S
3	1	L	24	S	5	G	28	C	5	P	22	A	24	T	8	N	24	O	29	V	20	S	29	G
5	29	L	22	G	3	C	25	Q	0	A	15	T	18	I	3	O	20	V	27	L	20	G	29	C
7	28	S	21	C	1	Q	20	P	24	A	9	I	12	N	28	O	17	L	25	S	19	C	27	Q
9	27	G	19	Q	28	Q	15	A	18	T	3	N	6	O	24	V	15	S	24	G	17	Q	24	P
11	26	C	16	P	24	P	10	T	12	I	27	N	1	V	21	L	13	G	23	C	14	P	20	A
13	25	Q	11	A	19	A	4	I	6	N	21	O	27	V	18	S	12	C	20	Q	10	A	14	T
15	21	P	6	T	13	T	27	I	0	O	17	V	24	L	17	G	10	Q	17	P	5	T	8	I
17	16	A	29	T	7	I	21	N	25	O	14	L	22	S	16	C	8	P	13	A	29	T	2	N
19	10	T	23	I	1	N	16	O	21	V	12	S	21	G	15	Q	5	A	9	T	23	I	26	N
21	3	I	18	N	25	N	13	V	19	L	12	G	21	C	13	P	0	T	3	I	17	N	20	O
23	27	I	13	O	21	O	11	L	19	S	13	C	21	Q	10	A	25	T	27	I	11	O	14	V
25	22	N	10	V	19	V	11	S	19	G	12	Q	18	P	5	T	19	I	20	N	5	V	10	L
27	18	O	8	L	17	L	11	G	19	C	10	P	14	A	29	T	13	N	15	O	1	L	7	S
29	15	V			17	S	10	C	18	Q	6	A	9	T	23	I	7	O	10	V	29	L	6	G
31	12	L			16	G			14	P			3	I	17	N			7	L			7	C

1987 BST: 29/3-25/10

date	Jan		Feb		Mar		Apr		May		Jun		Jul		Aug		Sep		Oct		Nov		Dec	
1	22	C	14	P	22	P	10	T	14	I	28	N	0	V	16	L	6	G	14	C	8	P	16	A
3	22	Q	12	A	20	A	6	I	8	N	22	O	24	V	12	S	4	C	13	Q	5	A	12	T
5	20	P	7	T	15	T	0	N	1	O	16	V	20	L	10	G	3	Q	12	P	3	T	8	I
7	16	A	2	I	10	I	24	N	25	O	11	L	16	S	9	C	3	P	10	A	29	T	3	N
9	11	T	26	I	4	N	18	O	20	V	8	S	15	G	9	Q	2	A	8	T	25	I	27	N
11	5	I	19	N	28	N	12	V	16	L	7	G	16	C	9	P	0	T	4	I	19	N	21	O
13	29	I	13	O	22	O	8	L	14	S	7	C	16	Q	8	A	26	T	29	I	13	O	15	V
15	23	N	8	V	17	V	5	S	13	G	7	Q	15	P	5	T	21	I	23	N	7	V	9	L
17	17	O	3	L	13	L	4	G	13	C	6	P	13	A	1	I	15	N	17	O	1	L	5	S
19	11	V	29	L	10	S	2	C	12	Q	3	A	9	T	25	I	9	O	11	V	27	L	2	G
21	6	L	27	S	7	G	1	Q	10	P	29	A	4	I	19	N	3	V	6	L	24	S	1	C
23	3	S	25	G	6	C	29	Q	6	A	24	T	28	I	12	O	27	V	2	S	23	G	1	Q
25	0	G	24	C	4	Q	26	P	2	T	19	I	22	N	6	V	23	L	29	S	22	C	1	P
27	0	C	23	Q	3	P	23	A	27	T	13	N	15	O	1	L	19	S	27	G	20	Q	29	P
29	0	Q			1	A	19	T	22	I	6	O	9	V	26	L	6	G	25	C	18	P	26	A
31	0	P			27	A			16	N			4	L	22	S			23	Q			22	T

1988 BST: 27/3-23/10

date	Jan		Feb		Mar		Apr		May		Jun		Jul		Aug		Sep		Oct		Nov		Dec	
1	5	I	21	N	11	O	25	V	29	L	17	G	25	C	19	P	11	T	17	I	4	O	5	V
3	29	I	14	O	5	V	20	L	25	S	15	C	24	Q	18	A	8	I	13	N	28	O	29	V
5	24	N	8	V	29	V	15	S	22	G	14	Q	23	P	15	T	4	N	7	O	21	V	23	L
7	17	O	2	L	23	L	11	G	19	C	12	P	21	A	12	I	28	N	1	V	15	L	18	S
9	11	V	26	L	18	S	8	C	17	Q	10	A	18	T	7	N	22	O	25	V	9	S	14	G
11	5	L	21	S	14	G	6	Q	16	P	8	T	15	I	1	O	16	V	18	L	5	G	11	C
13	0	S	19	G	12	C	5	P	14	A	5	I	10	N	25	O	9	L	13	S	1	C	9	Q
15	26	S	17	C	11	Q	4	A	12	T	1	N	4	O	19	V	3	S	8	G	28	C	7	P
17	24	G	18	Q	11	P	3	T	9	I	26	N	28	O	12	L	28	S	4	C	26	Q	5	A
19	24	C	18	P	11	A	1	I	5	N	20	O	22	V	7	S	24	G	1	Q	24	P	3	T
21	25	Q	17	A	9	T	27	I	0	O	14	V	16	L	2	G	21	C	0	P	23	A	1	I
23	24	P	15	T	6	I	22	N	24	O	8	L	10	S	28	G	20	Q	29	P	22	T	28	I
25	22	A	11	I	2	N	16	O	18	V	2	S	6	G	27	C	20	P	29	A	20	I	24	N
27	19	T	5	N	26	N	10	V	12	L	28	S	4	C	27	Q	21	A	28	T	16	N	19	O
29	14	I	29	N	20	O	4	L	7	S	26	G	4	Q	27	P	20	T	25	I	11	O	13	V
31	8	N			13	V			3	G			4	P	27	A			21	N			7	L

1989 BST: 26/3-29/10

date	Jan		Feb		Mar		Apr		May		Jun		Jul		Aug		Sep		Oct		Nov		Dec	
1	19	L	3	G	12	G	0	Q	8	P	1	T	10	I	0	O	17	V	19	L	4	G	8	C
3	13	S	0	C	8	C	29	Q	7	A	1	I	8	N	26	O	11	L	13	S	28	G	3	Q
5	9	G	28	C	6	Q	28	P	7	T	29	I	5	O	20	V	4	S	7	G	23	C	29	Q
7	6	C	27	Q	5	P	29	A	7	I	27	N	0	V	14	L	28	S	1	C	19	Q	26	P
9	4	Q	27	P	5	A	29	T	5	N	22	O	24	V	8	S	23	G	27	C	17	P	25	A
11	3	P	26	A	5	T	27	I	1	O	16	V	18	L	2	G	18	C	24	Q	16	A	25	T
13	2	A	24	T	4	I	23	N	26	O	10	L	12	S	27	G	16	Q	23	P	17	T	25	I
15	0	T	21	I	1	N	18	O	20	V	4	S	7	G	24	C	15	P	23	A	17	I	23	N
17	27	T	17	N	26	N	12	V	14	L	28	S	2	C	22	Q	15	A	24	T	15	N	20	O
19	24	I	12	O	21	O	5	L	89	S	24	G	29	C	21	P	15	T	23	I	12	O	15	V
21	20	N	6	V	15	V	29	L	2	G	20	C	27	Q	20	A	14	I	20	N	7	V	10	L
23	15	O	29	V	8	L	23	S	27	G	17	Q	26	P	19	T	11	N	16	O	1	L	3	S
25	9	V	23	L	2	S	18	G	23	C	15	P	24	A	17	I	7	O	10	V	25	L	27	S
27	3	L	17	S	26	S	13	C	20	Q	13	A	22	T	14	N	1	V	4	L	19	S	22	G
29	27	L			21	G	10	Q	18	P	12	T	20	I	9	O	25	V	28	L	13	G	17	C
31	21	S			17	C			17	A			17	N	4	V			22	S			13	Q

1990 BST: 25/3-23/10

date	Jan		Feb		Mar		Apr		May		Jun		Jul		Aug		Sep		Oct		Nov		Dec	
1	26	Q	18	A	28	A	22	I	29	N	17	V	21	L	4	G	19	C	22	Q	11	A	19	T
3	23	P	16	T	27	T	20	N	26	O	12	L	14	S	28	G	14	Q	19	P	11	T	20	I
5	21	A	15	I	25	I	16	O	21	V	6	S	8	G	23	C	11	P	18	A	11	I	20	N
7	20	T	13	N	23	N	11	V	15	L	0	G	2	C	19	Q	9	A	17	T	11	N	18	O
9	19	I	10	O	19	O	6	L	9	S	23	G	27	C	15	P	7	T	17	I	9	O	15	V
11	17	N	6	V	14	V	0	S	3	G	18	C	22	Q	13	A	6	I	15	N	6	V	10	L
13	15	O	1	L	9	L	24	S	26	G	12	Q	18	P	11	T	4	N	12	O	1	L	5	S
15	11	V	25	L	3	S	17	G	21	C	8	P	16	A	9	I	2	O	9	V	26	L	29	S
17	5	L	19	S	27	S	11	C	15	Q	5	A	14	T	8	N	29	O	4	L	20	S	22	G
19	29	L	13	G	21	G	6	Q	12	P	4	T	13	I	6	O	25	V	29	L	14	G	16	C
21	23	S	8	C	15	C	3	P	10	A	4	I	12	N	3	V	20	L	23	S	7	C	10	Q
23	17	G	3	Q	11	Q	1	A	10	T	4	N	11	O	29	V	15	S	17	G	1	Q	5	P
25	12	C	1	P	9	P	1	T	10	I	3	O	8	V	24	L	8	G	10	C	26	Q	1	A
27	9	Q	29	P	8	A	2	I	10	N	0	V	4	L	19	S	2	C	4	Q	22	P	28	A
29	6	P			8	T	2	N	8	O	26	V	29	L	12	G	26	C	0	P	19	A	27	T
31	4	A			8	I			5	V			23	S	6	C			27	P			28	I

1991

date	Jan		Feb		Mar		Apr		May		Jun		Jul		Aug		Sep		Oct		Nov		Dec	
1	13	N	4	V	12	V	1	S	4	G	18	C	20	Q	7	A	28	T	7	N	0	V	7	L
3	12	O	2	L	9	L	25	S	28	G	12	Q	15	P	4	T	26	I	5	O	27	V	3	S
5	10	V	27	L	5	S	19	G	21	C	6	P	11	A	1	I	25	N	3	V	24	L	29	S
7	7	L	22	S	0	G	13	C	15	Q	1	A	8	T	0	N	24	O	1	L	21	S	23	G
9	2	S	16	G	23	G	7	Q	10	P	29	A	6	I	0	O	23	V	28	L	15	G	17	C
11	26	S	9	C	17	C	2	P	7	A	28	T	6	N	0	V	20	L	24	S	9	C	11	Q
13	19	G	3	Q	12	Q	28	P	5	T	28	I	7	O	28	V	16	S	19	G	2	Q	4	P
15	13	C	28	Q	7	P	26	A	4	I	28	N	6	V	25	L	11	G	13	C	26	Q	29	P
17	7	Q	24	P	4	A	25	T	4	N	27	O	4	L	21	S	5	C	6	Q	21	P	25	A
19	2	P	21	A	1	T	25	I	3	O	25	V	0	S	15	G	29	C	1	P	17	A	23	T
21	28	P	19	T	0	I	23	N	1	V	20	L	24	S	9	C	23	Q	26	P	15	T	22	I
23	24	A	17	I	28	I	21	O	28	V	15	S	18	G	2	Q	18	P	23	A	14	I	22	N
25	22	T	16	N	26	N	18	V	23	L	9	G	12	C	26	Q	14	A	21	T	13	N	22	O
27	21	I	14	O	24	O	14	L	18	S	3	C	6	Q	22	P	11	T	19	I	12	O	21	V
29	21	N			21	V	9	S	12	G	27	C	0	P	17	A	9	I	18	N	10	V	18	L
31	20	O			18	L			6	C			25	P	14	T			16	O			13	S

1992 BST: 29/3–24/10

date	Jan		Feb		Mar		Apr		May		Jun		Jul		Aug		Sep		Oct		Nov		Dec	
1	26	S	11	C	1	Q	16	P	19	A	8	I	16	N	10	V	2	S	7	G	23	C	25	Q
3	20	G	4	Q	25	Q	11	A	16	T	7	N	16	O	9	L	29	S	3	C	17	Q	19	P
5	14	C	28	Q	19	P	6	T	13	I	6	O	15	V	7	S	24	G	27	C	11	P	13	A
7	7	Q	22	P	14	A	3	I	11	N	5	V	13	L	3	G	19	C	21	Q	5	A	8	T
9	1	P	17	A	10	T	0	N	9	O	3	L	10	S	27	G	12	Q	15	P	0	T	4	I
11	25	P	13	T	6	I	28	N	8	V	0	S	6	G	22	C	6	P	9	A	26	T	2	N
13	20	A	10	I	4	N	27	O	6	L	26	S	0	C	15	Q	0	A	4	T	23	I	0	O
15	17	T	8	N	2	O	26	V	3	S	21	G	25	C	9	P	24	A	29	T	20	N	29	O
17	15	I	8	O	2	V	24	L	0	G	16	C	18	Q	3	A	20	T	26	I	18	O	27	V
19	15	N	8	V	1	L	21	S	25	G	10	Q	12	P	27	A	16	I	23	N	16	V	25	L
21	15	O	8	L	0	S	17	G	20	C	3	P	6	A	23	T	13	N	21	O	15	L	22	S
23	15	V	6	S	27	S	12	C	13	Q	27	P	1	T	19	I	11	O	21	V	13	S	19	G
25	14	L	1	G	22	G	6	Q	7	P	22	A	27	T	18	N	11	V	20	L	10	G	14	C
27	10	S	26	G	16	C	29	Q	2	A	19	T	25	I	18	O	11	L	18	S	6	C	9	Q
29	5	G	19	C	9	Q	24	P	27	A	16	I	24	N	18	V	10	S	15	G	1	Q	3	P
31	29	G			3	P			24	T			24	O	18	L			11	C			26	P

CHAPTER FOUR

Mercury:
The way you think

How do you communicate? What kind of mind do you have?

The sign position of Mercury reveals how the individual `thinks. Mercury acts as a 'vehicle' for the thought process. It shows how the person arrives at a certain conclusion and describes the degree of mental speed and agility.

Mercury in the air signs, such as Gemini or Aquarius, denotes a thinking vehicle, equivalent to a jet plane with all the latest technology on board, and including apparatus that gives an objective overview of the terrain. Located in one of the practical earth signs, this position becomes a mental workhorse that is thorough and efficient - the family saloon of Mercuries.

When Mercury is found in one of the Water signs, imagination takes over. Mercury here is a gondola - romantic and inspirational, but not the most logistically sound mode of transport. When Mercury is in a fire sign, the person thinks in the manner of a hot air balloon - fired with energy, the thought patterns expand into action and soar until they run out of steam. Mercury in the fire signs can sometimes be full of hot air and easily deflated.

Mercury is the prime mover of the zodiac. It relates not only to the way we communicate, but also to the way we move. It gives an insight into our internal co-ordination so that we can see how we drive, dance, walk, play tennis and so on.

93

Because of the particular motion of the planet Mercury it will always fall either in the same sign as the Sun sign or in the one preceding or following it. It is very interesting to look at how Mercury affects people's self-expression, revealing both how they think, and what they like to talk about. It is easy to base our perception of someone on what they have to say. Yet, when we look at the sign Mercury is in and compare this to other planetary signs such as the Sun, we can see that how a person communicates is not always indicative of the underlying personality. Mercury can heed or hinder the expression of the self.

For instance, people with Sun in Gemini may exhibit many of the typical Gemini characteristics one would expect of these Sun signs, for example, always moving around, working in the communications field etc. Yet if they have Mercury in Taurus, their thinking process would be methodical rather than speedy. So, rather than being dazzled by the Geminian talk-show, one would notice a slower, more considered quality about these people, because the position of Mercury in Taurus would colour the expression of Sun in Gemini. Conversely, a down-to-earth, conventional Capricorn Sun will express in a highly intuitive and sometimes provocative manner if Mercury is in Aquarius.

MERCURY IN ARIES

Mercury here is usually quick thinking and alert. People with this placement can become very irritable with others who cannot keep up with their fast mental pace. Speech can come across as assertive and enthusiastic. These people are best as initiators, and good at stirring others to action with their impulsive ideas. However, plans tend to come and go as Mercury in Aries becomes fired up and then loses interest. These Mercury signs are very easily bored, and frequently leave others to pick up the pieces of their ideas after they have moved on to something else.

They can be argumentative because their mental energy is alive with a feisty quality. They hotly defend, challenge and discuss their ideas and often rouse opposition with their fighting talk. They are not ones to pussy-foot around, but come straight to the point, as wasting words and time prettying things makes them want to jump up and down with impatience.

They have the guts to call a spade a spade, and this honesty and directness is just what is needed to make things happen sometimes.

People with Mercury in Aries are also frustrated by anything that moves slowly and prefer to drive themselves or walk rather than rely on the idiosyncrasies of public transport. They are permanently in 'fast forward' mode, striding ahead in races of their own making.

MERCURY IN TAURUS

When Mercury falls in this sign, the tendency is for a cautious, deliberate stance to be taken. Ideas are formed slowly and carefully. Thinking is structured and well-organized in such a way that plans are made almost in the manner of creating form out of building blocks. This person will not make snap decisions, preferring to think things through in order to cover every eventuality.

The stubbornness of this placement means that these types will not alter their opinions just to make polite conversation. They are doggedly determined to stick to their guns and can arouse tension in others with their bull-headedness. They take time to assimilate what other people are saying because they sometimes get stuck on what they believe they hear, thereby missing any vital nuance that changes the meaning.

It is easy to engage these Mercury signs' interest on practical matters. They love to mull mentally over money or food and are able to capture touch, taste and smell in words because they express things primarily through the senses.

More interested in comfort than speed, people with Mercury in Taurus move at a sedate pace. Rushing anywhere causes great consternation to these placements who are like good wines that do not travel well. They amble rather than race, taking their time and enjoying the scenery.

MERCURY IN GEMINI

The planet Mercury has a great affinity with the sign of Gemini and functions easily in it, twisting and turning the thinking process with amazing dexterity. Whether the Sun is also in Gemini, or is in Taurus or Cancer, Mercury here lends enormous mental versatility. So much so, that often the other person in a conversation is left bewildered as Mercury in Gemini displays a kind of cut and run quality, skipping on to the next subject without a glance back.

Born communicators, people with Mercury in Gemini are entertaining companions. They appear to have a passing knowledge of just about any subject you care to bring up in conversation. They will never be caught out when questioned in depth because they can turn the tables so skilfully that you are manœuvred off a topic before you have time to scratch its surface.

Those with Mercury in Gemini never really stand still. They think on their feet and like to move constantly around. In fact, movement seems to stimulate the mental process. They can embody the image of the mobile communicator - ear to the carphone, tapping into the lap-top on the train or plane - and revel in transmitting their thought waves, or receiving information. These types have the gift of the gab and, to go with it, a logic that slices through life, carving it up into mental territories.

MERCURY IN CANCER

Mercury in Cancer sensitizes the thinking process to such an extent that differentiating between thinking and feeling becomes almost impossible. Ask people with Mercury in Cancer what they think about anything from the weather to the new boss and you will receive a barrage of impressions culled from their subjective feelings. However, what is lacking in logic is more than made up for in a rich imagination and a compassionate way with words. Mercury in Cancer is the listener of the zodiac and also has a gift for reading between the lines.

Mercury in Cancer signs enjoys mulling and musing over the nuances of human relationships and excel in their ability to express feeling in words, something which the air signs find difficult. They like to talk about the personal things in life. Confide your opinion about the state of the economy and they will be unable to connect, but pour out your soul over your difficult mother-in-law and you will engage them utterly.

Their experiences are distilled over the years and entered into an internal databank of memories and background information. They mop up the mental memorabilia that other signs discard. Like granny's attic, Mercury in Cancer types store the past and can bring back what others have forgotten - their recall of events and people is astounding.

MERCURY IN LEO

Lion dominated Mercury signs are forces to be reckoned with. Not only do they believe they are right, but they must convince you as well - winning arguments becomes a matter of pride. People with Mercury in Leo think from the position of 'top dog'; they speak with authority and have the ability to hold sway with their opinions.

The sign of Leo is focused on the idea of good quality and high standards. When Mercury is placed here, ideas are on a grand scale and designed to take effect without any concessions. Mercury in Leo types will not sacrifice their high standards for anyone. Even from a young age, the sparkle of Leo is evident - from the moment they grab the lion's share of the lines in the school play as the 'King', they begin to thrill to the power of words.

Leo signs conduct themselves regally. Even if their budget will not stretch to the Orient Express or Concorde, they still like to travel in style. Let others emerge from the underground hot and bothered, these Mercury types would prefer a black cab. They walk with dignity, straight back, head held high and they radiate their presence to the world. When they speak, others listen - whether they are discussing the world economy or the opening times of the local supermarket.

MERCURY IN VIRGO

In astrology, Virgo, like Gemini is 'ruled' by the planet Mercury. In other words, Mercury has a special relationship with these signs and sits comfortably here. Mercury in Virgo is noted for an ordered mind. Precision is everything to Mercury in Virgo - the 'getting it right' quality that permeates the thought process.

Mercury here denotes a tidy mind which means that nothing can be left to float freely. People with Mercury in Venus must pick over, sort through, sift and categorize the reasons why you forgot a birthday, left a partner or were made redundant. And, like a dog chewing on one's best shoes, they may not realize that all this critical appraisal and analysis may cause others considerable distress.

Their talent for taking things apart also applies to putting things together. They have practical minds and excel at mental organization. Nothing is left to chance, and every last detail has been thought of. Mercury in Virgo is constantly turning the pockets of life inside out to make sure that things do not get lost. Others may see it as worry, but Mercury in Virgo cannot switch off this mental machinery. Even if these types appear dreamy, they are probably pigeon-holing their thoughts, transferring ideas between the in and the out trays.

MERCURY IN LIBRA
Mercury in the sign of Libra exudes the objectivity and logical skills associated with the air signs. People with this placement have a certain gracefulness with words and movement that marks true

strategists. They will carefully select the tactics that will get an end result without disturbing the balance.

Those with this sign come from the particular brand of charm school that creates a smooth path, and always preface the presentation of their ideas with a 'What do you think about...?' or 'Would you mind if ....' They appear always to consider the other point of view and this diplomacy usually ensures their plans are well received. In fact, although they will listen to what others have to say, they are usually one step ahead. They have already weighed up all the alternatives and reached a conclusion, but they play their cards so that their companions will take credit for the idea.

These types are great social conversationalists, always able to find some area of interest where they can relate to others. They will even listen avidly to a monologue on train spotting and make all the right interested noises. After all, whatever their personal views, they figure that everyone has the right to theirs. They are essentially unbiased, which can be infuriating if you expect them to back you up in an argument - they will not necessarily take your side and are great believers in

giving others the benefit of the doubt.

MERCURY IN SCORPIO
When the planet Mercury is in the underwater sign of Scorpio we have a mental submarine, always on the look-out for what is beneath the surface. Scorpio is known for a penetrating insight into others, and, whether the Sun is in Libra, Scorpio or Sagittarius, Mercury in this sign will have an uncanny ability to know what is going on at a deeper level.

Because Scorpio is famous for being suspicious, the caricature of this Mercury placement questions everything. Even a straight forward 'Hello, how are you doing?' will elicit the Scorpionic response of wondering what exactly is meant by that! Nothing is taken at face value with this Mercury. In fact, they need to find an outlet for their capacity to delve so deeply and psychology and research work gives them the justification to probe.

Scorpio types move incognito. They try to be unobtrusive, but still draw attention, like a limousine with tinted glass windows that makes one wonder who is inside. It is hard to know what they are really thinking because they will not reveal much about themselves unless they feel really safe with a person. They like 'big talk', not small talk, and will hold the floor on any taboo subject such as sex and death. They will also prize information out of you that you would not confide to anyone else - it is just as well that Scorpio is good at keeping secrets!

MERCURY IN SAGITTARIUS

'Think big' could be the motto of this placement. Mercury in the expansive sign of Sagittarius always holds a vision of where things might lead. It is hard for people with this placement to keep their mental awareness in the here and now, because Sagittarius is apt to leap into the possibilities that the future might hold. Mercury here will project forward, seeing the cocoon as a butterfly, the baby as an adult. Of course, this ability can come in very useful for those who need to plan ahead, but the danger is of overlooking what is in front of one's nose.

A certain mental restlessness encourages people with Mercury in Sagittarius to become perpetual students. They love to discuss the meaning of life and an insatiable appetite for knowledge drives them on, devouring whole philosophies and cultures on the way. This enthusiasm translates into an inspirational way of speaking. In fact, Mercury in Sagittarius types are in their element whenever they get a chance to deliver their infectious optimism. Teaching, promoting or selling enable them to share with others their abundant perception of the universe.

These individuals have huge mental energy but, in keeping with the somewhat careless nature of the sign, their thoughts can wander all over the place. Sagittarians can appear ungainly because words charge out before sufficient thought has taken place. Tact and composure are not their forte - they are the archers shooting their arrows and where they fall they do not care.

MERCURY IN CAPRICORN

People with Mercury in Capricorn are solid thinkers. They arrive at conclusions after a long process of deliberation - no short cuts or instant answers for them. Studying is a serious business for them and they will often put in longer hours than any other sign. Capricorns like to be sure and the only way to be sure is to plod on. For them, the end result is only worth something if it reflects the amount of effort put in. They are never ones to conduct themselves with wild abandon, preferring to move in their own good time. They like to get the measure of things, so they walk and talk carefully, ensuring that they do not trip up.

The practical and cautious turn of mind of those with Mercury in Capricorn is a comfort to others of a more highly strung nature and their advice is often sought after. In a professional capacity, they have the ability to muster a suitable level of solemnity that adds weight to their words. They are steady rather than lightning thinkers, and they mean what they say. They are able to follow through on their ideas and will not get led off course by interruptions or alternative hare brained schemes.

One of these signs' favourite subjects is money. They have a good head for figures anyway, and the world of finance is a source of endless fascination for them. They find it more difficult to express their feelings partly because they cannot get to grips with things that they are unable to touch or see. Their minds revolve around tangible objects.

MERCURY IN AQUARIUS

The 'bolt out of the blue' quality of Aquarius is apparent in this Mercury sign. Thoughts pop into the head in a flash and temporarily illuminate everything. Mercury in Aquarius can be inspired by

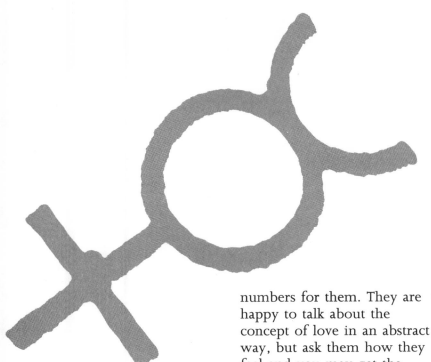

moments of perfect clarity and vision. Yet the electrical current can sometimes overload the system and create a kind of mental power cut. When this happens, even the most simple information appears to have been lost - a fault in the memory and thinking process creates a blank.

These Mercury signs are known for being ahead of their time. Their original turn of mind can lead to a breakthrough that upsets the old pattern of thought. They will never swallow the existing structure of ideas without questioning it - for them, rules are made to be broken. Their rational and broad perspective means that they like to discuss issues that affect people on a large scale. There is safety in numbers for them. They are happy to talk about the concept of love in an abstract way, but ask them how they feel and you may get the power cut!

Mercury in Aquarius types have a kind of contrariness and perversity about them. They will deliberately take the opposite viewpoint to add a little sparkle to the conversation, whatever their own feelings on the matter. It is the thrill of creating a line of thought that amuses and challenges them. They like to stir things up a bit and then calmly announce that they just wanted to see your reaction!

MERCURY IN PISCES

There is a thin line between fantasy and reality for people with Mercury in Pisces which allows them to disconnect from the facts in order to dream and imagining. Their creative thinking can blur the edges but they also need to 'unfocus' for a bit in order to move on. Often their best ideas come in this half-awake state. Instead of being truly in touch with the thinking process, like Mercury in the air signs, Mercury in Pisces finds the head and heart are interchangeable. These types feel what they think. They often cannot explain why they believe something, all they can tell you is that they simply feel it to be so. All the logic in the world will not change their minds when they are so bound to honour their inner emotions.

Those with the Mercury in Pisces placement can infuriate the air and earth signs with their inability to make concrete plans. It seems as if their ideas are pie in the sky, yet their very ability to enter other realms enables them to come into contact with the magical, whimsical thoughts that entrance and captivate others.

When they move they appear to float - walking several steps off the ground. They are fluid, and will never tie themselves down if they can just flow along with what comes. Their compassion and understanding give them a sympathetic ear - they are able to identify with your problems and, although they are the last to make a practical suggestion, they can soothe and heal with words.

YEAR	ARIES	TAURUS	GEMINI	CANCER	LEO	VIRGO	LIBRA	SCORPIO	SAGITTAR	CAPRIC	AQUARIUS	PISCES
1922	7/4-22/4	23/4-6/5	7/5-31/5	1/6-10/6	1/8-14/8	15/8-1/9	2/9-30/9	1/10-4/10	28/11-16/12	1/1-10/1	11/1-31/1	1/2-8/2
			11/6-13/7	14/7-31/7			5/10-8/11	9/11-27/11		17/12-31/12	9/2-17/3	18/3-6/4
1923	31/3-13/4	14/4-30/4	1/5-8/7	9/7-22/7	23/7-6/8	7/8-27/8	28/8-4/10	2/11-20/11	21/11-9/12	1/1-4/1	5/1-6/2	13/3-30/3
						5/10-11/10	12/10-1/11			7/2-13/2	14/2-12/3	
1924	22/3-5/4	6/4-12/6	13/6-28/6	29/6-12/7	13/7-29/7	30/7-6/10	7/10-23/10	24/10-11/11	12/11-2/12	1/1-13/2	14/2-4/3	5/5-12/3
										3/12-31/12		
1925	13/3-31/3	1/4-15/4	7/6-20/6	21/6-4/7	5/7-25/7	26/7-26/8	30/9-16/10	17/10-5/11	1/1-13/1	14/1-6/2	7/2-24/2	25/2-21/3
	16/4-16/5	17/5-6/6			27/8-10/9	11/9-29/9			6/11-31/12			
1926	6/3-12/5	13/5-28/5	29/5-11/6	12/6-28/6	29/6-5/9	6/9-21/9	22/9-9/10	10/10-30/10	1/1-10/1	11/1-30/1	31/1-17/2	18/2-5/3
								28/11-13/12	31/10-27/11			
									14/12-31/12			
1927	17/4-5/5	6/5-20/5	21/5-3/6	4/6-27/6	28/6-13/7	29/8-13/9	14/9-2/10	3/10-8/12	1/1-4/1	5/1-23/1	24/1-9/2	10/2-16/4
				14/7-11/8	12/8-28/8				9/12-28/12	29/12-31/12		
1928	11/4-26/4	27/4-10/5	11/5-28/5	29/5-4/8	5/8-18/8	19/8-4/9	5/9-26/9	27/9-24/10	1/12-20/12	1/1-6/1	7/1-2/2	3/2-28/2
							25/10-10/11	11/11-30/11		21/12-31/12		18/3-10/4
1929	4/4-18/4	19/4-2/5	3/5-11/7	12/7-26/7	27/7-10/8	11/8-29/8	30/8-4/11	5/11-23/11	24/11-13/12	1/1-7/1	8/1-15/3	16/3-3/4
										14/12-31/12		
1930	27/3-9/4	10/4-30/4	1/5-16/5	5/7-18/7	19/7-3/8	4/8-25/8	26/8-19/9	29/10-16/11	17/11-5/12	1/1	2/1-22/1	9/3-26/3
		17/5-13/6	14/6-4/7			20/9-10/10	11/10-28/10			23/1-14/2	15/2-8/3	
1931	19/3-2/4	3/4-10/6	11/6-25/6	26/6-10/7	11/7-28/7	29/7-3/10	4/10-21/10	22/10-9/11	10/11-1/12	6/12-31/12	11/2-1/3	2/3-18/3
									21/12-31/12			
1932	9/3-15/5	16/5-2/6	3/6-16/6	17/6-1/7	2/7-27/7	28/7-10/8	26/9-12/10	13/10-1/11	2/11-31/12	1/1-10/2	5/2-22/2	23/2-8/3
					11/8-8/9	9/9-25/9				2/12-20/12		
1933	3/3-25/3	10/5-24/5	25/5-7/6	8/6-26/6	27/6-1/9	2/9-17/9	18/9-5/10	6/10-29/10	1/1-7/1	8/1-28/1	29/1-13/2	14/2-2/3
	18/4-9/5							16/11-11/12	30/10-15/11			26/3-17/4
									12/12-31/12			
1934	15/4-1/5	2/5-16/5	17/5-31/5	1/6-8/8	9/8-24/8	25/8-9/9	10/9-29/9	30/9-5/12	6/12-24/12	1/1-19/1	20/1-5/2	6/2-14/4
										25/12-31/12		
1935	8/4-24/4	25/4-7/5	8/5-29/5	30/5-20/6	2/8-15/8	16/8-2/9	3/9-27/9	28/9-12/10	29/11-17/12	1/1-12/1	13/1-31/1	1/2-14/2
		21/6-13/7		14/7-1/8			13/10-9/11	10/11-28/11		18/12-31/12	15/2-17/3	18/3-7/4
1936	31/3-14/4	15/4-30/4	1/5-8/7	9/7-22/7	23/7-7/8	8/8-28/8	29/8-1/11	2/11-20/11	21/11-9/12	10/12-31/12	6/1-12/3	13/3-30/3

YEAR	-ARIES	TAURUS	GEMINI	CANCER	LEO	VIRGO	LIBRA	SCORPIO	SAGITTAR	CAPRIC	AQUARIUS	PISCES
1937	24/3-6/4	7/4-13/6	14/6-30/6	1/7-14/7	15/7-31/7	1/8-7/10	8/10-25/10	26/10-13/11	14/11-3/12	10/1-13/2	1/1-9/1	6/3-23/3
										4/12-31/12		
1938	15/3-31/3	1/4-23/4	8/6-21/6	22/6-6/7	7/7-26/7	27/7-2/9	1/10-17/10	18/10-6/11	7/1-12/1	1/1-6/1	14/2-5/3	27/2-14/3
	24/4-16/5	17/5-7/6			3/9-10/9	11/9-30/9			7/11-31/12	13/1-7/2	8/2-26/2	
1939	7/3-13/5	14/5-30/5	31/5-13/6	14/6-29/6	30/6-6/9	7/9-22/9	23/9-10/10	11/10-31/10	1/1-11/1	12/1-31/1	1/2-18/2	19/2-6/3
								3/12-13/12	1/11-2/12			
									14/12-31/12			
1940	3/3-8/3	7/5-20/5	21/5-4/6	5/6-25/6	26/6-20/7	29/8-13/9	14/9-2/10	3/10-8/12	1/1-5/1	6/1-24/1	25/1-10/2	11/2-2/3
	7/4-6/5			21/7-11/8	12/8-28/8				9/12-28/12	29/12-31/12		9/3-7/4
1941	12/4-28/4	29/4-12/5	13/5-28/5	29/5-5/8	6/8-20/8	21/8-6/9	7/9-27/9	28/9-29/10	3/12-21/12	1/1-16/1	17/1-2/2	3/2-6/3
							30/10-11/11	12/11-2/12		22/12-31/12	7/3-16/3	17/3-11/4
1942	5/4-20/4	21/4-4/5	5/5-11/7	12/7-28/7	29/7-12/8	13/8-30/8	31/8-6/11	7/11-24/11	25/11-14/12	1/1-8/1	9/1-16/3	17/3-4/4
										15/12-31/12		
1943	28/3-11/4	12/4-29/4	30/4-25/5	6/7-19/7	20/7-4/8	5/8-26/8	27/8-24/9	31/10-17/11	18/11-7/12	1/1-2/1	3/1-27/1	11/3-27/3
	16/4-10/5	26/5-13/6	14/6-5/7			25/9-11/10	12/10-30/10			28/1-14/2	15/2-10/3	
										8/12-31/12		
1944	19/3-2/4	3/4-10/6	11/6-26/6	27/6-10/7	11/7-27/7	28/7-4/10	5/10-21/10	22/10-9/11	10/11-30/11	1/1-11/2	12/2-7/3	3/3-18/3
									24/12-31/12	1/12-23/12		
1945	11/3-15/5	16/5-3/6	4/6-17/6	18/6-2/7	3/7-25/7	26/7-16/8	27/9-14/10	15/10-3/11	1/1-13/1	14/1-2/4	5/2-22/2	23/2-10/3
					17/8-9/9	10/9-26/9			4/11-31/12			
1946	4/3-31/3	11/5-26/5	27/5-9/6	10/6-26/6	27/6-2/9	3/9-18/9	19/9-7/10	8/10-29/10	1/1-8/1	9/1-28/1	29/1-14/2	15/2-3/3
	16/4-10/5							20/11-12/12	30/10-19/11	11/12-31/12		1/4-15/4
									13/12-31/12			
1947	16/4-3/5	4/5-17/5	18/5-1/6	2/6-9/8	10/8-25/8	26/8-10/9	11/9-30/9	1/10-6/12	1/1-2/1	3/1-20/1	21/1-7/2	8/2-15/4
									7/12-25/12	26/12-31/12		
1948	9/4-24/4	25/4-8/5	9/5-27/5	28/5-27/6	2/8-16/8	17/8-2/9	3/9-26/9	27/9-16/10	29/11-17/12	1/1-14/1	15/1-1/2	2/2-19/2
			28/6-10/7	11/7-1/8			17/10-9/11	10/11-28/11		18/12-31/12	20/2-17/3	18/3-8/4
1949	1/4-15/4	16/4-1/5	2/5-9/7	10/7-24/7	25/7-8/8	9/8-27/8	28/8-2/11	3/11-21/11	22/11-10/12	1/1-5/1	6/1-13/3	14/3-31/3
										11/12-31/12		
1950	24/3-8/4	9/4-13/6	14/6-1/7	2/7-15/7	16/7-1/8	2/8-26/8	27/8-9/9	27/10-14/11	15/11-4/12	15/1-13/2	1/1-14/1	8/3-23/3
							9/10-26/10			5/12-31/12	14/2-7/3	
1951	16/3-2/4	3/4-1/5	10/6-24/6	25/6-8/7	9/7-27/7	28/7-2/10	3/10-19/10	20/10-8/11	9/11-1/12	1/1-9/2	10/2-28/2	1/3-15/3
	2/5-15/5	16/5-9/6							13/12-31/12	2/12-12/12		

YEAR	ARIES	TAURUS	GEMINI	CANCER	LEO	VIRGO	LIBRA	SCORPIO	SAGITTAR	CAPRIC	AQUARIUS	PISCES
1952	8/3-14/5	15/5-31/5	1/6-14/6	15/6-30/6	1/7-7/9	8/9-23/9	24/9-11/10	12/10-1/11	1/1-13/1	14/1-3/2	4/2-20/2	21/2-7/3
									2/12-31/12			
1953	3/3-15/3	9/5-23/5	24/5-6/6	7/6-26/6	27/6-28/7	31/8-15/9	16/9-4/10	5/10-31/10	1/1-6/1	7/1-25/1	26/1-11/2	12/2-2/3
	18/4-8/5		29/7-11/8		12/8-30/8			7/11-10/12	11/12-31/12			16/3-17/4
1954	14/4-30/4	1/5-14/5	15/5-30/5	31/5-7/8	8/8-22/8	23/8-8/9	9/9-29/9	30/9-4/11	5/12-23/12	1/1-18/1	19/1-4/2	5/2-13/4
							5/11-11/11	12/11-4/12		24/12-31/12		
1955	7/4-21/4	22/4-6/5	7/5-13/7	14/7-30/7	31/7-14/8	15/8-1/9	2/9-7/11	8/11-26/11	27/11-15/12	1/1-10/1	11/1-17/3	18/3-6/4
										16/12-31/12		
1956	29/3-12/4	13/4-29/4	30/4-6/7	7/7-20/7	21/7-5/8	6/8-25/8	26/8-29/9	1/11-18/11	19/11-7/12	1/1-3/1	4/1-2/2	11/3-28/3
						30/9-10/10	11/10-31/10			3/2-14/2	15/2-10/3	
										8/12-31/12		
1957	21/3-4/4	5/4-6/12	13/6-28/6	29/6-12/7	13/7-29/7	30/7-6/10	7/10-23/10	24/10-11/11	12/11-1/12	1/1-11/2	12/2-3/3	4/3-20/3
									29/12-31/12	2/12-28/12		
1958	13/3-1/4	2/4-10/4	6/6-19/6	20/6-4/7	5/7-25/7	26/7-23/8	29/9-15/10	16/10-4/11	1/1-13/1	14/1-6/2	7/2-24/2	25/2-12/3
	11/4-16/5	17/5-5/6			24/8-10/9	11/9-28/9			5/11-31/12			
1959	6/3-12/5	13/5-28/5	29/5-11/6	12/6-28/6	29/6-4/9	5/9-20/9	21/9-8/10	9/10-30/10	1/1-10/1	11/1-30/1	31/1-16/2	17/2-5/3
								26/11-13/12	31/10-25/11			
1960	16/4-4/5	5/5-18/5	19/5-2/6	3/6-30/6	1/7-6/7	27/8-9/12	13/9-1/10	2/10-7/12	1/1-4/1	5/1-23/1	24/1-9/2	10/2-15/4
				7/7-10/8	11/8-26/8				14/12-31/12	28/12-31/12		
1961	11/4-26/4	27/4-10/5	11/5-28/5	29/5-3/8	4/8-18/8	19/8-4/9	5/9-27/9	28/9-22/10	8/12-27/12	1/1-4/1	5/1-1/2	2/2-24/2
						17/9-10/10	23/10-10/11	11/11-30/11		20/12-31/12	25/2-18/3	19/3-10/4
1962	3/4-18/4	19/4-5/3	4/5-11/7	12/7-26/7	27/7-10/8	11/8-29/8	30/8-4/11	5/11-23/11	24/11-12/12	1/1-7/1	8/1-15/3	16/3-2/4
									1/12-19/12	13/12-31/12		
1963	26/3-9/4	10/4-2/5	3/5-10/5	4/7-18/7	19/7-3/8	4/8-26/8	27/8-16/9	29/10-16/11	17/11-5/12	1/1-2/1	3/1-20/1	10/3-25/3
		11/5-14/6	15/6-3/7			17/9-10/10	11/10-28/10			21/1-15/2	16/2-9/3	
										6/12-31/12		
1964	17/3-1/4	2/4-8/6	9/6-24/6	25/6-8/7	9/7-27/7	28/7-2/10	3/10-20/10	21/10-8/11	9/11-30/11	1/1-10/2	11/2-29/2	1/3-16/3
									17/12-31/12	1/12-16/12		
1965	10/3-15/5	16/5-2/6	3/6-15/6	16/6-1/7	2/7-30/7	31/7-3/8	26/9-12/10	13/10-2/11	1/1-12/1	13/1-3/2	4/2-21/2	22/2-9/3
					4/8-8/9	9/9-25/9			3/11-31/12			
1966	3/3-22/3	10/5-24/5	25/5-6/6	7/6-26/6	27/6-1/9	2/9-17/9	18/9-5/10	6/10-29/10	1/1-7/1	8/1-26/1	27/1-13/2	14/2-2/3

YEAR	ARIES	TAURUS	GEMINI	CANCER	LEO	VIRGO	LIBRA	SCORPIO	SAGITTAR	CAPRIC	AQUARIUS	PISCES
1966	18/4-9/5							14/11-11/12	30/10-13/11			23/3-17/4
1967	15/4-1/5	2/5-16/5	17/5-31/5	1/6-8/8	9/8-24/8	25/8-9/9	10/9-29/9	30/9-5/12	12/12-31/12 6/12-24/12	1/1-19/1 25/12-31/12	20/1-5/2	6/2-14/4
1968	7/4-22/4	23/4-6/5	7/5-29/5 14/6-12/7	30/5-13/6 13/7-31/7	1/8-14/8	15/8-1/9	2/9-27/9 8/10-8/11	28/9-7/10 9/11-27/11	28/11-16/12	1/1-12/1 17/12-31/12	13/1-1/2	2/2-11/2
1969	31/3-14/4	15/4-30/4	1/5-7/7	8/7-22/7	23/7-6/8	7/8-27/8 8/10-9/10	28/8-7/10 10/10-1/11	2/11-20/11	21/11-9/12	1/1-4/1 10/12-31/12	12/2-17/3 5/1-12/3	18/3-6/4 13/3-30/3
1970	23/3-6/4	7/4-13/6	14/6-30/6	1/7-12/7	13/7-31/7	1/8-7/10	8/10-25/10	26/10-12/11	13/11-3/12	1/1-13/2 4/12-31/12	14/2-5/3	6/3-22/3
1971	15/3-1/4 19/4-17/5	2/4-18/4 18/5-7/6	8/6-21/6	22/6-6/7	7/7-26/7 30/8-11/9	27/7-29/8 12/9-30/9	1/10-17/10	18/10-6/11	2/1-14/1 7/11-31/12	15/1-7/2	8/2-26/2	27/2-14/3
1972	6/3-12/5	13/5-29/5	30/5-12/6	13/6-28/6	29/6-5/9	6/9-21/9	22/9-10/10	11/10-30/10 30/11-12/12	1/1-11/1 31/10-29/11 13/12-31/12	12/1-31/1	1/2-18/2	19/2-5/3
1973	17/4-6/5	7/5-20/5	21/5-4/6	5/6-27/6 17/7-11/8	28/6-16/7 12/8-28/8	29/8-13/9	14/9-2/10	3/10-8/12	1/1-4/1 9/12-28/12	5/1-23/1 29/12-31/12	24/1-9/2	10/2-16/4
1974	12/4-28/4	29/4-12/5	13/5-29/5 14/6-7/4	30/5-5/6	6/8-20/8	21/8-6/9 27/10-11/11	7/9-28/9 12/11-2/12	29/9-26/10	1/1-16/1 22/12-31/12	17/1-2/2	3/2-11/4	
1975	5/4-19/4	20/4-4/5	5/5-12/7	13/7-29/7	30/7-12/8	13/8-30/8	31/8-6/11	7/11-25/11	26/11-14/12	1/1-8/1 15/12-31/12	9/1-16/3	17/3-4/4
1976	27/3-10/4	11/4-29/4 20/5-13/6	30/4-19/5 14/6-7/4	5/7-18/7	19/7-3/8	4/8-25/8 22/9-10/10	26/8-21/9 11/10-29/10	30/10-16/11	17/11-6/12	1/1-2/1 27/1-15/2 7/12-31/12	3/1-26/1 16/2-9/3	10/3-26/3
1977	19/3-3/4	4/4-10/6	11/6-26/6	27/6-10/7	11/7-28/7	29/7-4/10	5/10-21/10	22/10-9/11	10/11-1/12 22/12-31/12	1/1-10/2 2/12-21/12	11/2-2/3	3/3-18/3
1978	11/3-16/5	17/5-3/6	4/6-17/6	18/6-2/7	3/7-27/7 14/8-9/9	28/7-13/8 10/9-26/9	27/9-14/10	15/10-3/11	1/1-13/1 4/11-31/12	14/1-4/2	5/2-22/2	23/2-10/3
1979	4/3-28/3 18/4-10/5	11/5-26/5	27/5-9/6	10/6-27/6	28/6-2/9	3/9-18/9	19/9-7/10	8/10-30/10 19/11-12/12	1/1-8/1 31/10-18/11 13/12-31/12	9/1-28/1	29/1-14/2	15/2-3/3 29/3-17/4
1980	15/4-2/5	3/5-16/5	17/5-30/5	31/5-9/8	10/8-24/8	25/8-10/9	11/9-30/9	1/10-5/12	1/1-2/1 6/12-25/12	3/1-21/1 26/12-31/12	22/1-7/2	8/2-14/4

YEAR	ARIES	TAURUS	GEMINI	CANCER	LEO	VIRGO	LIBRA	SCORPIO	SAGITTAR	CAPRIC	AQUARIUS	PISCES
1981	9/4-24/4	25/4-8/5	9/5-28/5	29/5-22/6	2/8-16/8	17/8-2/9	3/9-27/9	28/9-14/10	29/11-17/12	1/1-12/1	13/1-31/1	1/2-16/2
1982	1/4-15/4	16/4-1/5	23/6-12/7	13/7-1/8	25/7-8/8	9/8-28/8	15/10-10/11	11/11-26/11	22/11-12/12	18/12-31/12	17/2-18/3	19/3-8/4
			2/5-9/7	10/7-24/7							6/1-13/3	14/3-31/3
1983	24/3-7/4	8/4-14/6	15/6-1/7	2/7-15/7	16/7-1/8	2/8-29/8	30/8-6/9	27/10-14/11	15/11-4/2	1/1	2/1-12/1	8/3-23/3
						7/9-8/10	9/10 26/10			13/1-14/2	15/2-7/3	
										5/12-31/12		
1984	15/3-31/3	1/4-25/4	8/6-22/6	23/6-6/7	27/7-30/9	27/7-30/9	1/10-18/10	19/10-6/11	7/11-1/12	1/1-10/2	11/2-27/2	28/2-14/3
	26/4-15/5	16/5-7/6							18/12-31/12	2/12-7/12		
1985	7/3-14/5	15/5-30/5	31/5-13/6	14/6-29/6	30/6-6/9	7/9-22/9	23/9-10/10	11/10-31/10	1/1-11/1	12/1-1/2	2/2-18/2	19/2-6/3
								5/12-12/12	1/11-4/12			
									13/12-31/12			
1986	4/3-11/3	8/5-22/5	23/5-5/6	6/6-26/6	27/6-23/7	24/7-11/8	12/8-30/8	31/8-15/9	1/1-5/1	6/1-25/1	26/1-11/2	12/2-3/3
	18/4-7/5					16/9-4/10	16/9-4/10	5/10-10/12	11/12-29/12	30/12-31/12	30/12-31/12	12/3-17/4
1987	13/4-29/4	30/4-13/5	14/5-30/5	31/5-6/8	7/8-21/8	22/8-7/9	8/9-28/9	29/9-1/11	1/1-11/1	1/1-17/1	18/1-4/2	5/2-11/3
							2/11-11/11	12/11-3/12	4/12-22/12	23/12-31/12	12/3-13/3	14/3-12/4
1988	15/4-20/4	21/4-4/5	5/5-12/7	13/7-28/7	29/7-12/8	13/8-30/8	31/8-6/11	7/11-25/11	26/11-14/12	1/1-10/1	11/1-16/3	17/3-14/4
										15/12-31/12		
1989	29/3-11/4	12/4-29/4	30/4-28/5	7/7-20/7	21/7-6/8	7/8-26/8	27/8-26/9	31/10-18/11	19/11-7/12	1/1-2/1	3/1-29/1	11/3-26/3
		29/5-12/6	13/6-6/7			27/9-11/10	12/10-30/10			30/1-14/2	15/2-10/3	
										8/12-31/12		
1990	20/3-4/4	5/4-12/6	13/6-27/6	28/6-11/7	12/7-29/7	30/7-5/10	6/10-23/10	24/10-18/11	19/11-2/12	1/1-12/2	13/2-3/3	4/3-19/3
									26/12-31/12	3/12-25/12		
1991	12/3-16/5	17/5-5/6	6/6-19/6	20/6-4/7	5/7-26/7	27/7-19/8	29/9-15/10	16/10-5/11	1/1-14/1	15/1-5/2	6/2-24/2	25/2-11/3
					20/8-10/9	11/9-28/9			5/11-31/12			
1992	4/3-3/4	12/5-26/5	27/5-9/6	10/6-27/6	28/6-3/9	4/9-19/4	20/9-7/10	8/10-29/10	1/1-10/1	11/1-29/1	30/1-16/2	17/2-3/3
	15/4-11/5							22/11-12/12	30/10-21/11			4/4-14/4

CHAPTER FIVE

Venus:
Your love life

Who are you attracted to? Who and what do you find beautiful? How do you like to socialize?

The goddess of love manifests in our lives according to the sign Venus is in at birth. We both give and receive love in a way that resonates with the Venus sign, and we are attracted to those people that look and behave in a style that corresponds to our Venus placement. In a very real sense, Venus will tell us who exactly is 'our type'.

Astrological compatibility is a complex business, as there are many factors to be born in mind. However, with a knowledge of the signs of the planets it is possible to see the potential for relationship on all levels. Compatibility between the Sun, Moon and Venus signs is important, but other planets also play a part. For instance, two people might find their respective Sun, Moon and Venus signs in harmony, giving them a common purpose and mutual sense of comfort and attraction, but, if their Mercuries are incompatible, they might actually find it difficult to talk to each other!

However, for pure romantic attraction the sign position of Venus is of the utmost importance. If partners have the same signs prominently placed in his and her chart, either on the

Descendant, or as the Sun, Moon or Venus sign then there is a good chance that they will embody each other's ideal love in some way.

Venus in the fire signs (Aries, Leo and Sagittarius) is active and go-getting in the romantic stakes, but although seen in 'hot pursuit', can quickly go off the boil. Venus in the earth signs (Taurus, Virgo and Capricorn) is controlled and contained, looking for security and permanence. In the water signs (Cancer, Scorpio and Pisces) Venus is emotional and romantic, often looking for the dream lover. In the air signs (Gemini, Libra and Aquarius) Venus is after a meeting of minds, with communication the key to affection.

If two people have Venus in the same element, they will feel a similar power of attraction, and enjoy the same things. Air and fire Venus signs tend to produce positive romantic combustion, and earth and water Venus signs also fire Cupid's arrows at each other. Other combinations are more hit and miss!

Venus is tied up with the concept of money because it indicates personal magnetism - the sort of vibrations people put out in order to attract what they want. Venus is also indicative of the values of the individual in the sense that people tend to spend time and money on what they value. For example, Venus in Sagittarius might have an easy come, easy go relationship with people and money, whereas Venus in Capricorn has a tighter rein on its heart and purse strings.

Venus describes the things that look attractive to people - other people, clothes, furnishings, anything which activates our personal style and taste. It is useful to know someone's Venus sign when giving them a present, because it is easier to pick something that resonates with them. The sign position also indicates what gives pleasure, for example, whether someone is a party person or prefers quiet nights at home. The sign Venus is in at birth indicates favourite haunts and pastimes that a person really enjoys.

VENUS IN ARIES

A woman with Venus in Aries will impress you with her independence. She likes to choose her lover, and she is honest and direct in her negotiations! Cupid strikes very quickly when Venus is in this sign, and she is apt to fall 'instantly' in love. When the fire burns, the heat of her passion can be felt, but if she is 'put out' she goes cold. She enjoys 'doing her own thing', and needs time and space to pursue her own interests. Venus in Aries is attracted to strength in her man; both physical strength and strength of character. She despises weakness and enjoys testing men out to make sure they are on their mettle!

Men with Venus in Aries are attracted to strong women who will not cling or hang on to their every word. These men will not spend much time lingering over long romantic dinners, or wooing gradually with flowers. Venus in Aries is after his goal, and when he has someone in mind, she had better get ready to be carried off into the jungle. He is very pushy and views love as another opportunity to exercise his salesmanship. He believes that something worth having is worth fighting for and he loves to battle with the competition - a little rivalry heightens his ardour.

Both men and women with Venus in Aries love sport, so you may be inveigled into going motor-racing or go-karting on your first date. They enjoy 'doing' rather than talking and are often to be found at their exercise club or taking in the thrill of a game or race. They love to be around something that sets their pulses running, and their desire for adrenalin can make them feisty in relationships. They like a sparring partner and admire someone who can hold their own and stand up to them.

Because of their natural spontaneity, Venus in Aries types make new friends everywhere. They feel that rush of connection with others, who instantly become part of their circle. Their social lives are action-packed, and they like to do things at the drop of a hat, so people who have to check their diaries and plan two months ahead, in the manner of the Earth signs, can forget it - if they cannot keep up they will be dropped. Friendship with Venus in Aries is a matter of survival of the fittest!

Money tends to burn a hole in the pocket of these Venus signs - they are impulsive spenders. That rowing machine looked so good in the shop they just had to have it, although the bother of a routine and all that time spent pumping iron soon consigns it to the garage. People with Venus in Aries exude a definite sense of personal taste. They like to make a statement with what they wear and are attracted to bold colours. No matter how traditional the suit, the red tie adds that little touch of assertion that makes Venus in Aries feel good. And women with Venus in Aries frequently love to wear the trousers!

VENUS IN TAURUS

Women with Venus in Taurus convey a certain earthiness.

Relationships for them should be lasting and secure - in a sense the quantity of years put into a union overrides their quality. They are possessive, and expect total loyalty. In return they deliver the message that they will always be there for their partners. Venus in Taurus women are experts at making people feel comfortable. Like fertile empresses, they are at their best when allowed to nurture and indulge someone else.

Men with Venus in Taurus are concerned with making a sensible choice of partner. They take all practical matters into consideration before selecting prospective candidates. After they have examined your bank balance, and your feet, to make sure they are firmly on the ground they may invite you out. They like to be in control and recoil from advances made by women. Their image of the perfect woman is constant, feminine and nurturing. They do not want to play second fiddle to her high-powered job or feel over cast by her shadow.

The Venus in Taurus man loves to wine and dine. He will take you to his favourite restaurant where he may be unable to resist choosing your food for you, and putting the bill on his gold card. He has probably planned to have you for pudding. After that, he may want you to massage his shoulders!

Both sexes with this placement are very tactile and sensual. Love is experienced through the senses and, because hugging and touching are so important, they are not attracted to reed-slim types or those who prefer contact through the mind, like the air signs. The more there is of someone, the more to be enjoyed, and these Venus signs value solidity - in both frame and personality.

Socially, Venus in Taurus likes to stick to the tried and tested. These types hang on to their friends for dear life, and will always be there to help when lightning strikes. Staying with them can be an absolute pleasure as they encourage you to relax completely, whilst plying you with gourmet delights. Relaxation is really the key to a pleasant life for people with Venus in Taurus. They are not keen on strenuous or competitive activities and not the sort to join in running a marathon for charity - they would rather donate the money and recline somewhere comfortable.

Their taste tends towards the conservative. Venus in Taurus placements like the feel of natural fabrics against their skin, and would always prefer to look classically elegant rather than outrageously up-to-the-minute. They get pleasure out of spending money on art, their homes and gardens, silk shirts, good food and wine - anything that adds more quality to their comfort zone. They are also not averse to having a bit stashed away in the bank!

VENUS IN GEMINI

The female version of Venus in Gemini fashions herself on the image of the coquette, she is light, enticing and flirtatious. This lady is seemingly an amour without armour, yet, if you try to corner her, she will simply leave you standing, catching your breath, whilst she is already alighting on the next object of interest. She loves to play with ideas, and relationships are ideas to her - because they feed her mind.

She is a seeker of knowledge, and at her best when she is caught in the unpredictability of romance, rather than trapped as a wife or mother. To catch her, you must challenge her mind.

Men with Venus in Gemini have enormous curiosity about love, but may not want to find answers to their questions because life without the thrill of the unknown bores them. Venus in Gemini is the man who insists on talking to a woman on the plane or train only to disappear at the other end without leaving an address. These types like to keep their options open, and a certain duality can manifest itself as a desire for more than one relationship at once. There is a touch of philandering fickleness, but the prospect of too many emotional demands, particularly from the Water nymphs, keeps them just playing mind games rather than entering the fray. One thing is certain, you will never be bored with Venus in Gemini, and there are plenty of women who would give up the suffocating sameness of the slippers and pipe routine for the elusive enchantment of this smooth talker.

Both men and women with Venus in Gemini will

go out with someone primarily to talk to them. When they take you to see the film or the play, they will expect you to have formulated opinions about the lighting, plot and casting before you have even left the auditorium. For Venus in Gemini, any comment at all is preferable to no comment. They will not probe behind a wall of silence because they are intimidated by the prospect of plumbing the depths of another's psyche. They prefer to glance at the goods directly in the shop window.

There is safety in numbers for the Venus in Gemini, so a partner should be prepared to meet his friends. Double dating is the perfect way for him to keep things light and on the move. Venus in Gemini is a social creature, a butterfly actually. Both sexes are great mixers, spreading themselves thinly amongst many people. They usually have so many interests that their social lives are a constant juggling act of people to see and places to go.

In the financial stakes, Venus in Geminis can be the whiz-kids or the profligates. They are wheeler-dealers and see the currency of money as a language - a means of communication. For them money really does talk. They are not interested in amassing great wealth, in fact material things are not of great value because they are too static. Although objects such as books and cars are important to them, dinner services, lampshades and carpets are not! Sometimes a concept such as minimalist or bohemian might catch their fancy, but their tastes are ever changing.

VENUS IN CANCER
Venus in Cancer activates motherly feelings in a woman. She needs to pour her maternal, nurturing instincts into relationships. Gently encouraging, the Venus in Cancer woman is the one who enjoys her role behind a successful man. Her sensitivity to her partner's needs urges her to check out whether he is hungry, tired and in need of her tender loving care. Far from being a wet rag, she generates enough emotional energy to build a powerful support system. In return, she needs the man to acknowledge receipt of her feelings by opening up and sharing his own. Her constant desire for closeness makes her dependent on her relationships to a large extent.

A man with Venus in Cancer is attracted to women who will look after him emotionally. He can be on the look out for a mother figure, the big breasted, homely type who can offer solace on a dark night. Besides, he has that needy look about him that demands attention. Venus in Cancer men are seduced by the creation of home and family - until this happens for them, they are always searching for a missing link.

A vital part of the courtship for both sexes with this placement will be the test of whether they fit into the context of the other's family. By way of home-making, the male with Venus in Cancer will also often resort to asking his partner to 'put that feminine touch' into his bachelor pad. When she turns up, however, she will probably find herself tripping up over all the bits and pieces he has already collected. He loves to stay in and play house with his partner. Of course, this is after he has exhausted the possibilities of playing mummies and daddies!

People with Venus in Cancer create a family network from their friends. This provides an emotional safety net which can be wonderfully supportive for everyone. But, true to family life, squabbles and moods tend to erupt from time to time, and result in grievances that would not come to light in more detached relationships.

Venus in Cancer expect a tremendous amount of

emotional closeness from their friends - this often means ringing every day and keeping them informed about whatever is happening in your life. Sharing and caring makes the world go round for them, and they understand better than any other Venus sign the meaning of having a friend in need. Hot water bottles, chicken soup and a listening ear are all always available.

The home is sacred to Venus in Cancer, and they will never skimp on it. Their taste inclines towards cosiness and is largely influenced by their childhood homes. They love family photographs and collector's items. Financially, they can be hoarders but love to spend on the home, the clan and those they care about.

VENUS IN LEO

Venus in Leo women are ideal mates for men who like to put their partners on a pedestal. After all, this is the natural habitat of the female Venus in Leo. She wants to be given the full works by a man, desiring his total attention, and if he falls below standard he can expect trouble. The loving princess will turn into a pouting prima donna, refusing to perform for anything less than a standing ovation. If she is kept in style and handled with respect, she

will bestow the affectionate pampering of the lioness, and the company of a woman who turns heads everywhere.

Men with Venus in Leo are apt to display their magnificence with the pride of a peacock. They certainly believe in flaunting it if they've got it, and are crest-fallen if their champagne has made them look a Charlie. Flattery will get you everywhere with these men, and destinations are more likely to be the Ritz and Rio than Rotherham.

He loves to show a woman off to his friends, or even the people at the next table, so she will get nowhere if she is down at heel and heart. He wants to be proud of her. He will take her to all the best places, and no tacky back row smooching with him because they will be in the front seats. Once there, he might play footsie but he is probably only polishing his shoes on the back of her stockings.

Both male and female Venus in Leo attract people like bees to a honeypot. They usually revel in a large social circle and they want to be right at the centre of things. They entertain on a grand scale, and have the capacity to make their friends feel really special because they pull out all the stops and have a great sense

of occasion. The female Venus in Leo is the stunning hostess who emerges from the hairdressers just in time to don her new designer outfit while the caterers have been slaving over a hot stove. She is stage manager, not skivvy. Venus in Leo loves the drama of the theatre, and social events such as Royal Ascot and Glyndbourne, where to be seen is as important as to see.

Money is important to these Venus types - they have expensive lifestyles to keep up. They are generous to a fault, frequently going over the top because they would rather die than be accused of being mean. Quality is the trademark of all Venus in Leo possessions. They would rather not have something if they could not afford the best.

Venus in Leo loves dressing up, so a woman might have a fight on her hands for the bathroom mirror with her Venus in Leo man. Venus in Leo women adore putting on the glitz and looking a million dollars. They love the sparkle of jewellery and because they are consummate actors can put on quite a show even with the costume variety. Fake gems are only for fun though, darling; anyone who means business with this lady had better buy her the real thing.

VENUS IN VIRGO

Women with Venus in Virgo are quite unassuming, particularly about their own attractiveness. Although perhaps not the virginal innocents their symbol suggests, they are in a sense naïve about sexuality. Virgo is an earth sign and therefore is in touch with the physical body, but pleasure is not automatically on the same menu. For them, the body is to be honoured and looked after, and delight is to be found in the mind.

A woman with Venus in Virgo is looking for a man who lives up to her ideal of wit, repartee, mental sophistication and savoir faire. Her instinctual critical appraisal can also be her own worst enemy as she tots up all the reasons why the man is not quite right. Once she has spied a man who is a cut above the rest, however, her loyalty and willingness to make the relationship work usually ensure a long-lasting partnership.

Men with Venus in Virgo are not impressed by those that flaunt themselves or are ablaze with dynamism. For this reason, they are happy to let the Air signs steal their Fire, because they are searching for women who radiate intelligence, gentleness and common sense which are usually visible to the naked eye in the Air, Water and Earth signs They particularly admire women who have developed a skill or talent, and would much prefer to come home to a newly upholstered sofa than a set of manicured nails. Men with this placement can also be highly critical of their loved ones, pointing out the spinach stuck between their teeth even as midnight strikes on New Year's Eve.

Venus in Virgo is a people watcher, so favourite haunts are where they can analyse the situation and what makes people tick. They love to monitor the prices at auctions, and the form at race meetings. They are born to compare and contrast. On a first date with a male Venus in Virgo, a woman will be passed through his personal points system which is divided into sections for deportment, good conduct and effort. If she can stand this and is around to collect the seal of approval, the heat is off for a while, and she can be assured of convivial company and a supportive relationship.

Venus in Virgo types can be shy and private. They like to observe rather than bask in the social limelight. Others can count themselves lucky to be chosen as friends, because it means they are really valued. Friends will, however, be the recipients of endless Virgoan analysis which can be both helpful and hurtful. Venus in Virgo loves you warts and all (and do not imagine for one minute they have not noticed the warts).

Although Venus in Virgo will generously give friends time and attention, they are careful with their spending, being very fastidious with money. They value practicality above frivolity and are masters at finding that useful present. Their taste is for well-made clothes, tailored to fit. Their style is essentially clean cut, neat and tidy, and they will never buy something for its looks if it does not do the job efficiently.

VENUS IN LIBRA

Women with Venus in its own sign of romance are after a courtly type of love. They want polish, good manners and discretion rather than a hot-blooded Rambo. Love is fairly cerebral in the air signs, and the Libran version, particularly, can be more of a dalliance than a passion. Those with Venus in Libra drink but never get their lips wet. The women are concerned with appearances and, as long as others look good and act with some finesse, they are pleased to be in their company. They like to project an understated but attractive image that is 'socially acceptable'. They are charming, and know just what to say to win people over, but when all is said and done, they are cool-headed in the area of romance.

Men with Venus in Libra will not give you a second glance if they dislike what they see. This behaviour does not conform to the Libran model of justice, but all is fair in love for Venus in Libra. The more perfectly formed a woman is, in his opinion, the more appreciative he is. His vision of Aphrodite is beautiful and poised, so your version of the wild woman will not go down very well. He is charming and knows how to make a woman feel feminine. However, he is not seeking to explore the deep dark recesses of her mind because he feels safer on the surface. As long as things appear to be harmonious and they both look happy then, as far as he is concerned, this means that they *are* happy. He reads the lines, not what is between them.

The first date with a Venus in Libra man is devised for romance to blossom. He may arrive with flowers, take the woman for dinner by candlelight, and then round off the evening with the perfectly practised peck which leaves her interested but not overwhelmed. In fact, men with Venus in Libra are seldom pushy - they are far too refined for that. For them, romance has its own strategy that must be timed and implemented correctly.

Both men and women with Venus in Libra love to socialize. Beautiful people, well-presented food and pleasant conversation make a successful recipe for enjoying themselves. As friends, they will always remember birthdays, anniversaries and thoughtful thank yous. They do not, however, wish to know about your custody case or your irritable bowels - basically if you cannot say something nice, it is better to say nothing at all.

This placement handles money with dexterity, although an indulgence for beautiful things can sometimes cause a financial balancing act. Venus in Libra, unlike Venus in Virgo, is seduced into buying by appearance rather than functionality. That art nouveau clock graces the mantelpiece with style but has long since stopped ticking. People with Venus in Libra appreciate classical shapes and aim for harmony in an overall look rather than chancing an unusual choice of colour. They are always 'well turned out' and appropriately attired for an occasion.

VENUS IN SCORPIO
The image associated with the female Venus in Scorpio is a combination of siren and high priestess. But far from a vision in black, Venus in Scorpio is subtly seductive rather than blatantly salacious. However there is a chance that men looking for something casual will bite off more than they can chew here. She is a woman of passion with great insight into other's hearts, and is definitely not to be toyed with. Love is an all-or-nothing matter for Venus in Scorpio. The fated meetings, complications and intrigue that send Venus in Taurus a million miles in the opposite direction are proof to Venus in Scorpio that a relationship is 'meant to be'.

Men with Venus in Scorpio are attracted to women who exude intensity and passion; the more torrid the better. Venus in Scorpio likes to create an exotic ambience of secrecy and intimacy. After he has lulled a woman into imparting her inside story, and she has more or less bared her soul, he will then see if his magnetism can captivate her enough to expose anything else! Sex is very important to Venus in Scorpio as a vehicle for releasing passion that can get dammed up in the body. However intimately involved a relationship may seem, a Venus in Scorpio man usually reserves the right to withhold his feelings. He is afraid that if he discloses himself he will relinquish the upper hand - power is a big issue with this sign.

People with Venus in Scorpio can be very demanding of their friends. They want absolute loyalty and will drop you at the mildest hint of a defection. However, as friends, Venus in Scorpio receive you into their private inner world to share their psychological insights. They are not interested in those who bubble away on the surface, because they want to experience both the light and the dark in life. They can spot pretence and sham instantly, and will never flinch from you at your worst because they always admire the truth, no matter how painful. In keeping with the Scorpio proclivity for extremes, they either love you as a friend and will do anything for you, or they ignore you completely because you do not exist for them.

Venus in Scorpios have a distinctly dramatic style. They seldom go for anything that is middle of the road, and when not exhibiting their black and whiteness, are drawn to rich colours that create a sense of depth. With money, these Venus signs can be dark horses. They dislike being upfront and flashy, but are fascinated by the power of money. They can treat it as a means of control over others and tend to alternate between stinginess and generosity.

VENUS IN SAGITTARIUS

The female Venus in Sagittarius is a hard one to pin down. She is a gadabout, bright and breezy and not too keen on coming down to earth. She likes a relationship that broadens her horizons, and men who can take her beyond her normal realm of experience. Venus in Sagittarius is often attracted to over-the-top men, the larger-than-life variety who can keep the level of excitement alive with their reach-for-the-stars attitude. Unfortunately, this same type of man is the one who is so busy racing ahead that he often trips over his shoelaces and then the lady archer can take a tumble too. She is not the sort to stick things out for long. Love is a vehicle for her to 'get on with her life', and if she gets stuck she will wrestle to be free again.

Men with Venus in Sagittarius are usually big-hearted and generous-spirited. These men are attracted to active women, the doers of life who challenge themselves to experience everything to the full. For both sexes with Venus in Sagittarius, having fun is a main priority in relationships. They want a playmate, not someone who will make heavy emotional demands which weigh them down. Sagittarius is a journeyer and often Venus here will attract a person from another country or culture or an inveterate traveller. These Venus types cannot be contained within a given space; they need room to roam.

Because this placement signifies a great love of the outdoors, people may literally be asked 'out'. They would be well advised to take on board the motto of the boy scout and 'be prepared...' for anything. The male Venus in Sagittarius is the Indiana Jones of the zodiac, and a spontaneous adventure is what he has in mind so do not worry if your clothes aren't ironed (this presents quite a problem for Miss Virgo). He is not one to settle easily - however many times he is led to water he may not want to drink. When he does, of course, it will be champagne all the way.

As friends, people with Venus in Sagittarius are often like big brothers or sisters - constantly amazing others with their latest daring feats. They are terrible at remembering things like birthdays and do not want to be tied to being constantly in touch. They drop into other's lives like Alka Seltzer adding a healthy fizz to the proceedings, but such enthusiasm can be too much for the earth and water signs in particular, who find a little goes a long way.

Venus in Sagittarius types are big spenders. They are gamblers, loving the risk that comes with the promise of more. They play with money, enjoying a spending spree at Harrods or a flutter on the horses. Their personal tastes also reflect their largesse - they are always trading up for something bigger and better. The home itself is not especially important to those with Venus in Sagittarius. As long as it is large enough and comfortable enough, they use it purely as a base from which to explore the world.

VENUS IN CAPRICORN

Women with Venus in Capricorn need long-term security in their relationships. They are on the look out for men who can help them to feel deeply rooted and provide some kind of order and continuity for them. These women are very status conscious and view the world as being divided on many levels into a hierarchy. It is important for them to know where they fit in the structure, where their place is, which is why they like ambitious men who know where they are going. Venus in Capricorn is very contained, controlled and somewhat cool. These women can seem rather aloof and untouchable, they tend to repress rather than express their feelings. Believing that permanent relationships require hard work, they are often prepared to put a lot in on a practical level, and will never shirk responsibility. However, their serious attitude to love can be a dampener for the more volatile fire and air types.

Men with Venus in Capricorn are aware of the value of commitment. They see it as an anchor that helps them to stabilize their lives. What is the point of sowing fields of wild oats when all you want is a verdant corner to call your own? These men like to know where they stand, what the prospects are and whether potential partners are prepared to climb the same mountain. They are attracted to the 'working woman' who pulls her weight, whether she is running a million pound corporation or the household budget. These men believe people have to pay their dues in life and be useful.

Ever the pragmatist, Venus in Capricorn man will tread cautiously in the initial stages of a relationship. He sets great store by doing things properly, so he is not the type to seduce someone at an office party. He is formal, even a little stiff socially, and it takes a lot to loosen him up. He is quite prepared to take a woman out and discuss nothing more personal than how to divide the bill. His defence barrier will spring up if he is tackled on the issue of feelings before he is ready, and anyone he feels to be dangerous will be relegated to the scrap heap. Once he feels safe, however, he will try and clinch the deal and prove that he surpasses anything else on offer.

Socially, both men and women with Venus in Capricorn are often accused of climbing. This is not always the case, of course, but these placements do have an inbuilt set of rules and regulations that they live by, and they cannot admit people who do not conform to their acceptable guidelines. Not gregarious by nature, Venus in Capricorn holds on to a few trusted friends, but you may never know what they are really feeling. It is as if part of themselves is locked away, an area to which even they do not have instant access.

Capricorns can be mean with money because they deplore waste. They accumulate stocks because they are not given to extravagant impulses. They like to spend 'sensibly' on things that last and their taste is conventional, rather 'proper' but also conspicuously inclines towards the very best quality. They like to keep up appearances.

VENUS IN AQUARIUS

Women with Venus in Aquarius can be quite detached in relationships. They mentally peruse the whole issue of love, and conclude that it is just another word for friendship, mutual companionship and shared interests - these are concepts they understand and hold close to their heart. They are not about to abandon themselves to the image of 'the wife', or even 'the mistress', because they believe in creating themselves individually. In love, they require plenty of freedom and space to allow this flourishing of their individuality, and they do not give a damn what the neighbours think.

Men with Venus in Aquarius are looking for a relationship that will not cramp their style. If someone trys to bind them in chains, they strain to get free, obstinately defending their right to choose whatever they want to do, whoever they want to see, and fuelling the worst imaginings of a partner. In fact, Venus in Aquarius is not on the rampage for 1000 Arabian Nights, he just likes the company of other people, is genuinely interested in his friends and cannot bear any

relationship which makes his life predictable.

In keeping with the sudden nature of this sign, love strikes out of the blue in the most unexpected places. One minute there is no partner on the horizon, the next, Venus in Aquarius has catapulted into their life. And the excitement does not stop there. Often the relationship has a kind of stop/go, switch on/switch off quality which can be disconcerting for those who need continuity. People with Venus in Aquarius love to experiment, but if the relationship threatens to break out of the confines of the mental laboratory they are apt to distance themselves by behaving erratically, giving themselves (and their partners) time to cool off.

The Venus in Aquarius man will take a woman out somewhere completely different - he is thrilled by the new and unusual. Women who attract him are those who demonstrate independence and stand out from the crowd. He likes to start off as friends and take it from there - exactly where, only he knows, and often only split seconds before it happens.

Those with Venus in the sign of friendship act as magnets for different types of people, and they thrive on team spirit. Strangely,

although they may collect a myriad of friends, they can also be quite anti-social. They like to do things in their own way, and balk at being socially acceptable. Their honesty cuts through expectations and conventions, enabling him to achieve friendships that are uniquely their own.

In a sense, Venus in Aquarius types do not care about money which is purely a means to an end, buying them their freedom - the one thing they value most in the world. Their taste can be a touch eccentric - sometimes outrageous, but never bland. They have their own definite ideas about style and no one can tell him otherwise!

VENUS IN PISCES

Female fish are looking for the dream lover, and, being so wrapped up in their fantasies often avoid the reality of the person. They see the prince, the romantic charmer, not the ordinary man cutting his toe-nails and worrying about his bank balance. In love, the woman with Venus in Pisces wants above all, to give herself and her feelings. However, when it comes to commitment she may panic because, once the knot is tied, it cuts off the possibilities and 'what ifs?' that she loves to dream about. In her imagination both her partner and

relationship can be perfect. In comparison, the everyday nitty-gritty aspects of living with another person can be a disappointment.

The man with Venus in Pisces is attracted to women who are archetypically 'feminine', particularly those who need his help and support. Many times, he may try to rescue a mermaid from the sea only to find that she cannot exist on dry land. He is prone to falling in love with the unobtainable woman who keeps slipping through his fingers, returning to another man, or simply cannot make up her mind. Like his female counterpart, a man with

Venus in Pisces is often happier with the fantasy of a relationship than the reality. Both sexes can be selflessly devoted in love - giving so much and asking little in return. For them, receiving can sully the spiritual ideal of love. Attraction to those who are especially needy or unable to give in return is par for the course.

The man with Venus in Pisces is never obvious in his approach. He is not one to stride up and ask a woman what she is doing for the rest of her life. Although he plays things by ear, he often fails to hear what is said, for example, the fact that a woman has mentioned her

existing boyfriend. Venus in Pisces man may be equally economical with the truth about his own situation. He hangs loose even with four children, alimony payments and a heart lost to his childhood sweetheart years ago. He will not deliberately mislead his partner, he just likes to live in a world where all things are possible, including her. And, for him, it is possible to love someone even if it is entirely impractical.

Venus in Pisces types care about people in a way that reaches beyond their own personal experience. They feel compassion for, and acceptance of, humanity that transcends the boundaries that divide life into right and wrong, good and bad. Venus in Pisces gives out a healing energy that respects the soul. As friends, these people are unerringly thoughtful, kind and understanding. They are much in demand and, because they go to great lengths to help others, are sometimes left drained and over-stretched. It is hard for Venus in Pisces to say no.

Their financial situation can get into a muddle because they have lost their grip and let things drift. However, very few Pisceans worship the god of Mammon. Their style is refined, beautiful and often glamorous, creating a kind of magical image.

YEAR	ARIES	TAURUS	GEMINI	CANCER	LEO	VIRGO	LIBRA	SCORPIO	SAGITTAR	CAPRIC	AQUARIUS	PISCES
1922	13/3-6/4	7/4-30/4	1/5-25/5	26/5-19/6	20/6-14/7	15/7-9/8	10/8-6/9	7/9-10/10	11/10-28/11	1/1-24/1	25/1-16/2	17/2-12/3
1923	27/4-21/5	22/5-14/6	15/6-9/7	10/7-3/8	4/8-27/8	28/8-20/9	21/9-14/10	29/11-31/12 1/1 15/10-7/11	2/1-6/2 8/11-1/12	7/2-5/3 2/12-25/12	6/3-31/3 26/12-31/12	1/4-26/4
1924	13/2-8/3	9/3-4/4	5/4-5/5	6/5-8/9	9/9-7/10	8/10-2/11	3/11-26/11	27/11-21/12	22/12-31/12	15/1-7/2	1/1-19/1	20/1-12/2
1925	28/3-20/4	21/4-15/5	16/5-8/6	9/6-3/7	4/7-27/7	28/7-21/8	22/8-15/9	16/9-11/10	1/1-14/1 12/10-6/11	7/11-5/12	8/2-3/3 6/12-31/12	4/3-27/3
1926	7/5-2/6	3/6-28/6	29/6-23/7	24/7-17/8	18/8-11/9	12/9-5/10	6/10-29/10	30/10-22/11	23/11-16/12	17/12-31/12	1/1-5/4	6/4-6/5
1927	27/2-22/3	23/3-16/4	17/4-11/5	12/5-5/6	8/6-7/7	8/7-9/11	10/11-8/12	9/12-31/12	1/1-7/1	8/1	9/1-1/2	2/2-26/2
1928	12/4-5/5	6/5-29/5	30/5-23/6	24/6-17/7	18/7-11/8	12/8-4/9	5/9-28/9	1/1-3/1 29/9-23/10	4/1-28/1 24/10-16/11	29/1-22/2	23/2-17/3 12/12-31/12	18/3-11/4
1929	3/2-7/3 20/4-2/6	8/3-19/4 3/6-7/7	8/7-4/8	5/8-30/8	31/8-25/9	26/9-19/10	20/10-12/11	13/11-6/12	7/12-30/12	17/11-11/12 31/12	1/1-5/1	6/1-2/2
1930	13/3-4/5	6/4-30/4	1/5-24/5	25/5-18/6	19/6-14/7	15/7-9/8	10/8-6/9	7/9-11/10 22/11-31/12	12/10-21/11	1/1-23/1	24/1-16/12	17/2-12/3
1931	26/4-20/5	21/5-13/6	14/6-8/7	9/7-2/8	3/8-26/8	27/8-19/9	20/9-13/10	1/1-3/1 14/10-6/11	4/1-6/2 7/11-30/11	7/2-4/3 1/12-24/12	5/3-31/3 25/12-31/12	1/4-25/4
1932	12/2-8/3	9/3-3/4	4/4-5/5 13/7-27/7	6/5-12/7 28/7-8/9	9/9-6/10	7/10-1/11	2/11-25/11	26/11-20/12	21/12-31/12		1/1-18/1	19/1-11/2
1933	27/3-19/4	20/4-28/5	29/5-8/6	9/6-2/7	3/7-26/7	27/7-20/8	21/8-14/9	15/9-10/10	1/1-13/1 11/10-5/11	14/1-6/2 6/11-4/12	7/2-2/3 5/12-31/12	3/3-26/3
1934	6/5-1/6	2/6-27/6	28/6-22/7	23/7-16/8	17/8-10/9	11/9-4/10	5/10-28/10	29/10-21/11	22/11-15/12	16/12-31/12	1/1-5/4	6/4-5/5
1935	26/2-21/3	22/3-15/4	16/4-10/5	11/5-6/6	7/6-6/7	7/7-8/11	9/11-7/12	8/12-31/12	1/1-7/1	1/1-7/1	8/1-31/1	1/2-25/2
1936	11/4-4/5	5/5-28/5	29/5-22/6	23/6-16/7	17/7-10/8	11/8-4/9	5/9-27/9	1/1-2/1 28/9-22/10	3/1-27/1 23/10-15/11	28/1-21/2	22/2-16/3 11/12-31/12	17/3-10/4
1937	2/2-8/3 14/4-3/6	9/3-13/4 4/6-6/7	7/7-3/8	4/8-29/8	30/8-24/9	25/9-18/10	19/10-11/11	12/11-5/12	6/12-29/12	16/11-10/12 30/12-31/12	1/1-5/1	6/1-1/2
1938	12/3-4/4	5/4-28/4	29/4-23/5	24/5-18/6	19/6-13/7	14/7-8/8	9/8-6/9	7/9-13/10 15/11-31/12	14/10-14/11	1/1-22/1	23/1-15/2	16/2-11/3
1939	25/4-19/5	20/5-13/6	14/6-8/7	9/7-1/8	2/8-25/8	26/8-19/9	20/9-13/10	1/1-3/1 14/10-6/11	4/1-5/2 7/11-30/11	6/2-4/3 1/12-24/12	5/3-30/3 25/12-31/12	31/3-24/4
1940	12/2-7/3	8/3-3/4	4/4-5/5 5/7-31/7	6/5-4/7 1/8-8/9	9/9-5/10	6/10-31/10	1/11-25/11	26/11-19/12	20/12-31/12		1/1-18/1	19/1-11/2

YEAR	ARIES	TAURUS	GEMINI	CANCER	LEO	VIRGO	LIBRA	SCORPIO	SAGITTAR	CAPRIC	AQUARIUS	PISCES
1941	27/3-19/4	20/4-13/5	14/5-6/6	7/6-1/7	2/7-26/7	27/7-20/8	21/8-14/9	15/9-9/10	1/1-12/1	13/1-5/2	6/2-1/3	2/3-26/3
									10/10-5/11	6/11-4/12	5/12-31/12	
1942	6/5-1/6	2/6-26/6	27/6-22/7	23/7-16/8	17/8-9/9	10/9-3/10	4/10-27/10	28/10-20/11	21/11-14/12	15/12-31/12	1/1-4/4	6/4-5/5
1943	25/2-20/3	21/3-14/4	15/4-10/5	11/5-6/6	7/6-6/7	7/7-8/11	9/11-7/12	8/12-31/12		1/1-7/1	8/1-31/1	1/2-24/2
1944	10/4-3/5	4/5-28/5	29/5-21/6	22/6-16/7	17/7-9/8	10/8-2/9	3/9-27/9	1/1-2/1	3/1-27/1	28/1-20/2	21/2-16/3	17/3-9/4
								28/9-21/10	22/10-15/11	16/11-10/12	11/12-31/12	
1945	2/2-10/3	11/3-6/4	7/7-3/8	4/8-29/8	30/8-23/9	24/9-18/10	19/10-11/11	12/11-5/12	6/12-29/12	30/12-31/12	1/1-4/1	5/1-1/2
	7/4-3/6	4/6-6/7										
1946	11/3-4/4	5/4-28/4	29/4-23/5	24/5-17/6	18/6-12/7	13/7-8/8	9/8-6/9	7/9-15/10	16/10-7/11	1/1-21/1	22/1-14/2	15/2-10/3
								8/11-31/12				
1947	25/4-19/5	20/5-12/6	13/6-7/7	8/7-1/8	2/8-25/8	26/8-18/9	19/9-12/10	1/1-4/1	5/1-5/2	6/2-4/3	5/3-29/3	30/3-24/4
								13/10-5/11	6/11-29/11	30/11-23/12	24/12-31/12	
1948	11/2-7/3	8/3-3/4	4/4-6/5	7/5-28/6	8/9-5/10	6/10-31/10	1/11-25/11	26/11-19/12	20/12-31/12		1/1-17/1	18/1-10/2
			29/6-2/8	3/8-7/9								
1949	26/3-19/4	20/4-13/5	14/5-6/6	7/6-30/6	1/7-25/7	26/7-19/8	20/8-14/9	15/9-9/10	1/1-12/1	13/1-5/2	6/2-1/3	2/3-25/3
									10/10-5/11	6/11-5/12	6/12-31/12	
1950	5/5-31/5	1/6-26/6	27/6-21/7	22/7-15/8	16/8-9/9	10/9-3/10	4/10-27/10	28/10-20/11	21/11-13/12	14/12-31/12	1/1-5/4	6/4-4/5
1951	25/2-21/3	22/3-15/4	16/4-10/5	11/5-6/6	7/6-7/7	8/7-9/11	10/11-7/12	8/12-31/12		1/1-7/1	8/1-31/1	1/2-24/2
1952	10/4-4/5	5/5-28/5	29/5-21/6	22/6-16/7	17/7-9/8	10/8-3/9	4/9-27/9	1/1-2/1	3/1-27/1	28/1-20/2	21/2-16/3	17/3-9/4
								28/9-21/10	22/10-15/11	16/11-10/12	11/12-31/12	
1953	2/2-13/3	14/3-31/3	8/7-3/8	4/8-29/8	30/8-24/9	25/9-18/10	19/10-11/11	12/11-5/12	6/12-29/12	30/12-31/12	1/1-5/1	6/1-1/2
	1/4-5/6	6/6-7/7										
1954	12/3-4/4	5/4-28/4	29/4-23/5	24/5-17/6	18/6-13/7	14/7-8/8	9/8-6/9	7/9-22/10	23/10-27/10	1/1-22/1	23/1-15/2	16/2-11/3
								28/10-31/12				
1955	25/4-19/5	20/5-13/6	14/6-7/7	8/7-1/8	2/8-25/8	26/8-18/9	19/9-13/10	1/1-6/1	7/1-5/2	6/2-4/3	5/3-30/3	31/3-24/4
								14/10-5/11	6/11-3011	1/12-24/12	25/12-31/12	
1956	12/2-7/3	8/3-4/4	5/4-7/5	8/5-23/6	9/9-5/10	6/10-31/10	1/11-25/11	26/11-19/12	20/12-31/12		1/1-17/1	18/1-11/2
			24/6-4/8	5/8-8/9								
1957	26/3-19/4	20/4-13/5	14/5-6/6	7/6-1/7	2/7-26/7	27/7-19/8	20/8-14/9	15/9-9/10	1/1-12/1	13/1-5/2	6/2-1/3	2/3-25/3
									10/10-5/11	6/11-6/12	7/12-31/12	
1958	6/5-31/5	1/6-26/6	27/6-22/7	23/7-15/8	16/8-9/9	10/9-3/10	4/10-27/10	28/10-20/11	21/11-14/12	15/12-31/12	1/1-6/4	7/4-5/5
1959	25/2-20/3	21/3-14/4	15/4-10/5	11/5-6/6	7/6-8/7	9/7-20/9	10/11-7/12	8/12-31/12		1/1-7/1	8/1-31/1	1/2-24/2
					21/9-24/9	25/9-9/11						

YEAR	ARIES	TAURUS	GEMINI	CANCER	LEO	VIRGO	LIBRA	SCORPIO	SAGITTAR	CAPRIC	AQUARIUS	PISCES
1960	10/4-3/5	4/5-28/5	29/5-21/6	22/6-15/7	16/7-9/8	10/8-2/9	3/9-26/9	1/1-2/1; 27/9-21/10	3/1-27/1; 22/10-15/11	28/1-20/2; 16/11-10/12	21/2-15/3; 11/12-31/12	16/3-9/4
1961	3/2-5/6	6/6-7/7	8/7-3/8	4/8-29/8	30/8-23/9	24/9-17/10	18/10-11/11	12/11-4/12	5/12-28/12	29/12-31/12	1/1-5/1	6/1-2/2
1962	11/3-3/4	4/4-28/4	29/4-22/5	23/5-17/6	18/6-12/7	13/7-8/8	9/8-6/9	7/9-31/12		1/1-21/1	22/1-14/2	15/2-10/3
1963	24/4-18/5	19/5-12/6	13/6-7/7	8/7-31/7	1/8-25/8	26/8-18/9	19/9-12/10	1/1-6/1; 13/10-5/11	7/1-5/2; 6/11-29/11	6/2-4/3; 30/11-23/12	5/3-29/3; 24/12-31/12	30/3-23/4
1964	11/2-7/3	8/3-4/4	5/4-9/5; 18/6-5/8	10/5-17/6; 6/8-8/9	9/9-5/10	6/10-31/10	1/11-24/11	25/11-19/12	20/12-31/12		1/1-16/1	17/1-10/2
1965	26/3-18/4	19/4-12/5	13/5-6/6	7/6-30/6	1/7-25/7	26/7-19/8	20/8-13/9	14/9-9/10	1/1-12/1; 10/10-5/11	13/1-5/2; 6/11-7/12	6/2-1/3; 8/12-31/12	2/3-25/3
1966	6/5-31/5	1/6-26/6	27/6-21/7	22/7-15/8	16/8-8/9	9/9-2/10	3/10-26/10	27/10-19/11	20/11-13/12	7/2-25/2; 14/12-31/12	1/1-6/2; 26/2-6/4	7/4-5/5
1967	24/2-20/3	21/3-14/4	15/4-10/5	11/5-6/6	7/6-8/7; 10/9-1/10	9/7-9/9; 2/10-9/11	10/11-7/12	28/12-31/12		1/1-6/1	7/1-30/1	31/1-23/2
1968	9/4-3/5	4/5-27/5	28/5-20/6	21/6-15/7	16/7-8/8	9/8-2/9	3/9-26/9	1/1; 27/9-21/10	2/1-26/1; 22/10-14/11	27/1-20/2; 15/11-9/12	21/2-15/3; 10/12-31/12	16/3-8/4
1969	3/2-6/6	7/6-6/7	7/7-3/8	4/8-28/8	29/8-22/9	23/9-17/10	18/10-10/11	11/11-4/12	5/12-28/12	29/12-31/12	1/1-4/1	5/1-2/2
1970	11/3-3/4	4/4-27/4	28/4-22/5	23/5-16/6	17/6-12/7	13/7-8/8	9/8-7/9	8/9-31/12		1/1-21/1	22/1-14/2	15/2-10/3
1971	24/4-17/5	18/5-12/6	13/6-6/7	7/7-31/7	1/8-24/8	25/8-17/9	18/9-17/10	1/1-7/1; 18/10-5/11	8/1-5/2; 6/11-29/11	6/2-4/3; 30/11-23/12	5/3-29/3; 24/12-31/12	30/3-23/4
1972	11/2-7/3	8/3-3/4	4/4-10/5; 12/6-6/8	11/5-11/6; 7/8-7/9	8/9-4/10	5/10-30/10	31/10-24/11	25/11-18/12	19/12-31/12		1/1-16/1	17/1-10/2
1973	25/3-18/4	19/4-12/5	13/5-5/6	6/6-30/6	1/7-25/7	26/7-19/8	20/8-13/9	14/9-9/10	1/1-11/1; 10/10-5/11	12/1-4/2; 6/11-7/12	5/2-28/2; 8/12-31/12	1/3-24/3
1974	5/5-31/5	1/6-25/6	26/6-21/7	22/7-14/8	15/8-8/9	9/9-2/10	3/10-26/10	27/10-19/11	20/11-13/12	30/1-28/2; 14/12-31/12	1/1-29/1; 1/3-6/4	7/4-4/5
1975	24/2-19/3	20/3-13/4	14/4-9/5	10/5-6/6	7/6-9/7; 3/9-4/10	10/7-2/9; 5/10-9/11	10/11-7/12	8/12-31/12		1/1-6/1	7/1-30/1	31/1-23/2
1976	9/4-2/5	3/5-27/5	28/5-20/6	21/6-14/7	15/7-8/8	9/8-1/9	2/9-26/9	1/1; 27/9-20/10	2/1-26/1; 21/10-14/11	27/1-19/2; 15/11-9/12	20/2-15/3; 10/12-31/12	16/3-8/4
1977	3/2-6/6	7/6-6/7	7/7-2/8	3/8-28/8	29/8-22/9	23/9-17/10	18/10-10/11	11/11-4/12	5/12-27/12	28/12-31/12	1/1-4/1	5/1-2/2
1978	10/3-2/4	3/4-27/4	28/4-22/5	23/5-16/6	17/6-12/7	13/7-8/8	9/8-7/9	8/9-31/12		1/1-20/1	21/1-13/2	14/2-9/3
1979	24/4-18/5	19/5-11/6	12/6-6/7	7/7-30/7	31/7-24/8	25/8-17/9	18/9-11/10	1/1-1/7	8/1-5/2	6/2-3/3	4/3-29/3	30/3-23/4

YEAR	ARIES	TAURUS	GEMINI	CANCER	LEO	VIRGO	LIBRA	SCORPIO	SAGITTAR	CAPRIC	AQUARIUS	PISCES
1979								12/10-4/11	5/11-28/11	29/11-22/12	23/12-31/12	
1980	10/2-6/3	7/3-3/4	4/4-12/5; 6/6-6/8	13/5-5/6; 7/8-7/9	8/9-4/10	5/10-30/10	31/10-24/11	25/11-18/12	19/12-31/12		1/1-16/1	17/1-9/2
1981	25/3-17/4	18/4-12/5	13/5-5/6	6/6-29/6	30/6-24/7	25/7-18/8	19/8-12/9	13/9-8/10	1/1-11/1; 9/10-5/11	12/1-4/2; 6/11-8/12	5/2-28/2; 9/12-31/12	1/3-24/3
1982	5/5-30/5	31/5-25/6	26/6-20/7	21/7-14/8	15/8-7/9	8/9-2/10	3/10-26/10	27/10-18/11	19/11-12/12	24/1-2/3; 13/12-31/12	1/1-23/1	7/4-4/5
1983	23/2-19/3	20/3-13/4	14/4-9/5	10/5-6/6	7/6-10/7; 28/8-5/10	11/7-27/8; 6/10-9/11	10/11-6/12	7/12-31/12		1/1-5/1	3/3-6/4	30/1-22/2
1984	8/4-2/5	3/5-26/5	27/5-20/6	21/6-14/7	15/7-7/8	8/8-1/9	2/9-25/9	1/1; 26/9-20/10	2/1-25/1; 21/10-13/11	26/1-19/2; 14/11-9/12	6/1-29/1	15/3-7/4
1985	3/2-6/6	7/6-6/7	7/7-2/8	3/8-28/8	29/8-22/9	23/9-16/10	17/10-9/11	10/11-3/12	4/12-27/12	28/12-31/12	20/2-14/3; 10/12-31/12	5/1-2/2
1986	10/3-2/4	3/4-26/4	27/4-21/5	22/5-15/6	16/6-11/7	12/7-7/8	8/8-7/9	8/9-31/12	1/1-20/1	1/1-20/1	1/1-4/1	14/2-9/3
1987	23/4-27/5	18/5-11/6	12/6-5/7	6/7-30/7	31/7-23/8	24/8-16/9	17/9-10/10	1/1-7/1; 11/10-3/11	8/1-5/2; 4/11-28/11	6/2-3/3	21/1-13/2; 4/3-28/3	29/3-22/4
1988	10/2-6/3	7/3-3/4	4/4-17/5; 28/5-6/8	18/5-27/5; 7/8-7/9	8/9-4/10	5/10-29/10	30/10-23/11	24/11-17/12	18/12-31/12	29/11-22/12	23/12-31/12	16/1-9/2
1989	24/3-16/4	17/4-11/5	12/5-4/6	5/6-29/6	30/6-24/7	25/7-8/8	9/8-12/9	13/9-8/10	1/1-10/1; 9/10-5/11	11/1-3/2; 6/11-10/12	1/1-15/1	28/2-23/3
1990	5/5-30/5	31/5-25/6	26/6-20/7	21/7-13/8	14/8-7/9	8/9-1/10	2/10-25/10	26/10-18/11	19/11-12/12	17/1-3/3; 13/12-31/12	4/2-27/2; 11/12-31/12	7/4-4/5
1991	23/2-18/3	19/3-13/4	14/4-9/5	10/5-6/6	7/6-11/7; 22/8-6/10	12/7-21/8; 7/10-9/11	10/11-6/12	7/12-31/12		1/1-5/1	1/1-16/1; 4/3-6/4	30/1-22/2
1992	8/4-1/5	2/5-26/5	27/5-19/6	20/6-13/7	14/7-7/8	8/8-31/8	1/9-25/9	26/9-19/10	1/1-25/1; 20/10-13/11	26/1-18/2; 14/11-8/12	6/1-29/1; 19/2-13/3; 9/12-31/12	14/3-7/4

CHAPTER SIX

Mars:
Your way of working

How do you get what you want? What type of work appeals to you? How assertive are you?

People could not achieve anything in life without using the energy of the planet Mars. They simply would not get out of bed in the morning, get dressed, go anywhere or choose to do anything. Mars is invoked the minute a person decides to do something, and is the carrier of the energy that brings actions to fruition. It gives people the will to accomplish and achieve what they want, and is linked to the principle of desire. Mars demands that we assert our will, and therefore brings into play our competitive instincts and aggressive energies. If we want something we must move forward to get it. If we are blocked from taking action, we can become angry or depressed because our natural healthy urge to move has been suppressed.

The sign that Mars occupies at birth will show the way in which people express their drives. It shows what motivates them, how they do things and make them happen. Mars demonstrates how we run our lives, the ways in which we manage or organize ourselves. According to the element Mars is in at birth, some may find it easy to apply themselves to practical matters (Mars in the earth signs), while others may be impatient to achieve their desires (Mars in the fire signs). Mars in the water signs acts in a way that 'feels right', and in the air signs Mars wants to put ideas into operation.

Some signs find it easier to express their assertive energy than others. The level of vitality, vigour and vibrancy in individuals alters according to how effectively they can express themselves and 'be who they are'. If their inner selves cannot connect with the activities or work that they engage in, then the denial of self can lead to health problems. Mars is a tool at the disposal of each individual and the sign it is in will reflect the nature of this tool. It is then up to the worker to use it skilfully in life.

The Mars sign can be seen in the kind of work we do, and the way in which we go about it. For example, although not all Mars in Gemini types are salesmen, some kind of outlet will be needed in their lives to express their desire to move around and communicate with people. Mars in Aries has a fiery, impulsive quality and if there is not enough scope in their activities to let off steam, individuals with this sign may get very angry. Yet with the right amount of challenge in their lives they can forge ahead and use their forthright Mars to get things done quickly.

The kind of Mars people have is in motion every time they take an action. Do they plan shopping lists with precision like Mars in Virgo, putting all the goods in neat piles in the trolley, ready for packing? Or do they succumb to impulse buys like Mars in Sagittarius, racing round at the last minute, throwing everything in and ending up with double quantities? How do they behave in queues? Those with Mars in Taurus wait patiently for their turn, whilst Mars in Pisces may let others go first - probably people with Mars in Aries who have pushed their way to the front!

MARS IN ARIES

Mars in Aries types are fired with the idea of being heroes and heroines. They thrill to challenge, and need to overthrow obstacles because winning is important. They like to be first, and get very impatient if they are held back from doing things quickly. When they want something, they want it yesterday.

People with Mars in Aries are good at motivating others. They have high energy levels and exude a go-getting quality that stirs up action and gets things done. They will not sit quietly or take no for an answer and are prepared to do battle with anyone who stands in their way. At work, Mars in Aries types are primarily initiators. They have quick bursts of enthusiasm, but get bored with detail and routine. They make good leaders and pioneers. It is best if they allow others to follow through what they have started.

They believe in doing things their way, and dislike being in subordinate positions so they are ideal candidates for running their own businesses. Their courage and daring sometimes pushes them to rush in where angels fear to tread, but they are capable of taking the rough with the smooth. They approach what they want very directly and decisively, and need fast results or they lose interest in what they are doing. They will not want to wait around for the market to pick up, but will try something else, find a quicker route or take a short cut.

MARS IN TAURUS

These types are happy to stay with jobs that are comfortable, in preference to ones that challenge them. They are the sort of people who will not let you down and can be relied upon to sort things out, but they usually need someone else to supply the ideas or motivation. They are the completers of the zodiac, and understand the meaning of 'getting stuck in' to something. They will immerse themselves and wade through tasks, lumbering on in bull-like way. It is not easy to stop them once they have decided to do something.

People with Mars in Taurus are a combination of placidity and strong will. They are determined to get what they want and go about it slowly, in a measured way. They do not chop and change in careers because their tendency is to get entrenched where they are. These Mars types manage to hold on to their goals, clients and job. They have great staying power and will still be there when others have fallen by the wayside.

They prefer to put their energies into something that is already established and solid, because they are not generally risk-takers. What they may lack in imagination, they make up for in practicality and stability. Mars in Taurus is often motivated by money rather than anything else, and work must be lucrative and reasonably secure. There can also be a rather lazy, indolent way of going about their business. Let the other Mars signs rush about and burn themselves out, Taurus conserves energy, keeping something in store for a rainy day.

MARS IN GEMINI

Mars in Gemini will often talk about something rather than do it. In fact there is rarely enough time to do all the things that come up on the Gemini agenda, and Mars in Gemini compromises by doing, discussing and thinking about different activities simultaneously. It can be unnerving to be in the middle of a passionate moment with someone with Mars in Gemini who suddenly expresses a desire to move house.

It is important for those with Mars in Gemini to channel energy into communicating. These types need to work with ideas, and distribute information. They feel trapped if they cannot move around in what they do, either physically or metaphorically.

Mars in Gemini are salespeople at heart and, although not always the travelling variety, like to see their ideas go forward.

There is a skittish quality to Mars in Gemini. It can be hard for them to focus and concentrate because they feel they might be missing out elsewhere. Work that entails plenty of variety suits them. Although they will not apply themselves to one task with intensity, they have the facility to keep a running score of their proceedings in their head. It can come as a surprise to others who have seen Mars in Gemini appearing to wander to find that they have actually not missed a trick. Mars in Gemini are skilful in getting what they want. They are light in their approach and move very quickly, more than able to outwit the opposition.

MARS IN CANCER

When Mars is in Cancer, the person wants to be emotionally involved in what he or she is doing. Work that is connected with looking after people is highly satisfying for Mars in Cancer.

Although not all with this sign choose the caring or catering professions, they usually find some means of taking people under their wing. Wherever those with Mars in Cancer find their niche in life, they will attach great importance to establishing strong bonds with colleagues and clients, reminiscent of a family set up. Whatever it is they chose to do, they do it with feeling.

When people with Mars in Cancer decide they want something, they become very attached to it in mind, body and soul. It is hard for them to be objective about their desires because they are completely wrapped up in attaining them. If they are blocked in any way from reaching goals, they take it as a personal affront. Even if, for example, the bus is too full to take them or the grocery shop has run out of bread, Mars in Cancer feels very hard done by and upset. Their whole world can cave in if they are passed over for promotion.

If Mars in Cancer can harness their emotions, they can be very effective. When they ask for something they can make an appeal that tugs at the heartstrings. When they put their hearts into things they can touch people in a way that elicits the desired response. This is an excellent position to be in for professions that involve contact with the public.

MARS IN LEO

The Leonine Mars is a strong beast with powerful energy and vitality. People of this type take pride in everything they do and want above all to be recognized and appreciated for their efforts. If applause is not forthcoming, they can feel crushed. The urge to be magnificent, to put on a show that stuns the world, is characteristic of Mars in Leo who love to perform. They will pull out all the stops to do something with style and flair, and can be rather grand.

Mars in Leo types are assertive and enthusiastic about what they want and, if they cannot get it, they roar ferociously. They make natural chiefs rather than indians, assuming their position as king pin, and highly aware of their own wants and desires. They work well when they can express themselves creatively. They are bursting with a zest to live out their own roles in life. Sometimes autocratic in their methods, they genuinely believe no one else can do things with as much flair as them.

Despite all the bluster, Mars in Leo is unfailingly generous and loves to see others basking in their reflected glory. Their spontaneity can be a catalyst to light fires and often energizes other people. They are aware of the playful child within themselves and can encourage others to lose their inhibitions and sing, rather than pay, for their supper.

MARS IN VIRGO

People with Mars in Virgo have very precise methods of going about their business. They can be nit-pickers, fussing over details, but are also efficient to the last. They do not put energy into waving their own flag. They hang back, but are like beavers, working away to make sure that they accomplish what they have set out to do.

When confronting difficulties in achieving their goals, those with Mars in Virgo tend to worry rather than assert themselves. They are mental analysts, and will endlessly review a situation rather than blast their way through it. If their desires are blocked, their unspent energy goes round and round in their digestive system making them prone to stomach ulcers. However, if they are able to pursue their ambitions and are free to 'do it properly', their results will testify to an astounding competence. Mars in Virgo types are essentially craftsmen. They are brilliant at executing the finishing touches that make all the difference.

Both sexes of Mars in Virgo are attracted to work that satisfies their minds, has a definite purpose and makes them feel useful. They gain pleasure from tasks that other signs would consider unglamourous, such as totting up figures or overhauling a system. They are naturals for jobs in the service industries. They love to wade through the mire, working out what is worthwhile and casting aside the rest. They really come into their own sorting out the mess that other people have made.

MARS IN LIBRA

People with Mars in Libra like to do things beautifully. They are packagers, presenters - often the middle men, ensuring things flow smoothly between supplier and customer.

Mars in Libra types are public relations people, and want to be seen to be doing the right thing. They have a tremendous need to be liked and therefore find it difficult to assert themselves if it means endangering their popularity. They will smile at a waiter even if the soup is cold and late: they would hate to cause a fuss in such a lovely place - it would spoil the atmosphere and run them the risk of being mistaken for one of those brash, aggressive Aries types.

Those with Mars in Libra often do not know what they want. They cannot make up their minds between the cruise down the Nile or the trek in the Himalayas. In fact, they have difficulty deciding between a 60 or 100 watt light bulb. They find it much easier when others make decisions - then they have a yardstick to go by and can give satisfaction.

To a large extent, people with Mars in Libra want what others want, but if they are basically untrue to themselves they will find ways of tipping the scales back. With charm of course!

MARS IN SCORPIO

People with Mars in Scorpio want something either intensely or not at all. Nothing is allowed to stand in their way, and they will out-manœuvre an opponent without relinquishing their self-control. They find it hard to be direct about what they want and their methods are subtle and sometimes manipulative. It is not surprising that their underground tactics are often met with suspicion. The cloak of mystery is hardly conducive to a team atmosphere.

Mars in Scorpio types will often take a sledgehammer to crack a nut because their very survival is tied up with being able to pull off what they want. They sometimes do not know their own inner strength because they excel in keeping it hidden, even from themselves. Because the Scorpio energy is contained deep inside, it can be hard to find the key that lets it out. They often anticipate struggles, but their most important battles are with themselves. A lot of energy can be trapped in their own internal wrestling matches.

Once they have gained access into their own volcanic power, they can pour it into work that feeds their need for deep involvement. They are often catalysts for transformation from one level to another. They will challenge other people, perhaps stripping away their illusions in an effort to revitalize them. They are the alchemists forever engaged in changing base matter into gold.

MARS IN SAGITTARIUS
People with Mars in Sagittarius usually have energy to spare and are rarely to be found kicking their heels while there is something left to conquer. The source of this energy is enthusiasm which they are able to channel into action. If they believe in something, they will crusade for it against the odds, but if it loses its truth their balloon will burst.

Mars in Sagittarius types are fired by the thought of where something might lead. They are always putting two and two together and getting five and, for this reason, can inspire others to go beyond the limits. Archers live on the hoof. They are permanently en route towards their latest goal, but actually winning the gold star is momentary bliss compared with the buzz they get from galloping towards it.

People with Mars in Sagittarius have a natural ability to spread the word and promote and arouse interest. With their expansive drive, they want to get messages across to the widest audience possible. Today, Weston-super-Mare, tomorrow the world - ever the optimist, these Mars signs always have their sights set on the main chance.

Those with Mars in Sagittarius have to watch a tendency to overstretch themselves. They bite off more than they can possibly chew and leave others to pick up the bits. They have a problem standing still long enough to see reality, but this is also their gift - there is no limit to what is possible.

MARS IN CAPRICORN
Mars in Capricorn is essentially a 'steady Eddie' - capable, careful and conscientious. These types are in their element adding

the practical touch to financial matters or tasks that require self-discipline and organization. Their serious approach equips them well in the business world. They are load-bearing, but sometimes the weight of responsibility sits so heavily on them that there is no room for them to experiment or dream.

People with Mars in Capricorn are planners. They will not buy into any get rich quick schemes because they have their own plans already worked out over a period of years - and calculated with interest! They are also concerned that everything they do exudes professionalism, so they never risk damaging their reputation by impulsively reaching out for what they want. They are hard taskmasters, but this applies equally to themselves.

Mars in Capricorn types are familiar with the idea of delays or limits being imposed on them. In fact, if they get what they want too easily they are convinced they have missed out on something.

They work well when pitted against difficulties - they need something to push against. They are attracted to work that gives them responsibility. From the moment they are made School Prefects they realize that belonging to the higher order more than compensates for the obligation to play by the rules.

MARS IN AQUARIUS
People with Mars in Aquarius will often go out on a limb to get what they want. They have some wacky ways of going about their business, but are not necessarily completely off the wall. There is a definite method in this madness. Aquarius is, after all, the sign of the awakener, and when Mars is placed here something new, unusual and different is set to take the old way of doing things by storm. It was probably Mars in Aquarius who went on to invent the wheel, despite the raised eyebrows of contemporaries.

Because Mars in Aquarius types are non-conformist, they appear to threaten the *status quo*. They are not the ones to bash their head against brick walls; they find a way to explode the structure. Needless to say, Mars in Aquarius is often felt as a 'disruptive influence', but change is inevitable if something new is to happen.

They are happiest operating within a large network of people because they believe in finding a common purpose. But do not give them a title or job description - that would really cramp their style. They like to work at both the forefront, and on the fringe of, developments so they are at once pioneers and outsiders. This gives them the freedom to experiment without the clutter of other people's expectations. Whether people with Mars in Aquarius are concocting a new recipe or an antidote to Aids, they thrill to the excitement of breaking new ground.

MARS IN PISCES
In order to get their energies flowing, people with Mars in Pisces have to align their desires with a purpose that goes beyond themselves. The trouble is that they often feel guilty about putting their own wants above anyone else's. They can always block themselves from achieving

something by thinking that another person deserves or needs it more than they do. Sometimes, the only way these Mars signs in Pisces can actually pursue their goal is if they achieve it for other people. This is why they are so well suited to work that enables them to help others.

Mars in Pisces types are poetic, rather than assertive, in their desires. They are in touch with the poignancy of not having what they want, and value the longing rather than the having. This is not to say that they are ineffectual, far from it. But they find the urge to grab for something rather primitive and must 'feel right' about what they do.

They are not ones to impose their will on others, and, as such, they find it difficult to confront people who stand in their way. Fish need to flow with the current. They know when the timing is right for them to make a move, and also when to let things wash over them. Although it looks as though they are avoiding and escaping action - and admittedly it is a fine line - these signs cannot be pushed into activity. Mars in Pisces placements are not the most organized or down-to-earth, nor are they natural authority figures, but they have the capacity to inspire other people with their vision.

YEAR	ARIES	TAURUS	GEMINI	CANCER	LEO	VIRGO	LIBRA	SCORPIO	SAGITTAR	CAPRIC	AQUARIUS	PISCES
1922								1/1-18/2	19/2-13/9	14/9-30/10	31/10-11/12	12/12-31/12
1923	21/1-3/3	4/3-15/4	16/4-30/5	31/5-15/7	16/7-31/8	1/9-17/10	18/10-3/12	4/12-31/12	20/1-6/3	7/3-24/4		1/1-20/1
1924	19/12-31/12							1/1-19/1	28/12-31/12		25/4-24/6	25/6-24/8
1925	1/1-4/2	5/2-23/3	24/3-9/5	10/5-25/6	26/6-12/8	13/8-28/9	29/9-13/11	14/11-27/12	1/1-8/2	9/2-22/3	23/3-3/5	4/5-14/6
1926	15/6-31/7	1/8-31/12							8/12-31/12			
1927	1/1-21/2	1/1-21/2	22/2-16/4	17/4-5/6	6/6-24/7	25/7-10/9	11/9-25/10	26/10-7/12	1/1-18/1	19/1-27/2	28/2-7/4	
1928	17/5-25/6	26/6-8/8	9/8-2/10	3/10-19/12								8/4-16/5
1929			20/12-31/12	11/3-12/5	13/5-3/7	4/7-21/8	22/8-5/10	6/10-18/11	19/11-28/12	29/12-31/12		
			1/1-10/3		30/3-10/6							
1930	25/4-2/6	3/6-14/7	15/7-27/8	28/8-20/10	21/10-31/12		2/8-16/9	17/9-30/10	31/10-9/12	1/1-6/2	7/2-16/3	17/3-24/4
1931				17/2-29/3	1/1-16/2	11/6-1/8				10/12-31/12		
					30/3-10/6							
1932	3/4-11/5	12/5-21/6	22/6-4/8	5/8-30/9	1/10-13/11	14/11-31/12				1/1-17/1	18/1-24/2	25/2-2/4
1933						1/1-6/7	7/7-25/8	26/8-8/10	9/10-18/11	19/11-27/12	28/12-31/12	
1934	14/3-22/4	23/4-2/6	3/6-15/7	16/7-30/8	31/8-17/10	18/10-10/12	11/12-31/12				1/1-3/2	4/2-13/3
1935							1/1-29/7	30/7-16/9	17/9-29/10	30/10-7/12	8/12-31/12	16/1-22/2
1936	23/2-2/4	3/4-13/5	14/5-26/6	27/6-10/8	11/8-27/9	28/9-15/11	16/11-31/12				1/1-15/1	23/12-31/12
1937							1/1-6/1	7/1-13/3	14/3-15/5	1/10-12/11	13/11-22/12	
								16/5-9/8	10/8-30/9			
1938	1/2-13/3	14/3-24/4	25/4-8/6	9/6-23/7	24/7-8/9	9/9-26/10	27/10-12/12	13/12-31/12				1/1-31/1
1939								1/1-30/1	31/1-22/3	23/3-25/5	26/5-22/7	21/11-31/12
										23/7-25/9	26/9-20/11	
1940	5/1-18/2	19/2-2/4	3/4-18/5	19/5-4/7	5/7-20/8	21/8-6/10	7/10-21/11	22/11-31/12				1/1-4/1
1941	4/7-31/12							1/1-5/1		19/2-3/4	4/4-17/5	18/5-3/7
1942	1/1-12/1	13/1-8/3	9/3-27/4	28/4-15/6	16/6-2/8	3/8-18/9	19/9-2/11	3/11-16/12	17/12-31/12			
1943	29/5-8/7	9/7-24/8	25/8-31/12	30/3-23/5	24/5-13/7	14/7-30/8	31/8-14/10	15/10-26/11	1/1-27/1	28/1-9/3	10/3-18/4	19/4-28/5
1944			1/1-29/3	9/9-12/11	13/11-27/2				27/11-31/12			
				28/12-31/12								
1945	4/5-12/6	13/6-24/7	25/7-8/9	1/1-23/4	24/4-21/6	22/6-10/8	11/8-25/9	26/9-7/11	1/1-6/1	7/1-15/2	16/2-26/3	27/3-3/5
1946									8/11-18/12	19/12-31/12		
1947	13/4-22/5	23/5-30/6	1/7-14/8	15/8-2/10	3/10-2/12	3/12-31/12				1/10-26/1	27/1-5/3	6/3-12/4
1948					14/2-19/5	1/1-13/2	19/7-4/9	5/9-18/10	19/10-27/11	28/11-31/12		

YEAR	ARIES	TAURUS	GEMINI	CANCER	LEO	VIRGO	LIBRA	SCORPIO	SAGITTAR	CAPRIC	AQUARIUS	PISCES
1948						20/5-18/7						
1949	23/3-1/5	2/5-11/6	12/6-24/7	25/7-8/9	9/9-28/10	29/10-27/12	28/12-31/12			1/1-5/1	6/1-12/2	13/2-22/3
1950						30/3-12/6	1/1-29/3; 13/6-11/8	12/8-26/9	27/9-7/11	8/11-16/12	17/12-31/12	
1951	2/3-9/4	10/4-20/5	21/5-3/7	4/7-17/8	18/8-4/10	5/10-23/11	24/11-31/12				1/1-22/1	23/1-1/3
1952							1/1-19/1	20/1-26/8	27/8-11/10	12/10-21/11	22/11-30/12	31/12
1953	8/2-19/3	20/3-30/4	1/5-13/6	14/6-28/7	29/7-14/9	15/9-1/11	2/11-20/12	21/12-31/12				1/1-7/2
1954								1/1-9/2	10/2-12/4; 4/7-24/8	13/4-3/7; 25/8-21/10	22/10-3/12	4/12-31/12
1955	15/1-25/2	26/2-10/4	11/4-25/5	26/5-10/7	11/7-26/8	27/8-12/10	13/10-28/11	29/11-31/12				1/1-14/1
1956	7/12-31/12							1/1-13/1	14/1-28/2	29/2-14/4	15/4-2/6	3/6-6/12
1957	1/1-28/1	29/1-17/3	18/3-4/5	5/5-20/6	21/6-7/8	8/8-23/9	24/9-8/11	9/11-22/12	23/12-31/12			
1958	7/6-20/7	21/7-20/9; 30/10-31/12	21/9-29/10						1/1-3/2	4/2-16/3	17/3-26/4	27/4-6/6
1959		1/1-10/2	11/2-10/4	11/4-31/5	1/6-19/7	20/7-5/9	6/9-20/10	21/10-3/12	4/12-31/12			
1960	11/5-19/6	20/6-1/8	2/8-20/9	21/9-31/12					1/1-13/1	14/1-22/2	23/2-1/4	2/4-10/5
1961				1/1-5/5	6/5-28/6	29/6-16/8	17/8-1/10	2/10-13/11	14/11-24/12	25/12-31/12		
1962	20/4-28/5	29/5-8/7	9/7-21/8	22/8-11/10	12/10-31/12					1/1-1/2	2/2-11/3	12/3-19/4
1963					1/1-2/6	3/6-26/7	27/7-11/9	12/9-25/10	26/10-4/12	5/12-31/12		
1964	29/3-6/5	7/5-16/6	17/6-30/7	31/7-14/9	15/9-5/11	6/11-31/12				1/1-12/1	13/1-19/2	20/2-28/3
1965						1/1-28/6	29/6-20/8	21/8-3/10	4/10-13/11	14/11-22/12	23/12-31/12	
1966	9/3-17/4	18/4-28/5	29/5-10/7	11/7-25/8	26/8-12/10	13/10-3/12	4/12-31/12				1/1-29/1	30/1-8/3
1967							1/1-12/2; 1/4-19/7	13/2-31/3; 20/7-9/9	10/9-22/10	23/10-1/12	2/12-31/12	
1968	17/2-27/3	28/3-8/5	9/5-20/6	21/6-4/8	5/8-21/9	22/9-8/11	9/11-29/12	30/12-31/12			1/1-8/1	9/1-16/2
1969								1/1-24/2	25/2-20/9	21/9-4/11	5/11-15/12	16/12-31/12
1970	25/1-6/3	7/3-18/4	19/4-1/6	2/6-17/7	18/7-2/9	3/9-19/10	20/10-6/12	7/12-31/12				1/1-24/1
1971	27/12-31/12							1/1-23/1	24/1-12/3	13/3-3/5	4/5-6/11	17/11-26/12
1972		11/2-27/3	28/3-12/5	13/5-28/6	29/6-15/8	16/8-30/9	1/10-15/11	16/11-30/12	31/12			
1973	21/6-12/8; 30/10-24/12	13/8-29/10; 25/12-31/12							1/1-12/2	13/2-26/3	27/3-8/5	9/5-20/6
1974		1/1-27/2	28/2-20/4	21/4-8/6	9/6-27/7	28/7-12/9	13/9-28/10	29/10-10/12	11/12-31/12			
1975	22/5-1/7	2/7-14/8	15/8-16/10	17/10-25/11					1/1-21/1	22/1-3/3	4/3-11/4	12/4-21/5

YEAR	ARIES	TAURUS	GEMINI	CANCER	LEO	VIRGO	LIBRA	SCORPIO	SAGITTAR	CAPRIC	AQUARIUS	PISCES
1975			26/11-31/12									
1976			1/1-18/3									
1977	28/4-5/6	6/6-17/7	18/7-31/8	19/3-16/5	17/5-6/7	7/7-24/8	25/8-8/10	9/10-20/11	21/11-31/12	1/1-9/2	10/2-19/3	20/3-27/4
1978				1/9-26/10	27/10-31/12 1/1-26/1	14/6-4/8	5/8-19/9	20/9-1/11	2/11-12/12	13/12-31/12		
				27/1-10/4	11/4-13/6							
1979	7/4-15/5	16/5-25/6	26/6-8/8	9/8-24/9	25/9-19/11	20/11-31/12				1/1-20/1	21/1-27/2	28/2-6/4
1980						1/1-11/3	11/7-28/8	29/8-12/10	13/10-21/11	22/11-30/12	31/12	
					12/3-3/5	4/5-10/7						
1981	18/3-25/4	26/4-5/6	6/6-18/7	19/7-2/9	3/9-21/10	22/10-16/12	17/12-31/12				1/1-6/2	7/2-17/3
1982							1/1-3/8	4/8-20/9	21/9-31/10	1/11-10/12	11/12-31/12	
1983	25/2-5/4	6/4-16/5	17/5-29/6	30/6-13/8	14/8-29/9	30/9-18/11	19/11-31/12				1/1-17/1	18/1-24/2
1984							1/1-11/1	12/1-17/8	18/8-5/10	6/10-15/11	16/11-25/12	26/12-31/12
1985	3/2-15/3	16/3-26/4	27/4-10/6	11/6-25/7	26/7-10/9	11/9-27/10	28/10-14/12	15/12-31/12				1/1-2/2
1986								1/1-2/2	3/2-29/3	29/3-9/10	10/10-26/11	27/11-31/12
1987	9/1-20/2	21/2-5/4	6/4-21/5	22/5-6/7	7/7-22/8	23/8-8/10	9/10-24/11	25/11-31/12				1/1-8/1
1988	14/7-23/10							1/1-8/1	9/1-22/2	23/2-6/4	7/4-22/5	23/5-13/7
	2/11-31/12											24/10-1/11
1989	1/1-19/1	20/1-11/3	12/3-29/4	30/4-16/6	17/6-3/8	4/8-19/9	20/9-4/11	15/11-18/12	19/12-31/12			
1990	1/6-12/7	13/7-31/8	1/9-14/12						1/1-29/1	30/1-11/3	12/3-20/4	21/4-32/5
		15/12-31/12										
1991		1/1-21/1	22/1-3/4	4/4-26/5	27/5-15/7	16/7-1/9	2/9-16/10	17/10-29/11	30/11-31/12			
1992	6/5-14/6	15/5-26/7	27/7-12/9	13/9-31/12					1/1-9/1	10/1-18/2	19/2-28/3	29/3-5/5

CHAPTER SEVEN

Jupiter: The luck in your life
Saturn: Your fears and insecurities

Are you an optimist or a pessimist? Where are you fortunate and where do you fail? Do you take chances or tread cautiously?

Jupiter and Saturn are two planets that are connected in astrology by virtue of their opposite natures. They are a necessary balance to each other, Jupiter being associated with luck, optimism, expansion and travel, and Saturn with fear, limitation, 'tightening one's belt' and the internal resources we have at our disposal to meet set-backs.

These two are as necessary to each other as breathing in and out, and provide a balance in life. When people have either a strongly placed Jupiter or Saturn, then their lives tend to be coloured by one of these attitudes. Looking to see if there are other planets in the signs of Sagittarius or Capricorn also helps to assess the level of Jupiterian expansion or Saturnian repression. There are those who look on the bright side and those who fear the worst - the risk-taker or the wet blanket.

The sign position of Jupiter and Saturn indicates the way in which we will express our confidence and our self-doubt. It shows which areas of our life will be prone to exaggeration and which we worry about. Will we push the

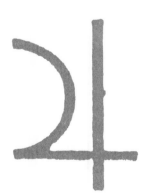

boat out or tread cautiously? Will we trust to luck or put in every effort? Jupiter and Saturn display very different attitudes.

In the areas in which Jupiter is placed, we feel fortunate, things come easily to us and we can count our blessings. Seen from a reincarnationist viewpoint, people with a well-placed Jupiter might believe that karmically they are reaping the rewards from a past life. The sign position of Saturn can be where there is a thorn in our side. We feel we must work especially hard in these difficult areas and that life throws us challenges here which cause us struggle - but ultimately self-knowledge, perhaps a karmic lesson to be learnt.

In the Monopoly game of life, Jupiter is when people pass 'Go' and collect £200, Saturn is when they are sent to 'Jail'. However, interpreting Jupiter and Saturn demands more than examining a series of events; these planets depict a frame of mind. People's personal philosophies and what they expect to happen to them plays a large part in determining their destiny.

JUPITER IN ARIES

People with Jupiter in Aries are impulsive to the point of recklessness. They see life as one long opportunity that must be taken advantage of. It is very difficult to get them to listen to others who attempt to slow them down, so they charge ahead on their own regardless. These people are outwardly self-confident and fearless. Never backward about coming forward, they are always first in line and can trample on others in the process, with their philosophy of 'every man for himself'.

Jupiter in Aries types believe in themselves and their ability to create their own luck, and it is this motivation and drive that seem to get them noticed and promoted, so they are able to manifest good fortune for themselves simply by pushing ahead. They are adventurous travellers - activity holidays are definitely best for them, to keep their energy channelled. People with Jupiter in Aries rugby-tackle life; the rough and tumble is just play for them, although to others they can seem excessive in their energy.

SATURN IN ARIES

Saturn in Aries casts a veil over the spontaneity of this sign. Although people with this placement are frequently highly ambitious, they are reticent and unforthcoming about themselves. There is a basic shyness and defensiveness that they must struggle with in order to assert who they really are. Assertion - the birthright of Aries - does not come easily when Saturn is in this sign. Its subjects can be brusque with others, stand-offish and aloof thus giving an impression of strength which is really a mask for their vulnerability.

Those with Saturn in Aries need to test themselves to gain access to their inner strength. Through confrontation with their own will they learn how to stand up for themselves - it is as if they have been given blunt swords that they need to sharpen in order to be effective.

JUPITER IN TAURUS

The expansion associated with Jupiter tends to flow through the material area of life when this planet is in the earthy sign of Taurus. People with Jupiter in Taurus like to measure their well-being through the accumulation of possessions and money. They may have the Midas touch when it comes to acquiring financial reward, but their desire for material comfort can make them very self-indulgent. Jupiter here inflates the need to be cocooned from material hardship, and, for all the common sense associated with the sign of Taurus, the tendency is to go over the top.

These people do, however, have a practical streak. They are earthed in the ground and do not look up to the clouds for meaning in life. They prefer to travel in the lap of luxury - you will not find this type struggling with a back-pack. Jupiter in Taurus is a also a connoisseur of good food and wine, and believes in the spirit of abundance.

SATURN IN TAURUS

Like Jupiter in Taurus, those with Saturn in Taurus are also accumulators but, unlike the former, they never think of themselves as well-off in the material sense. Even with the crown jewels in the bank, they would still be scratching their heads wondering where their next meal is coming from. Certainly, Saturn in Taurus suggests that the individual has some lessons to learn in the material sphere, and material deprivation of some sort can be part of this at some stage in life. But the gauntlet that is layed down to this sign challenges them to develop an internal sense of security.

Saturn in Taurus types are truly afraid of loss, and equate their identity with what they possess. Therefore they are constantly shoring themselves up against losing themselves. Life often deals them cards which teach them about their standing in life and, most importantly, where they stand with themselves.

JUPITER IN GEMINI

People with Jupiter in Gemini expand the sphere of the mind to include many diverse interests. Their minds buzz with ideas, and those which never get off the ground are quickly replaced. These people can talk their way into anywhere, possessing the patter that opens doors and brings opportunities. Their way with words often brings them luck, and they can capitalize on bright ideas. With so many people to see and places to go, they rarely stand still and are always absorbing information, reading and mentally digesting knowledge. They know a little about most things but, as mental wanderers, are easily bored if confined to one subject.

Jupiter in Gemini types are restless, but mainly travel in order to learn. Unless there is a huge stack of reading material they will not sit on a beach for long. Their curiosity encourages them to explore the environment, and their facility for communication will not be dimmed by a language barrier.

SATURN IN GEMINI

When the seriousness of the planet Saturn is found in the sign that is most noted for its ability to skip lightly, there is bound to be a bit of a bump as Gemini comes down to earth. Saturn here expresses itself through disciplining the mind. This planet is like the traditional school teacher who drums lessons home through repetition rather than creative play. The individual with Saturn in Gemini often has to learn things the hard way. The intelligence of Gemini is still very much in evidence, but often communication is like driving a car with the brakes on. People with Saturn in Gemini have to work hard at expressing what goes on inside their heads and their insecurity stems from a fear of looking stupid.

This placement needs time to form ideas, but is noted for its logic and capacity to work a concept through to completion. They need to really apply their minds to something, and come into their own tackling complex puzzles that require mental skill.

JUPITER IN CANCER

Jupiter in Cancer expands the capacity to relate to others on an emotional level. This individual instinctively reaches out to people and possesses strong resources that can sustain, support and protect. Good luck or providence is often connected with the family in some way. Either the individual receives material gain as an inheritance, or a good sense of humour, philosophy of life or religious values are instilled in childhood that stand the person in good stead.

Jupiter in Cancer usually derives great pleasure from home and family, and does not feel comfortable when taken away from familiar surroundings. These types do not travel well unless they have a home from home in which to flourish. Their outlook on life is emotionally subjective and their optimism is dependent on how secure they feel within themselvs at any one time.

SATURN IN CANCER

Saturn in Cancer is a placement that binds together the realms of emotion and duty. Therefore those with this birth sign often feel that family and affairs of the heart come with a price to pay. A fear of separation can inhibit the ability to get close to others from the start, and the individual has to work hard at learning to trust others and to open up.

Saturn can place a barrier that creates circumstances in childhood that generate a sense of self-reliance. Even as children, Saturn in Cancer types can feel alienated from support and, thus their safety comes from providing security for themselves rather than depending on others. As adults, this can be translated as a desire for material security (particularly property, with Cancer's emphasis on the home) that is valued as having the power to provide emotional sustenance.

JUPITER IN LEO

The Jupiterian spirit residing in the sign of Leo promotes the natural exuberance of this planet. These people find it easy to 'play', to express their natural creativity and enthusiasm. Jupiter encourages risk-taking, and placed in Leo the desire to gamble can be inflated out of a sense of proportion. Jupiter in Leo sits permanently at the roulette wheel of life taking chances.

The lifestyles of this sign can be grandiose, and they certainly have a sense of the dramatic and the ability to put on a good show. Jupiter in Leo can have problems getting a sense of proportion in life as the tendency is to overplay their hands. They attract positions of power and oscillate between generosity and autocracy.

SATURN IN LEO

When Saturn is in Leo, the radiance and self-confidence of this sign have to be forced out from the shade. Although Leo naturally loves the limelight, with Saturn here it is as if there is a fear of being noticed, a self-consciousness that prevents people from revelling in their individuality. These types have to escape from themselves to act spontaneously and enjoy pleasure without it becoming something of an ordeal. They are not real party poopers, but it is difficult for them to relax and they are often the ones found stage-managing events, as if they can only justify fun by making an effort.

Saturn in Leo people are shy but secretly want to be admired. They can resent others who are capable of pushing themselves forward into the attention zone while they still dally on the sidelines, with a one step forwards, two steps backwards shuffle. Ambition is strongly marked in this placement but it is the issue of recognition from others that presents the greatest challenge to this person.

JUPITER IN VIRGO

Fun-loving Jupiter sits uncomfortably in precise Virgo. Jupiter tends to expand the qualities of whatever sign it is in, thus analysis and emphasis on usefulness becomes exaggerated in Virgo. People with Jupiter in Virgo can go overboard examining the whys and wherefores and end up tying themselves into knots. This prominence of common sense and a critical faculty can often keep large ideas grounded. However, Jupiter in Virgo types can apply concepts to a purpose because they are naturally able to weed out the wheat from the chaff. This is their gift.

Because Jupiter in Virgo placements are so concerned with productiveness, they will often travel in the course of their work. They travel with a particular purpose in mind, and everything they encounter is passed through their personal points system and graded accordingly.

SATURN IN VIRGO

Saturn in Virgo is a stickler for detail, and fearful of not getting everything exactly right. These birth signs spend hours engaged in meeting their standards of perfection, convinced that they will stand or fall on the tiniest point. Saturn here can be obsessive in the pursuit of excellence, and determined to find fault where others might see blandness or normality. These types are hard taskmasters, pushing others and themselves to the limit.

They are not ones to bellow when things go wrong. They stew over it all and express their worry through nagging and carping, and at the bottom of it all is the fundamental insecurity of doubting Thomas. Never trusting that they are acceptable just as themselves, they are anxious that everything they do must be perfect. Their health is the barometer of their well-being. The constant tabulation that takes place in their minds registers in the body, and their challenge is to let go of the 'never good enough' critic and listen to another voice that allows and accepts.

JUPITER IN LIBRA
Jupiter in Libra is a people person, with the gift of being able to share. This highly sociable placement believes in the idea of the more the merrier. Jupiter in Libra types thrive in partnerships, both romantic and business, and fortunate openings are often derived through their partners.

People with Jupiter in Libra will rarely travel alone; they need a companions. They will usually spread their share of risks amongst others rather than stepping out of line on their own, and they will never act without carefully weighing up their options. The danger with Jupiter in Libra is of

relying too heavily on others. However, their positive attitude towards partnerships and their spirit of co-operation drop rewards into their laps.

SATURN IN LIBRA
It is through the area of relationships that Saturn's lessons are extended when the sign of Libra is occupied by this planet. This is not to say that people with this sign are constantly thwarted in their attempts to form partnerships, but relationships are really opportunities for self-discovery and psychological insight rather than joy rides. Wherever Saturn is placed, some kind of responsibility comes into view, and, in Libra, relationships are a serious business. Through the give and take, the working out of the balance in partnerships, Saturn teaches it subjects much about who they are, and what kind of partner they attract to complete the picture.

With Saturn in Libra it is tempting for individuals to blame their problems on others, when they have in fact set it up this way themselves, albeit unconsciously. The challenge is for them to see their own contribution, and recognize their own reflection in the behaviour in others.

JUPITER IN SCORPIO
Jupiter enlarges the Scorpionic desire for trawling the depths to bring self-understanding to the surface. This placement has a strong need to understand the meaning behind any belief system or religion, and has considerable depth of insight into others. Jupiter encourages the excessive nature of Scorpio to express itself with intensity leading to an all-or-nothing approach. Jupiter in Scorpio holds strong beliefs and can find it hard to see another point of view.

Sometimes a powerful change is brought about by travel, as Scorpio weaves its transformational magic in the process of venturing further afield, but this can also occur through broadening the mental horizons. Jupiter in Scorpio is a great fatalist and believer in change wrought by destiny. It seems that certain lucky breakthroughs are just 'meant to be'.

SATURN IN SCORPIO
Saturn in Scorpio builds an internal brick wall that prevents easy access to self-understanding. As a result, many of the fears and insecurities that block growth are brought about by resistance to change and repression of deep feelings. This placement hides

obstacles well and truly within. Saturn here often fosters a great fear of intimacy that stems from an earlier rejection. People with this placement may find it easier to control matters by shutting off altogether from a passion that threatens to overwhelm them.

Combining the discipline of Saturn with the power of Scorpio produces enormous strength of purpose. These people can become fixated with achieving their goals and have to watch a tendency towards manipulation. Truly, these placements can gain a unique insight into the uses and abuses of power, and the capacity for walls to be broken down and transformed, even their own.

JUPITER IN SAGITTARIUS

When Jupiter is found in its natural home sign of Sagittarius, an energy is cast that appears over the top and reckless to some, and delightfully playful and rumbustious to others. Jupiter here is brimming with optimism and expectancy that something better is around the corner. This placement is a great traveller, and ever ready to risk the familiar in exchange for something more promising.

Jupiter in Sagittarius embodies the spirit of free enterprise. People with this sign act on hunches, take advantage and usually come up smelling of roses. It is not so much that Lady Luck smiles more on this placement, but that Jupiter in Sagittarius is ready to grab the opportunity. Many buses may come along in life but if a person is rooted to the bus stop and does not step aboard then it is hard to go anywhere. Jupiter in Sagittarius almost always hops on just for the ride.

SATURN IN SAGITTARIUS

Saturn in Sagittarius is searching for a code by which to live. Those with this placement seek answers to the questions of their existence and usually have a long hard road to travel before they can piece it altogether. They cannot swallow one body of thought alone, but have to distil a sense of meaning from many avenues and experience some culs-de-sac in the process.

Ultimately, their fear may be that there is no meaning, and this is what drives them on, sometime setting them back into a kind of inner emptiness. They can feel pulled between a need to stick things out and an urge to be free of responsibility which seem to present an eternal conundrum. Saturn in Sagittarius types are challenged to discover their own philosophy of life, which will provide a sense of purpose that synthesises all other goals.

JUPITER IN CAPRICORN

People with Jupiter here have good business sense which slowly enables them to climb the ladder of success. Practicality and shrewdness are combined with a drive to expand that prevents them getting stuck for too long on one level. Because Capricorn is an earth sign, a desire for material gain often prompts a move forward, but Jupiter here is not a great risk-taker and footsteps are measured carefully.

With this placement, people are likely to believe very strongly in the concept of creating their own luck through effort. Jupiter in Capricorn is a double edged sword which can be seen in a tendency to vacillate between a kind of rigid optimism in the face of limiting situations and a melancholia that strikes even when the outlook is bright. The key to any kind of expansion with this placement is to apply oneself. On the other hand Jupiter in Capricorn can find it hard to relax and let go.

SATURN IN CAPRICORN

Saturn in its own sign of Capricorn facilitates self-discipline and the formation of a personal regime that

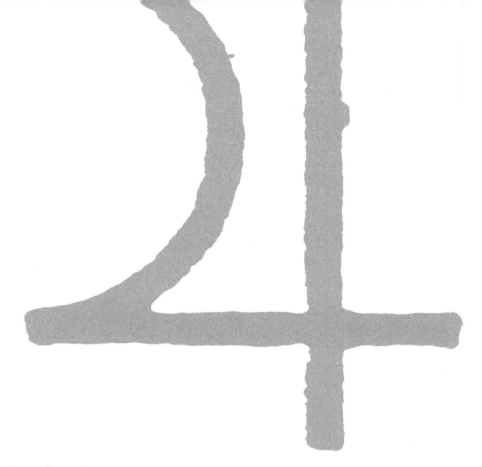

structures life. In the process, the drive of Saturn in Capricorn can appear as sacrifice and self-denial. Is the end worth the means? Only those with Saturn in Capricorn can find out the answer as they pound a treadmill which keeps them on the straight and narrow at the expense of their self-expression.

Ambition is prominent with these placements. It is as if only the recognition of their work can give them a true sense of identity, and, of course, people who are so strongly identified with their role in life cannot easily know themselves without it. So Saturn in Capricorn can become a workaholic as a kind of defence mechanism. Paradoxically, the hardest task for them might be not to work at all.

JUPITER IN AQUARIUS

Jupiter in Aquarius is tolerant, broad-minded and generous. Aquarius is attuned to the idea of groups and causes and Jupiter here allows expression of these humanitarian instincts. These signs are free-thinkers, and therefore will not go with the mainstream but choose for themselves who is deserving of their support. When Jupiter is in the unconventional sign of Aquarius, benefits can flow back and forth from some unusual and unexpected places!

Friendships are plentiful and fortuitous with these placements. Many contacts from all walks of life provide a network of ideas and opportunities for them, and Jupiter in Aquarius types appreciate the differences between people, espousing a philosophy of 'each to his own'. They are spur of the moment travellers, who delight in looking up friends and making new ones on their journeys.

SATURN IN AQUARIUS

The inhibiting energy of Saturn residing in the sign of

groups and friendships can cut individuals from their sense of connection with others. Saturn here can be a loner, or at the least feel alienated and unable to find common ground with others. Sometimes these types will compensate for this state by literally surrounding themselves with other people, working for large organizations, and joining societies and clubs. But as, team members, they have to work at coming in from the outside.

In many cases, people with Saturn in Aquarius will actually choose to differentiate themselves by taking responsibility for the group as leaders. Caught up in the organising process, they feels they have a place.

Ultimately, Saturn's lesson here is to teach about the nature of loneliness and friendship, and the choices tobe made in pursuing isolation or inclusion.

JUPITER IN PISCES

The capacity to give is emphasized when Jupiter is in Pisces. Compassion and sensitivity are extended to others, yet, as Pisces embodies the opposite qualities to Virgo's discriminating nature, Jupiter in Pisces can be gullible. These people are idealists and immensely open to persuasion and influence. Even if they are taken for a ride, however, they will usually view the matter philosophically - testimony to the Piscean power of forgiveness.

People with Jupiter in Pisces are guided by intuition rather than rationality and, whatever their circumstances, feel protected by and connected to some kind of spiritual source. Jupiter in Pisces types are able to bring hope to others through their own faith and trust in life, but they can also live on the border between spiritual hope and daydreaming. They have a romantic longing to be 'taken away from all this.' Being close to water soothes their souls and recharges their batteries, these are the types who dream of exchanging Manchester for Mustique.

SATURN IN PISCES

The challenge for people with Saturn in Pisces is to combine their sensitivity with practicality. These people can become overwhelmed with feelings of hopelessness and have to work to cultivate positive attitudes. They can sabotage themselves from moving on from their difficulties with their self-sacrificing attitude. In some form or other, Saturn in Pisces must confront the intertwined themes of the martyr, the rescuer and the victim.

Whether these types are doing the bailing out or remaining despondently stuck in difficulties, they are set the test of realising that they have a choice.

If they can combine the imagination of Pisces with the realism of Saturn, then they can put across their message to others. It is a fine line to walk: too much Pisces and they are left floating, too much Saturn and their feet become leaden. They need to direct the proceedings, blending both aspects as they go along.

Jupiter

YEAR	DATES	SIGN	YEAR	DATES	SIGN	YEAR	DATES	SIGN
				18/5-31/12	TAU		16/2-5/8	VIR
1922	1/1-26/10	LIB	1941	1/1-27/5	TAU		6/8-31/12	LIB
	27/10-31/12	SCO		28/5-31/12	GEM	1958	1/1-14/1	LIB
1923	1/1-24/11	SCO	1942	1/1-11/6	GEM		15/1-15/3	SCO
	25/11-31/12	SAG		12/6-31/12	CAN		16/3-5/9	LIB
1924	1/1-17/12	SAG	1943	1/1-30/6	CAN		6/9-31/12	SCO
	18/12-31/12	CAP		1/7-31/12	LEO	1959	1/1-9/2	SCO
1925	ALL YEAR	CAP	1944	1/1-27/7	LEO		10/2-20/4	SAG
1926	1/1-5/1	CAP		28/7-31/12	VIR		21/4-5/10	SCO
	6/1-31/12	AQU	1945	1/1-26/8	LIB		6/10-31/12	SAG
1927	1/1-17/1	AQU		27/8-31/12	VIR	1960	1/1-29/2	SAG
	18/1-5/6	PIS	1946	1/1-26/9	LIB		1/3-7/6	CAP
	6/6-10/9	ARI		27/9-31/12	SCO		8/6-21/10	SAG
	11/9-31/12	PIS	1947	1/1-25/10	SCO		22/10-31/12	CAP
1928	1/1-11/6	TAU		26/10-31/12	SAG	1961	1/1-16/3	CAP
	12/6-31/12	GEM	1948	1/1-16/11	SAG		17/3-11/8	AQU
1930	1/1-26/6	GEM		17/11-31/12	CAP		12/8-31/10	CAP
	27/6-31/12	CAN	1949	1/1-12/4	CAP		1/11-31/12	AQU
1931	1/1-16/7	CAN		13/4-28/6	AQU	1962	1/1-25/3	AQU
	17/7-31/12	LEO		29/6-30/11	CAP		26/3-31/12	PIS
1932	1/1-10/8	LEO		1/12-31/12	AQU	1963	1/1-4/4	PIS
	11/8-31/12	VIR	1950	1/1-16/4	AQU		5/4-31/12	ARI
1933	1/1-9/9	VIR		17/4-16/9	PIS	1964	1/1-9/4	ARI
	10/9-31/12	LIB		17/9-3/12	AQU		10/4-31/12	TAU
1934	1/1-10/10	LIB		4/12-31/12	PIS	1965	1/1-20/4	TAU
	11/10-31/12	SCO	1951	1/1-20/4	PIS		21/4-20/9	GEM
1935	1/1-8/11	SCO		21/4-31/12	ARI		21/9-15/11	CAN
	9/11-31/12	SAG	1952	1/1-26/4	ARI		16/11-31/12	GEM
1936	1/1-2/12	SAG		27/4-31/12	TAU	1966	1/1-5/5	GEM
	3/12-31/12	CAP	1953	1/1-10/5	TAU		6/5-27/9	CAN
1937	1/1-20/12	CAP		11/5-31/12	GEM		28/9-31/12	LEO
	21/12-31/12	AQU	1954	1/1-21/5	GEM	1967	1/1-16/1	LEO
1938	1/1-15/5	AQU		22/5-31/12	CAN		17/1-23/5	CAN
	16/5-30/7	PIS	1955	1/1-10/6	CAN		24/5-19/10	LEO
	31/7-30/12	AQU		11/6-20/11	LIO		20/10-31/12	VIR
	31/12	PIS		21/11-31/12	VIR	1968	1/1-27/2	VIR
1939	1/1-12/5	PIS	1956	1/1-10/1	VIR		28/2-15/6	LEO
	13/5-30/10	ARI		11/1-5/7	LIO		16/6-15/11	VIR
	31/10-20/12	PIS		6/7-15/12	VIR		16/11-31/12	LIB
	21/12-31/12	ARI		16/12-31/12	LIB	1969	1/1-30/3	LIB
1940	1/1-17/5	ARI	1957	1/1-15/2	LIB		31/3-15/7	VIR

YEAR	DATES	SIGN	YEAR	DATES	SIGN	YEAR (S)	DATES	SIGN
	16/7-16/12	LIB		20/1-31/12	CAP	1937	1/1-25/4	PIS
	17/12-31/12	SCO	1985	1/1-6/2	CAP		26/4-18/10	ARI
1970	1/1-30/4	SCO		7/2-31/12	AQU		19/10-31/12	PIS
	1/5-15/8	LIB	1986	1/1-20/2	AQU	1938	1/1-15/1	PIS
	16/8-31/12	SCO		21/2-31/12	PIS		16/1-31/12	ARI
1971	1/1-14/1	SCO	1987	1/1-2/3	PIS	1939	1/1-7/7	ARI
	15/1-5/6	SAG		3/3-31/12	ARI		8/7-23/9	TAU
	6/6-11/9	SCO	1988	1/1-8/3	ARI		24/9-31/12	ARI
	12/9-31/12	SAG		9/3-21/7	TAU	1940	1/1-20/1	ARI
1972	1/1-6/2	SAG		22/7-30/11	GEM		21/1-31/12	TAU
	7/2-24/7	CAP		1/12-31/12	TAU	1941	ALL YEAR	TAU
	25/7-25/9	SAG	1989	1/1-11/3	TAU	1942	1/1-9/5	TAU
	26/9-31/12	CAP		12/3-30/7	GEM		10/5-31/12	GEM
1973	1/1-23/2	CAP		31/7-31/12	CAN	1943	ALL YEAR	GEM
	24/2-31/12	AQU	1990	1/1-18/8	CAN	1944	1/1-21/6	GEM
1974	1/1-8/3	AQU		19/8-31/12	LEO		22/6-31/12	CAN
	9/3-31/12	PIS	1991	1/1-12/9	LEO	1945	ALL YEAR	CAN
1975	1/1-18/3	PIS		13/9-31/12	VIR	1946	1/1-3/8	CAN
	19/3-31/12	ARI	1992	1/1-10/10	VIR		4/8-31/12	LEO
1976	1/1-26/3	ARI		11/10-31/12	LIB	1947	ALL YEAR	LEO
	27/3-23/8	TAU				1948	1/1-20/9	LEO
	24/8-16/10	GEM		**Saturn**			21/9-31/12	VIR
	17/10-31/12	TAU	YEAR (S)	DATES	SIGN	1949	1/1-4/4	VIR
1977	1/1-3/4	TAU	1922	ALL YEAR	LIB		5/4-30/5	LEO
	4/4-20/8	GEM	1923	1/1-19/12	LIB		31/5-31/12	VIR
	21/8-31/12	CAN		20/12-31/12	SCO	1950	1/1-21/11	VIR
1978	1/1-11/4	GEM	1924	1/1-5/4	SCO		22/11-31/12	LIB
	12/4-5/9	CAN		6/4-13/9	LIB	1951	1/1-7/3	LIB
	6/9-31/12	LEO		14/9-31/12	SCO		8/3-13/8	VIR
1979	1/1-1/3	LEO	1925	ALL YEAR	SCO		14/8-31/12	LIB
	2/3-20/4	CAN	1926	1/1-2/12	SCO	1952	ALL YEAR	LIB
	21/4-29/9	LEO		3/12-31/12	SAG	1953	1/1-20/10	LIB
	30/9-31/12	VIR	1927-1928	ALL YEAR	SAG		21/10-31/12	SCO
1980	1/1-27/10	VIR	1929	1/1-14/3	SAG	1954-1955	ALL YEAR	SCO
	28/10-31/12	LIB		15/3-4/5	CAP	1956	1/1-10/1	SCO
1981	1/1-27/11	LIB		5/5-29/11	SAG		11/1-20/5	SAG
	28/11-31/12	SCO		30/11-31/12	CAP		21/5-10/10	SCO
1982	1/1-26/12	SCO	1933-1934	ALL YEAR	AQU		11/10-31/12	SAG
	27/12-31/12	SAG	1935	1/1-13/2	AQU	1957-1958	ALL YEAR	SAG
1983	ALL YEAR	SAG		14/2-31/12	PIS	1959-1960	ALL YEAR	CAP
1984	1/1-19/1	SAG	1936	ALL YEAR	PIS	1961	1/1-30/4	CAP

YEAR (S)	DATES	SIGN	YEAR (S)	DATES	SIGN				
1961	1/5-31/5	AQU		22/9-31/12	LIB				
	1/6-31/12	CAP	1981	ALL YEAR	LIB				
1962-1963	ALL YEAR	AQU	1982	1/1-29/11	LIB				
1964	1/1-24/3	AQU		30/11-31/12	SCO				
	25/3-15/9	PIS	1983	1/1-6/5	SCO				
	16/9-15/12	AQU		7/5-24/8	LIB				
	16/12-31/12	PIS		25/8-31/12	SCO				
1965-1966	ALL YEAR	PIS	1984	ALL YEAR	SCO				
1967	1/1-3/3	PIS	1985	1/1-17/11	SCO				
	4/3-31/12	ARI		18/11-31/12	SAG				
1968	ALL YEAR	ARI	1986-1987	ALL YEAR	SAG				
1969	1/1-29/4	ARI	1988	1/1-13/2	SAG				
	30/4-31/12	TAU		14/2-10/6	CAP				
1970	ALL YEAR	TAU		11/6-12/11	SAG				
1971	1/1-18/6	TAU		13/11-31/12	CAP				
	19/6-31/12	GEM	1989-1990	ALL YEAR	CAP				
1972	1/1-10/1	GEM	1991	1/1-6/2	CAP				
	11/1-21/2	TAU		7/2-31/12	AQU				
	22/2-31/12	GEM	1992	ALL YEAR	AQU				
1973	1/1-1/8	GEM							
	2/8-31/12	CAN							
1974	1/1-7/1	CAN							
	8/1-18/4	GEM							
	19/4-31/12	CAN							
1975	1/1-17/9	CAN							
	18/9-31/12	LEO							
1976	1/1-14/1	LEO							
	15/1-5/6	CAN							
	6/6-31/12	LEO							
1977	1/1-16/11	LEO							
	17/11-31/12	VIR							
1978	1/1-5/1	VIR							
	6/1-26/7	LEO							
	27/7-31/12	VIR							
1979	ALL YEAR	VIR							
1980	1/1-21/9	VIR							

CHAPTER EIGHT

The Outer Planets:
Uranus, Neptune and Pluto

How are you affected by the signs of the times?
The birth Signs of Uranus, Neptune and Pluto cover timespans of seven years or more, so when we observe these signs we must look beyond the individual to a whole generation of people, both those who were born within these timespans - all of whom will have those planets in the same sign - and those who lived through them. So the meanings of the sign positions are less personal, more collective, but nonetheless fascinating. The signs of Uranus, Neptune and Pluto reflect the prevailing trends of the time and how these affect groups of people.

The exciting new ideas that transform society, the dreams and images that capture the longings of an era, the powerful beginnings and endings of cycles in the world all correspond to the movement of Uranus, Neptune and Pluto through the signs.

Uranus: your desire for change

Uranus is known as the awakener. This planet is connected with sudden change and new experiences that alter existing circumstances. Uranus spends approximately seven years in any one sign and during its residency new ideas emerge that reflect the nature of this sign. Everyone born within a set of seven years of Uranian occupancy in a single sign will carry a similar seed potential for change, and those living within each seven year span will also be affected by the Uranian mood. Their ways of 'catching on' to what is new, their desire for personal freedom and independence will be expressed through the sign.

Uranus is also connected with the higher mind and originality, in that ideas that come about under the influence of Uranus can seem unusually enlightened and 'bright'. Uranus is the threshold, marking the edge of the unknown, where people often have to face the unexpected, react to changes which disturb them from their pattern but are thrilling and exciting just the same. Things happen suddenly with Uranus - people are taken by surprise, the past is swept away and they feel a new pulse beating in their lives. The sign position of Uranus can point to the type of changes individuals can expect. Our attitude to change is also tempered by the sign position of Uranus. Some might be restless types, always wanting to instigate change, others dislike being uprooted and having to step into the unknown.

It is important to realize that the extent to which an individual resonates to Uranus depends on its exact location in the birth chart by house and the degree to which it harmonizes or clashes with other planets. Its relationship to other chart factors will either bring Uranian issues into sharp focus, or allow them to recede into the background.

URANUS IN PISCES

Uranus in Pisces is idealistic and visionary. There is a desire for a new order that is compassionate and sensitive to suffering. Changes are often sensed before they happen, and on a personal level Uranus in Pisces can 'tune in' to find which way the wind is blowing and act accordingly. There is an open approach to spirituality that embraces all.

URANUS IN ARIES

These people tend to assert their independence and are strongly individualistic in their approach to life. Uranus in Aries gives rise to impulsive action that can sever connections with the past in an abrupt manner. When challenged, these types often form an isolationist position and prefer to go it alone rather than compromise.

URANUS IN TAURUS

Those with this birth sign find it hard to let go of the past, and tend to clutch on to permanency at the expense of personal growth. When they do make changes it is usually because of the practical advantages in doing so. Originality is often expressed around the areas of property and finance.

URANUS IN GEMINI

This can be a highly strung placement, where changes are made that take a toll on the nervous system. These types are very quick on the uptake of new ideas, possessing an intuition that enables them to forge ahead. Caution is needed to temper this 'off with the old and on with the new' mentality.

URANUS IN CANCER

Uranus here can throw the baby out with the bathwater. These people particularly need freedom within the family situation, and can experience sudden changes in their personal and domestic lives. Both emotional stability and a high level of independence are sought.

URANUS IN LEO

This placement encourages the individual to make changes that allow for greater self expression. Those with Uranus in Leo will not put up with rules that force

them to live in the shade, and they believe in living life creatively. They will make changes themselves rather than allow someone else to orchestrate their lives.

URANUS IN VIRGO

This birth sign is open to changes in attitudes towards health, diet and fitness. People with Uranus in Virgo experiment with alternative living and are aware of the effects that man can have on his environment. It is important for these individuals to express their social conscience through introducing new methods and techniques that are productive, efficient and useful rather than wasteful or self-seeking.

URANUS IN LIBRA

These individuals want the Uranian energy to exist within relationships - in other words, independence, excitement and spontaneity are important. Uranus in Libra is stifled within a partnership that does not feel alive, and changes in relationships are provoked if the interchange begins to freeze up. Partnerships are based on a sense of mutual understanding and co-operation rather than duty or tradition. Uranus in Libra has a strong desire for legal justice and freedom, and wants changes in society to be reflected in the law.

URANUS IN SCORPIO

This placement recognizes that change involves a kind of symbolic death and rebirth. They go whole-heartedly into new beginnings and often burn their bridges behind them. Not for them a surface change; they desire a total transformation or reconstruction. Uranus in Scorpio believes in making deep seated changes in society.

URANUS IN SAGITTARIUS

Uranus in Sagittarius believes in global change, and the breaking down of walls between countries. On an individual level, there is a need to make elbow room for new ideas that give a greater sense of freedom and choice. This person tends to make far-sweeping changes in life, seizing opportunities without a backward glance.

URANUS IN CAPRICORN

Uranus here witnesses the breakdown of old structures and makes moves to rebuild solid foundations for future security. There is a questioning of tradition and convention, particularly where it might diminish individuality. This placement is the reorganizer and shape of things to come.

Neptune: your dreams

Because Neptune spends approximately 14 years in a sign its expression tends to reflect a generation of people rather than the individual. The sign it is in represents the creativity, fashions, dreams and urge to be glamorous that pertain to a particular timespan of 14 years.

When we look at the sign that Neptune occupies in the birth chart of individuals, we are given a glimpse of what was thought to be magical and uplifting at the time they were born. Neptune's capacity to 'rise above' can take a spiritual or creative form. The longings and fantasies of a generation are translated into life in the form of fashion, music, art, film, and so on. A certain image captures the popular imagination, and then fades as Neptune passes on to the next sign. Neptune might move on, but the planet has left an imprint in its subjects, who respond to the vision connected with the sign Neptune is in at their birth for the rest of their lives.

NEPTUNE IN LEO

This generation was born just prior to or during the roaring Twenties: a time of enormous self-expression, in keeping with the sign of Leo. The extrovert nature of Leo can be seen in the image of the flapper. Exuberant art deco and the energy of the Jazz Age all combined to present an image that was designed to dazzle and enthral. Neptune in Leo is essentially romantic and spirited, and carries an enthusiasm for 'having a good time'.

NEPTUNE IN VIRGO

The Thirties and early Forties saw Neptune in Virgo, and people wanted to look chic and well-groomed. Virgo is the sign of fastidiousness rather than frippery, and fashionable styles became more tailored during this period. Both the depression of the Thirties and the rationing of the Forties put Neptune in Virgo to task, resulting in an admiration for economy, and efficiency. It is interesting that the expression 'to tighten one's belt' was actually reflected in the trim waisted fashions of the period. Neptune in Virgo is a thrifty sign, and quite capable of making a silk purse out of a sow's ear.

NEPTUNE IN LIBRA

Neptune in peace-loving Libra characterized the post-war years up to the mid-Fifties. Even in the early Forties, the Libran penchant for style and charm was embodied by Rita Hayworth. Whether people were 'Dreaming of a White Christmas' or identifying with the girl next-door images of Doris Day and

Debbie Reynolds, Libra's pleasant, harmonious and sugar sweet tones rubbed off on even its youngest subjects and were the order of the day. Neptune in Libra longs to play Happy Families and for all things 'nice' and serene.

NEPTUNE IN SCORPIO

The late Fifties and the whole of the Sixties heralded a desire for more intense experience, with Neptune residing in the deeper recesses of Scorpio. An explosion of sexuality, drug use, mysticism and the dawning of the nuclear age reflected the yearning to go beyond, to transgress the borders of nice Libran acceptability. This was the age of flower power, mini skirts, 'gurus', sensual music and a collective longing to find salvation through any other means than the 'safe' route. Those who were born with Neptune in Scorpio, although too young to participate in the age of experimentation, share a powerful creativity and a tendency to walk on the wild side.

NEPTUNE IN SAGITTARIUS

Throughout the Seventies and up until the mid-Eighties, Neptune was in Sagittarius. A tremendous mix of images characterized this period as fashion evolved quickly through the mini to the midi

to punk to new romantic, metamorphosing into Laura Ashley and Habitat. As usual, Sagittarius encourages the expression of a planet to run away with itself. This generation soon became avid travellers, with foreign culture fertilizing its appetite for lasagne, pizza and wine. They discarded their blankets in favour of 'continental quilts' or duvets and Freddie Laker caught our Sagittarian spontaneity, making it possible to cross oceans on standby. When people came home, it was to acres of Sagittarian-style pine furniture - a reminder of the great outdoors. Neptune in Sagittarius longs for freedom and expansion.

NEPTUNE IN CAPRICORN

Neptune came down to earth when it entered Capricorn in 1984 where it will stay until 1999. Capricorn is the sign of materialism. The Yuppie dream and boom time of the mid-Eighties reflect the longing for financial security. Fashions hark back to the past and nostalgia for the good old days has sparked many consumer products boasting of their traditional origins. At the same time as society moves forward there is a great consumer longing for the Aga, the conservatory, old-fashioned lemonade, original-style jeans, and so on. Capricorn tends to look backwards and value the past.

Pluto: your inner strength — How you handle crisis

Pluto is the planet of transformation, marking the end of a lifecycle and a subsequent rebirth. The slow passage of Pluto through the signs of the zodiac again reveals more about a generation of people than the individual. Pluto travels in an erratic orbit, taking between 12 and 30 years to pass through a sign.

Looking at Pluto's movement through the signs gives us an insight into what sort of shifts in consciousness resulted from major turning points in history. The sign corresponds with outer events that transform collective awareness. The drive for power has often been the catalyst for world events that have affected millions of people's lives. Pluto is connected with the use and abuse of power, and our ability to contact an inner strength that enables us to survive challenges in life.

When the position of Pluto by house and aspect is known, we can see the areas of life where a person is likely to undergo Plutonian transformation. Pluto's power is an overwhelming force that clears away the past, enabling people to 'survive' the crisis of change. In other words, those people strongly attuned to Pluto tend to develop a deep inner power. They often display a need to control the environment as a measure of self protection against circumstances which are by their very nature beyond control. Determination and inner grit are characteristic of a prominent Pluto in the birth chart.

PLUTO IN CANCER

Between 1913 and 1938-39 the Pluto in Cancer generation was born. There was an upsurge in protective feeling as World War I triggered off the need to defend home and country. During the Depression period many people were engaged in keeping their families together in the face of tough pressures from the outside world. Pluto in the sign of the family heralded major disruption and change within domestic life.

PLUTO IN LEO

The years between 1938-9 and 1956-7 saw a massive swing from death to rebirth in the world at large. Pluto in Leo intensified the need for power and this era saw a battle for supremacy between world leaders. The Fifties emerged as a time of new life after the dark days of the war and, in Leo style the age of consumerism began.

PLUTO IN VIRGO

As Pluto slid into Virgo between 1956 and 1972, many changes took place in employment. The constant analysis of values in the Sixties changed forever the dominance of the Puritan work ethic. Trade unions and the National Health Service were gaining strength during this time, reflecting Pluto's power to magnify Virgo's domain.

PLUTO IN LIBRA

Relationships between people and countries underwent significant change during the time Pluto was in Libra (1971-1984). This period witnessed the revolution of the family unit as people divorced in droves, became single parents, chose to live together rather than marry and altered the existing balance of relationships. Alliances between countries and political parties were also a feature of this time, reflecting Pluto in amicable Libra.

PLUTO IN SCORPIO

The years between 1983 and 1995, when Pluto is in Scorpio, have already set off some major changes in the world of a Scorpionic nature. Pluto destroys and transforms old structures that have outlived their purpose and to date this era has witnessed some of the most remarkable and dramatic endings and beginnings. The sign of Scorpio and Pluto have a special affinity in their association with life or death issues, hence the large scale battle with Aids and a transformation in attitudes to nuclear armament.

	Uranus		YEAR(S)	DATES	SIGN	YEAR(S)	DATES	SIGN
YEAR(S)	DATES	SIGN		23/5-24/6	VIR		7/11-31/12	SAG
1922-1926	ALL YEAR	PIS		25/6-31/12	LIB	1971-1983	ALL YEAR	SAG
1927	1/1-30/3	PIS	1970-1973	ALL YEAR	LIB	1984	1/1-18/1	SAG
	31/3-4/11	ARI	1974	1/1-21/11	LIB		19/1-22/6	CAP
	5/11-31/12	PIS		22/11-31/12	SCO		23/6-21/11	SAG
1928	1/1-12/1	PIS	1975	1/1-1/5	SCO		22/11-31/12	CAP
	13/1-31/12	ARI		2/5-8/9	LIB	1985-1992	ALL YEAR	CAP
1929-1933	ALL YEAR	ARI		9/9-31/12	SCO			
1934	1/1-5/6	ARI	1976-1980	ALL YEAR	SCO		Pluto	
	6/6-9/10	TAU	1981	1/1-17/2	SCO	YEAR(S)	DATES	SIGN
	10/10-31/12	ARI		18/2-20/3	SAG	1922-1936	ALL YEAR	CAN
1935	1/1-27/3	ARI		21/3-16/11	SCO	1937	1/1-8/10	CAN
	28/3-31/12	TAU		17/11-31/12	SAG		9/10-15/11	LEO
1936-1940	ALL YEAR	TAU	1982-1987	ALL YEAR	SAG		16/11-31/12	CAN
1941	1/1-8/8	TAU	1988	1/1-14/2	SAG	1938	1/1-5/8	CAN
	9/8-6/10	GEM		15/2-26/5	CAP		6/8-31/12	LEO
	7/10-31/12	TAU		27/5-2/12	SAG	1939	1/1-7/2	LEO
1942	1/1-15/5	TAU		3/12-31/12	CAP		8/2-15/6	CAN
	16/5-31/12	GEM	1989-1992	ALL YEAR	CAP		16/6-31/12	LEO
1943-1947	ALL YEAR	GEM				1940-1955	ALL YEAR	LEO
1948	1/1-31/8	GEM		Neptune		1956	1/1-19/10	LEO
	1/9-13/11	CAN	YEAR(S)	DATES	SIGN		20/10-31/12	VIR
	14/11-31/12	GEM	1922-1927	ALL YEAR	LEO	1957	1/1-16/1	VIR
1949	1/1-11/6	GEM	1928	1/1-20/9	LEO		17/1-18/8	LEO
	12/6-31/12	CAN		21/9-31/12	VIR		19/8-31/12	VIR
1950-1954	ALL YEAR	CAN	1929	1/1-19/2	VIR	1958-1970	ALL YEAR	VIR
1955	1/1-15/8	CAN		20/2-23/7	LEO	1971	1/1-4/10	VIR
	16/8-31/12	LEO		24/7-31/12	VIR		5/10-31/12	LIB
1956	1/1-3/2	LEO	1930-1941	ALL YEAR	VIR	1972	1/1-17/4	LIB
	4/2-31/5	CAN	1942	1/1-4/10	VIR		18/4-30/7	VIR
	1/6-31/12	LEO		5/10-31/12	LIB		31/7-31/12	LIB
1957-1960	ALL YEAR	LEO	1943	1/1-19/4	LIB	1973-1982	ALL YEAR	LIB
1961	1/1-31/10	LEO		20/4-3/8	VIR	1983	1/1-20/11	LIB
	1/11-31/12	VIR		4/8-31/12	LIB		21/11-31/12	SCO
1962	1/1-15/1	VIR	1944-1955	ALL YEAR	LIB	1984	1/1-20/5	SCO
	16/1-31/7	LEO	1956	1/1-30/4	SCO		21/5-29/7	LIB
	1/8-31/12	VIR		1/5-15/10	LIB		30/7-31/12	SCO
1963-1967	ALL YEAR	VIR		16/10-31/12	SCO	1985-1992	ALL YEAR	SCO
1968	1/1-28/9	VIR	1957-1969	ALL YEAR	SCO			
	29/9-31/12	LIB	1970	5/1-2/5	SAG			
	1/1-22/5	LIB		3/5-6/11	SCO			

CHAPTER NINE

Astrology in action

Let us see how a knowledge of the signs of the ten planets and Ascendant gives us a far greater depth of understanding than can be gained just from the Sun sign.

ASCENDANT	*SAGITTARIUS*
SUN	*CANCER*
MOON	*AQUARIUS*
MERCURY	*CANCER*
VENUS	*TAURUS*
MARS	*VIRGO*
JUPITER	*AQUARIUS*
SATURN	*CAPRICORN*
URANUS	*LEO*
NEPTUNE	*SCORPIO*
PLUTO	*VIRGO*

The friendliness of Sagittarius rising is apparent in the way Princess Diana opens up to the people she meets. It is easy to forget that seeing a Royal kneeling with children on the floor and embracing the dying was unheard of until she broke down these barriers. Sagittarius is renowned for the ability to put others at their ease and, with this sign on the Ascendant, that is what we see in the Princess. We are also made aware of her spontaneity and warmth, and her sense of humour which can sometimes produce Sagittarian fits of the giggles at inopportune moments. However, strongly placed

Saturn in Capricorn in the first house keeps her royally in check and determined to prove the seriousness of her commitment. What is not visible is the extent to which Princess Diana has to struggle to keep these two sides of her nature working in harmony. How far can she go? When should she hold back? The warring partners of Sagittarius and Capricorn see-saw between expression and repression. The Sun and Mercury in Cancer point to the sensitivity that fuels her ability to form an emotional rapport with the public, and particularly with children. Cancer lives, eats and

Aquarius helped her to survive this difficult time by enabling her to 'switch off' and put aside her anguish. This ability to shut off has its uses in her life today. Although Princess Diana's Cancer Sun instantly connects with the suffering of children, the Moon in Aquarius helps her to carry out her job by enabling her to stand back from becoming too involved in and swamped in the pain. Princess Diana is in touch with her own need to channel her caring, nurturing energy out into the world, embodying the Cancerian potential to be a universal mother. Personally and publicly her role as mother of the heir to the throne is, of course, her prime raison d'être. However, with both the Moon and Jupiter in the unconventional sign of Aquarius, we can expect the unexpected. In other words, Princess Diana will not be hidebound to tradition, but has an experimental and independent approach that finds expression in her personal life and particularly in motherhood. Not for her the formality and closeted quality of educating her children with a governess. An Aquarian breath of fresh air introduced them to school and to as ordinary and normal a life as possible. There she is

dropping them off in her baseball cap, winning the mothers' race and taking them out to a rugby match or for a hamburger - personal freedom is important for Moon in Aquarius and Jupiter in Aquarius wants to help others to be free.

The element of surprise generated by the Moon and Jupiter in Aquarius is tempered by the solidity of Venus in Taurus, Mars in Virgo and Saturn in Capricorn - these three earth signs keep Princess Diana's feet on the ground so that she is able to stay the course. As long as the outgoing Sagittarian and Aquarian sides of her personality have room to manoeuvre, she can keep going. Although she needs excitement there is also a desire for stability and permanence. So the restrictions of being a Royal pay off in terms of providing a solid structure that the Princess's Venus in Taurus particularly needs, even though her Moon in Aquarius may at times find it frustrating.

Mars in Virgo and Saturn in Capricorn enable her actually to enjoy the discipline and duty that comes with her public role. Behind the easiness and breeziness of Sagittarius on the Ascendant is a tremendous attention to detail and desire to get everything right.

breathes feelings - so for Princess Diana emotion is the raw material that forms the basis of life. As a five-year—old, Lady Diana Spencer experienced the pain and loss of her mother leaving the family. Her Moon in

THE DUCHESS OF YORK

ASCENDANT	*SCORPIO*
SUN	*LIBRA*
MOON	*ARIES*
MERCURY	*SCORPIO*
VENUS	*VIRGO*
MARS	*LIBRA*
JUPITER	*SAGITTARIUS*
SATURN	*CAPRICORN*
URANUS	*LEO*
NEPTUNE	*SCORPIO*
PLUTO	*VIRGO*

It is fascinating to note that the Duchess of York's planetary picture bears some resemblance to Margaret Thatcher's. Both have Sun and Mars in Libra and the sign of Scorpio on the Ascendant, denoting an intriguing mix of charm and steel. However, Margaret Thatcher's chart has a grittier tone to it with Saturn, the planet of ambition and control, lined up on the Ascendant giving her a desire for position and responsibility coupled with the Scorpio drive for power. In contrast, the Duchess's chart has a lighter flavour. Jupiter in Sagittarius in the first house tends to bowl people over with enthusiasm rather than tread on them, and the Moon in Aries adds a certain volatility to the emotions.

Scorpio on the Ascendant usually makes its mark through some powerful changes that bring about the realization of inner strength. The break up of her parents' marriage in her teens and the departure of her mother must have thrown the Duchess back on her own resources. It is rare for Scorpio rising to enter into a new phase of life gently; it can often seem more like a dramatic plunging into the unknown. The past is left by the wayside as this Ascendant moves along the road of self discovery.

Sarah Ferguson's marriage into the Royal Family heralded another vastly important new chapter in her life, because it challenged her to find her own power and cement a new image for herself. Over the last few years a physical transformation has taken place, the old style 'Fergie' being replaced by a sleeker, more glamorous version. The changes on the outer level have pointed to the inner change that has also been brewing below the surface. Now the eruption has taken place, she is faced with the death of one particular identity as wife of a royal prince. The shedding of the skin of royal life is a transformation that will eventually allow her to emerge in true Scorpionic style as a new person.

The Sun and Mars in personable, relationship oriented Libra enables her to find a bridge between herself and others. Although Libra likes people, it is hard for her to maintain balance when her Aries Moon is constantly stirring it up, making her emotionally volatile. The Libran part of her wants an easy life - enjoyable, sociable and harmonious - yet Moon in Aries is forthright and direct and often leads to confrontation.

Her exuberant side is instantly transmitted to others, despite Saturn in Capricorn laying down the the rules and regulations and calling for duty and discipline. Saturn can be a hard taskmaster, hitting us just where it hurts and calling us into line. Just as Jupiter in Sagittarius encourages her to travel, spread her wings and fly, both literally and symbolically, Saturn in Capricorn wags his cautionary finger.

The tension caused by the conflicting demands of these opposite qualities is also a contributory factor that has led to a crisis point in her life.

The Duchess's particular combination of birth signs shows exactly how we can be pulled in many directions. One part of us wants one thing, another part of us needs something completely different. Sun in Libra wants to 'fit in', Venus in Virgo is always analysing how to make a relationship 'perfect', Moon in Aries wants to take a risk, Mars in Libra wants to co-operate and so on. It is this constant interplay that creates the complexity of the human being.

JOHN CLEESE

ASCENDANT	*VIRGO*
SUN	*SCORPIO*
MOON	*ARIES*
MERCURY	*SCORPIO*
VENUS	*SCORPIO*
MARS	*AQUARIUS*
JUPITER	*ARIES*
SATURN	*ARIES*
URANUS	*TAURUS*
NEPTUNE	*VIRGO*
PLUTO	*LEO*

The sign of Virgo on the Ascendant, which describes physical appearance, denotes a rather dapper presentation. John Cleese's wiry frame reflects Virgo rising's tendency towards the lean side. What is also immediately apparent is the Virgo-style attention to detail and precise timing that creates Cleese's finely worked characterizations. Interestingly, much of the comedy revolves around the themes of order and chaos reflecting a strongly-felt Virgo theme. Even Basil Fawlty's excruciating attempts to make a perfect impression echo the Virgoan

concern to get things right in the face of 'circumstances beyond your control'. Through his training videos, John Cleese is able to combine acting with educational techniques designed to improve the effectiveness of salesmen. This is certainly a reflection of the Virgoan desire to be useful and provide service to others.

When we look beyond the Virgo Ascendant to other placements we begin to see the man behind the mask. John Cleese is evidently a very deep thinker and there is much more to him than meets the eye, with the Sun, Mercury and Venus in soul-searching Scorpio. It is not surprising that he has developed his interest in psychology, and co-written a book entitled *Families and How to Survive Them*. This reflects his Mercury in Scorpio delving into the deeper workings of the psyche. However, with the Sun and Venus in Scorpio, this delving is not just a hobby. John Cleese's desire for self-knowledge has beckoned him below the surface of life, to discover and release himself from old patterns through analysis. Venus in Scorpio suggests that he values depth more than surface appearance. His comedy asks why Manuel cannot help dropping the plates, why Basil cannot face

up to his incompetence and what it all means?

Again, with Venus, the planet of love, in sizzling Scorpio, affairs of the heart have included their share of crisis and passion. With the Moon in forthright Aries at odds with Venus in Scorpio John Cleese is apt to blow hot and cold, impulsive one minute and reticent the next. Many of the characters he plays seem to provide an outlet for his Moon in Aries, rushing headlong into situations without sufficient thought, feeling something and acting on it impulsively. Mars in Aquarius reveals the zany quality and originality of John Cleese's work. Monty Python was shocking in its day, and he doubtless enjoyed being part of the team with his Mars in group-minded Aquarius. He has the Aquarian capacity to surprise others with his sketches. Even when advertising that bastion of 'social arrival', the American Express card, he donned high heels, lipstick and a red feather boa for the magazine campaign pictures. John Cleese has both Jupiter and Saturn in Aries, an inherent contradiction that produces an interesting tension between the need to take the reins as an individual and an uncertainty and insecurity about doing so.

JANE FONDA

ASCENDANT	*CAPRICORN*
SUN	*SAGITTARIUS*
MOON	*LEO*
MERCURY	*CAPRICORN*
VENUS	*SAGITTARIUS*
MARS	*AQUARIUS*
JUPITER	*AQUARIUS*
SATURN	*PISCES*
URANUS	*TAURUS*
NEPTUNE	*VIRGO*
PLUTO	*CANCER*

Jane Fonda embodies the Capricorn work ethic with this sign on the Ascendant. The concept of pushing your body to the limit, and 'going for the burn' reflects the Capricorn fascination for defining and reworking boundaries. This rising sign exemplifies self-discipline, and Jane Fonda's punishing exercise regime broadcasts the message loud and clear that here is someone with outward self control.

As an Earth sign, Capricorn is drawn towards building material security and, with Capricorn rising and Mercury also in this sign, one would expect to find a shrewd business sense and financial flair. A fairly serious, professional image is typical of Capricorn on the Ascendant, and Jane Fonda has always striven to position herself away from the Hollywood glamour machine. She does, however, manifest the driving

ambition and need to prove her capability in her own right, as distinct from her well known father, an issue that frequently spurs Capricorns on to achievement.

The Sun and Venus in energetic Sagittarius produce a scattering of interests in many different directions. Jane Fonda has therefore created an identity that encompasses keep–fit queen, actress and political activist. With the Sagittarian zest for life she has pursued her goals and allowed no one to stand in the way of her adventurous search for her ideals. The world is a small place for Sagittarians, and Jane Fonda has never confined herself to the country of her birth.

Her Moon in Leo needs an enormous amount of appreciation and attention on the emotional front, something that was perhaps lacking in her childhood. Being up there on screen as someone special fulfils the emotional longing for recognition that is a fundamental source of security to Moon in Leo. This placement indicates that, in her personal life, Jane Fonda needs the lion's share of love, admiration and respect. Now she has thrashed out the Capricornian contracts and financial arrangements with Ted Turner, she is seeking the Leo fire and warmth in her marriage that eventually burnt out with Roger Vadim and Tom Hayden. However independent and self-assured Sun and Venus in Sagittarius appears to the outside world, Moon in Leo is vulnerable to insecurity. Continual reassurance of affection is required to feed the emotional ego, and playing second fiddle to another person or political ideology is not Moon in Leo's idea of nourishment.

Jane Fonda's Mars in Aquarius pulls her activities away from the subjective stance of Leo and into the more objective realm of ideas and belief systems. Saturn in Pisces also ingrains a desire to help the underdog. Both Mars and Jupiter reside in Aquarius making a combination that is perfect for promoting a controversial cause. She brought this planetary configuration vividly to life when she earned the nickname 'Hanoi Jane' for flying off to war-torn Vietnam in order to pursue her political vision. Stripping off as space age Barbarella also caused a stir.

Despite her conventional Capricorn on the Ascendant, Mars and Jupiter in Aquarius invite Jane Fonda close to the edge. She needs to make points, to shock and expose. With the Sagittarian emphasis on 'going for it' and taking a risk, she is not pre-disposed to maintaining the Capricorn veneer of puritanism further than her Ascendant. The outer discipline of the body masks the exuberance and fire underneath.

Birth Charts in Action

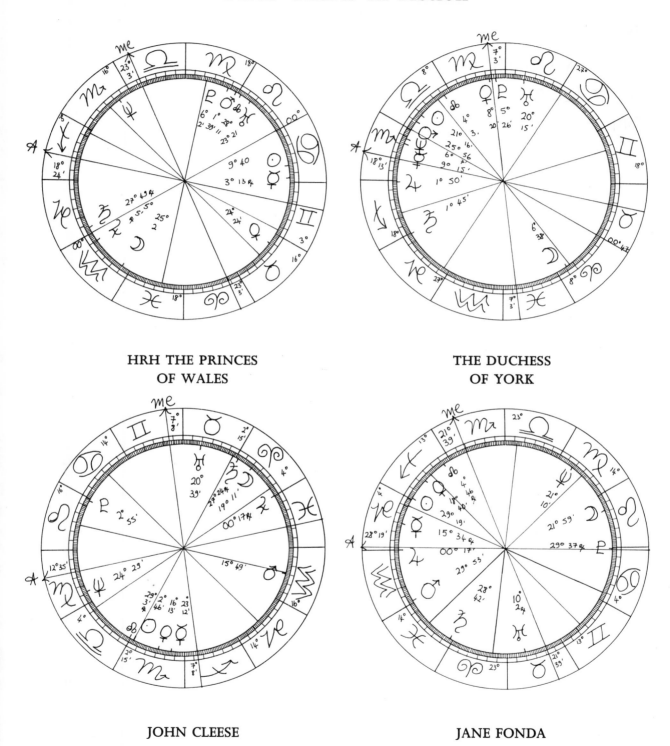

HRH THE PRINCES
OF WALES

THE DUCHESS
OF YORK

JOHN CLEESE

JANE FONDA

Jo

Aug. 14/69   6:40pm (B.S.T.)
              (approx.)

SUN — LEO

ASC. — AQUARIUS

DES. — LEO

MOON —